D1029348

HUNTING'S *Best*

SHORT STORIES

HUNTING'S *Best*

SHORT STORIES

Edited by Paul D. Staudohar

CHICAGO
REVIEW
PRESS

Library of Congress Cataloging-in-Publication Data

Hunting's best short stories / edited by Paul D. Staudohar.
    p. cm.
    Includes bibliographical references.
    ISBN 1-55652-402-1
    1. Hunting stories, American.   I. Staudohar, Paul D.

PS648.H86 H86 2000
813'.0108355–dc21

00-029470

Published by Chicago Review Press, Incorporated
814 North Franklin Street
Chicago, Illinois 60610
ISBN 1-55652-402-1

Printed in the United States of America
5 4 3 2 1

CONTENTS

ACKNOWLEDGMENTS

Outstanding people at several organizations provided guidance in creating this book, including Monte Burke at *Sports Afield*, C. Michael Curtis and Lucie Prinz at the *Atlantic Monthly*, Karen Donahue at Safari Club International, Robert K. Olson from the Listening Point Foundation, Carolee Green from *Field and Stream*, Robert Scheffler from *Esquire*, Charles Scribner and Lydia Zelaya from Charles Scribner's Sons, and Melissa DeMeo from the *New Yorker*. Michael Salmon, librarian at the Amateur Athletic Foundation in Los Angeles, uncovered ample resources. At California State University, Hayward, Lynne LeFleur managed to track down library materials from around the country, and librarians Kristin Ramsdell and Michele Buda were helpful. Also from Cal State, Florence Bongard assisted in the administration of the project. Writer Neil McMahon gave wise counsel. I'm further indebted to publisher Linda Matthews, executive editor Cynthia Sherry, and managing editor Gerilee Hundt from Chicago Review Press for their many insights. Thanks also to Drew Hamrick for suggesting two stories and for his editorial work.

—Paul D. Staudohar

INTRODUCTION

This collection of hunting stories has a companion volume called *Fishing's Best Short Stories*. They are the fifth and sixth in a series of collected sports fiction from the same editor and publisher. The first was *Baseball's Best Short Stories* (1995), followed by collections of stories on golf (1997), football (1998), and boxing (1999). Throughout the series, the goal has remained the same: to present the very best short fiction about favorite sports.

Although hunting and fishing are complementary "frontier" sports, there is today a controversial side to hunting that raises ethical questions not generally found with other sports, except perhaps boxing. Like boxing, hunting is a blood sport. Just as certain people would like to see boxing banned, some are appalled by hunting. Yet both these sports have inspired a graphic and compelling literature, especially of short fiction. An impressive number of outstanding authors have written superlative short stories about hunting. Unlike boxing, many of whose stories date prior to 1960, a good deal of fine hunting fiction is recent.

Twenty-one outstanding tales appear in this collection. Among the vintage writers, it's hard to beat Ernest Hemingway, Guy de Maupassant, and Irvin S. Cobb. A somewhat more recent group includes heralded authors Wallace Stegner, Corey Ford, and Thomas McGuane. Leading contemporary storytellers are also represented: Rick Bass, T. Coraghessan Boyle, Tony Earley, Richard Ford, David Guterson, E. Annie Proulx, David Quammen, and others. This relatively youthful group indicates that hunting retains a powerful grip on today's literary imagination.

Many of these stories were originally published in top-quality magazines that appeal not only to the hunting set but to a wider audience as well. Thus, while one might expect to see selections from *Field and Stream, Sports Afield,* and *Sports Illustrated,* there are also stellar choices from the *Atlantic Monthly,* the *New Yorker, Playboy, Harper's, TriQuarterly,* and the *Hudson Review.* Many of the stories are prizewinners, and some, like Hemingway's *The Short Happy Life of Francis Macomber* and Lawrence Sargent Hall's *The Ledge,* have been ranked among the greatest short fiction of the twentieth century.

An ample range of hunting types is presented here. Several stories illustrate the patience, freezing cold, fast shooting, and big potential bags of duck hunting. There are some nice entries on deer hunting, including one told from the perspective of a big buck; a couple of selections on hunting elk and moose; and a pleasing depiction of fox hunting in the South. Big-game hunting in Africa, for lion and buffalo, is chronicled in the marvelous Hemingway story. Boyle's "Big Game," set at a hokey man-made preserve in California, presents an interesting contrast—the real thing versus the contrived. An attractive zinger is "The Most Dangerous Game," a classic in which man hunts man.

The book is arranged for the most part in an alternating sequence of bird-hunting yarns and those of hunting larger animals. "Walking Out," by David Quammen, and "The Harlows' Christmas Dinner," by "Escohos," offer absolutely masterful characterizations of youngsters. Realism abounds; a few of the stories are rather hard on hunters, who wind up as objects of pity or, worse, as cadavers. Their authors seem to both love and hate the sport. Even the most shattering selections dramatize the bonds that hold friends and families together, a deep respect for nature, and an acceptance of life as it yields to the inevitability of death.

Every reader's attention will be held fast by the talent of these authors. For dedicated huntsmen who love and understand their sport, the book will certainly strike home. Readers who do not hunt will thrill to the action and adventure. As Charles Dickens said, "There is a passion for hunting . . . deeply implanted in the human breast." Let's cut to the chase!

This wonderful duck-hunting story shows a fine feel for the sport, especially for shooting. Drawing strongly on family relationships, it is narrated by a middle-aged man hunting with his father and his son. The story was origi-nally published in Sports Illustrated. *David Guterson's first novel,* Snow Falling on Cedars *(1995), won the PEN/Faulkner Award and was the American Booksellers' Book of the Year for 1995. His second novel,* East of the Mountains *(1999), has also been widely praised.*

David Guterson

OPENING DAY
(1989)

WE WAITED FOR MORNING in a sad little motel where you could smell hunters skulking in every direction. I lay listening to vague presences in the next room, strangers playing lonely rounds of five-card draw, until it seemed all right to dispense with the minor pretense of the clock and, gently, wake up my father and son. Pop couldn't turn himself over or sit upright first thing; he wheezed once and guessed he didn't want to be spry; everything hurt and it was no use pretending otherwise. But Sean, yawning, made a clean break from his dreams, spun from the bed, wheeled toward the bathroom, and after he had let loose a brash stream of night water, sprawled like a prince on his motel pillows stuffing shells into the pockets of his field jacket. "Come on, Pop," he said. "Up and at them."

Pop grunted, blinking, and fished for his glass of teeth, words leaking from the corner of his mouth, sour ire. "You thlow down, Thawn. Take afther your damn dad. Tho damn frithky firth thing like that."

I shook my head: they were both immoderate. "That was a long time ago," I reminded Pop. "Besides, any other morning you couldn't roust Sean out with anything short of TNT."

Pop fixed his teeth in place. "Not so long," he said, trying them out, his jaw working them over, the long crevices in his cheeks churning. "Where are we going to get breakfast?"

We drove through a silent and frosted darkness with the sage desert just beyond the pale of the road. Along the strip of autumnal, shameless motels, hunters loaded gear in lots lit by running lights, steam spewing from their mouths. The dogs circling just beyond the tires, the bald fences enclosing vacant guest pools, the last of the good willow leaves, the distant odor of the slaughterhouses, neon, all beneath lonesome heavens. "What did we forget?" Pop wondered aloud. "There's no Seven-Eleven in this sage desert." Everybody, all the businesses, had thrown themselves open at four o'clock in the morning, small pools of comforting light at the verge of Moses Lake, hawking last-minute wares. Faint in the west, toward the dark mountains and home, a loose, silky band of clouds wandered the long route of the horizon—Pop pointed them out to us readily. "We'll get flurries at noon," he predicted. "It just might help."

At breakfast we inhabited a world solely of hunters, some of them in camouflage, all of them interested in eating swiftly, most of them younger than myself it seemed, though not as young as Sean, and most of them waxing and waning through a studied, dark calm that belied an unspeakable eagerness. Pop tried to give away his pancakes three or four times before Sean took them off his hands uncomfortably. "You need them," Pop explained. "Eat them up. Go on, son."

"You sure?"

"Sure I'm sure."

"Keep half."

"Don't want half."

"You'll be hungry later."

"Take them." Pop pushed the plate away with his knife blade. "Now eat them up. Go on."

He watched without concealing the pleasure he took in it: an unbridled appetite was something he celebrated, for better or for worse. Sean, oblivious, clenching the tines of his fork between his big teeth, drowned everything in warm maple syrup.

Pop, with his pipe lit, had the waitress fill his thermos with sugared coffee for the day ahead. On the way out we found the tight foyer wedged with hunters, and in the parking lot more were adjusting their caps and talking to their dogs beneath the lights. "Smell that sage," I said to Sean. "It's the strongest smell you've got out here. It's everywhere."

"Some sage'll live for a hundred fifty years," Pop reflected. "Same sage Chief Joseph smelled, you're smelling now."

"Smells good," Sean said. "Let's get out into it."

I drove out on Dodson Road. To the left, desert, to the right, irrigated wheat fields under a heaven of cold stars. Canoes were putting in where the road crossed the wasteway. The sidelots were filled with stirring hunters, campers, vans, trailers, pickup trucks, lantern lights in curtained windows. Some, distant phantoms, had already set off into the desert with their flashlights wavering at their sides. The autumn wheat had been threshed down to stubble, but still stood high enough for birds to lie in; they would run in front of you in fields like this, refusing to put up unless they had to. "A lot of grain out there," Pop noted. "Sunny weather's been good to these wheatmen." We passed a lone pintail set down on a gutter pond. "They've got about an hour and a half left to do that," Sean said, swiveling to watch as we passed by.

We pulled off at the gate and began to parcel out the decoys. Pop couldn't seem to get his load just right; Sean held the light for him while he made it up slowly, a burlap sack and two pack straps of manila cord, the same rigging he'd employed for more than fifty hunting seasons. We picked up our weapons, I dragged low the top strand of barbed wire beside the gate and the three of us stepped over the range fence into the sage desert, following the twin ruts of a fading cattle road.

"Trail gets worse every year," Pop said. "No cattle in it anymore."

Sean said, "You don't need a trail out here, though. Just make a bee-line for the wasteway."

"Trouble with that is a bee don't have to walk. He doesn't get sand in his boots."

A quarter-mile in, Pop's load went; it sprang away from his back without warning and flopped down into the bunch grass. We waited while he got his knots just so, Sean gouging the sand with his boot heel and weighing the shells in his pockets. I was overdressed and heating up quickly, so I unbuttoned my jacket and took off my cap. The three of us hiked through chickweed and Johnson grass. The sky had already gone from black to purple when Pop pointed out the morning's first birds—a flight of mallards wheeling toward the northwest, eleven or twelve in silhouette. "They're coming in from The Potholes," he told us, following their sleek dip and swerve. "Those birds are definitely looking for a place to set."

"Let's go up there," Sean said. "Come on."

He moved on ahead of us. Pop and I sat against the base of a sand bluff for a while.

"How's the knee? Bothering you?"

Pop rubbed once or twice beside the outside tendon. "Not too bad. Not yet."

We followed a ridge, conjuring everywhere the bustle of pheasants in the sage. We climbed over a black dune, worked down to a section marker, then crossed between two pieces of cattail marsh where for years we'd gotten creditable jumpshooting just by splitting up and combing the shallow margins. Pop had put in plenty of good days here; I'd watched him get a triple more than once. I was driven to recall a flight of mallards that got up in the south pond, scattering, twenty years ago, Pop taking a left and then a right and at the end, incredibly, a going-away. I wondered if he remembered it. If all the ducks and even the upland hunting faded together in his brain.

It was light enough to move without the flashlights now. Strands of honkers, broken Vs, skated past darkly a thousand feet overhead. It didn't matter how many times you witnessed them in flight, their speed, their unity of purpose, their impressive altitude, the faint but audible sound from fifty throats—it left you with a pounding in the rib cage. Pop watched them, too, from under his pack load. I could hear him breathing. We traversed the last black dune side by side, slowly, and stood gazing out across the wasteway.

"There it is," Pop said. "Damn."

Marsh reeds, golden cattails, pockets of gray water for as far as you could see north and south. The sage desert, impossibly large, rolled away to the east and behind. While we watched a string of teal angled in, just where we'd had our set so many years. We heard shooting, first shots of the day, a teal plummeted like a ball of coal, and soon, shooting from every quarter.

"We're a little late," I said. "It's open season."

"What happened to Sean?"

"Getting into his waders."

"Channel moves further out every year. Deeper, too."

"We can lay our set this side of it, Pop. No reason to try and cross."

We scrambled out a point of sedge and worked our waders on. Sean had his things beneath a thorn willow, neatly. "Let's go," he said to us. "Come on."

I let him lead. Bunched tight we followed the bracken margins, hip high a quarter-mile or so, going laterally with the pull of the wasteway. We were in it, guns aloft. You could feel it sucking against the backs of your waders. I watched while a pair of trout shot away, more silently than in dreams I'd once had of them, moving in tandem toward the reeds.

Pop found us a dependable set—high marsh just upwind, good drift, thick bracken; we anchored the decoys at the low end, down current but well out in the open. It was belly-high work to get them placed so I did the deep wading myself. Pop had his pipe lit and stood in the reeds, tossing the decoys out to me; then each of us took up a twenty-yard stretch and faded into the camouflage.

The first ducks came in before an hour had gone by; there had been shooting everywhere, and now it was our turn. They were mallards, a group of four wheeling over too high to be heard, jumping across from the wheat fields having fed beneath the stars, and skittish because all the familiar places swarmed, this day, with the echoes of desperate gunshots. I beckoned them first with a feeding call, a series of low, gradual chuckles, and then with the harsh cry of hen to drake. They circled twice, wide arcs in order to cover the high reeds to the north; on the third pass all four set their wings beautifully and rode in with the wind bucking them up a bit. I saw them fluff up their breast feathers; there was some splashing confusion about the decoys. Sean stood in and took the lead bird with a close wing shot, and I took a hen going away to the left. She zagged once, then plummeted head over heels with her wings folded up, propelled away from me for a half-second, no more, by the violent thrust of the shot. The two remaining singles veered off climbing powerfully; Sean wasted a second shell on the hind one.

"Yours is swimming," Pop called from his blind. "Go on, son. Finish what you started."

Sean sluiced his wounded drake, looking sheepish, I thought, and reloaded afterward on the spot. We let the two birds drift out past the decoys until in the end they were awash against the cattails.

"Can I go around and pick them up?" Sean called. "I want to see how big mine is."

"They aren't going anywhere," Pop answered. "Leave them be, why don't you?"

The battle went forth all around through midmorning; hunters were gunning away at the high flyers, and Pop cursed them once or twice. Nothing would come down in this rain of steel shot; the ducks were going to stay skittish. I tried calling in a stray set of teal, but they weren't falling for it and scurried away over the bluffs. Everything else was dumbfounded high flyers.

Then at noon, sure enough, we got the winds Pop had prophesied, and suddenly, funneling low and hugging the terrain, no fewer than thirty teal passed through our set with their wings drumming the air above the water, a whole flurry of them, dark and flashing, and nobody getting a shot off but Sean, who emptied his gun at them to no avail. They peeled off to the east with a unified grace, climbing in a long bank of silhouettes, until distance erased them from sight.

"What happened?" Sean asked.

"Caught me sleeping," I said. "They were moving too fast. I never got shouldered."

"Working on my pipe," Pop called out. "Damn!"

When the air teased down a bit we stood out for lunch—sliced beef sandwiches, a wedge of pie each. Pop lit his pipe and held his knee in his hand. The sun had come up strong over the desert—bad for hunters, but pleasant at lunchtime. We opened our jackets and passed the water around, cold and tinted with the canteen taste. Pop watched while Sean lit into his pie, and so did I, pouring from the thermos.

"I wonder if we shouldn't try some jumpshooting," Sean said. "Maybe that'll be the ticket."

"Better not wander," answered Pop, sipping coffee. "Some of these skyshooters might mistake you for a stray and try to pot you in the brush."

"There's ponds over yonder." Sean pointed toward the southeast. "Nobody's shooting down that way. Singles have been going in all day over there. The strays get confused and end up along the margins. I'll bet we get some shooting down there. I'll bet we do, Pop."

"How much?" asked Pop. "You might and you might not. But you go ahead and find out, why don't you?"

"With three of us we just might get one up."

"You can do it just as easy with two, boy."

Sean and I tracked down a nice string of ponds to walk, and I took another mallard hen going off on the diagonal. She had trouble gaining altitude and gave me plenty of time to establish my lead and squeeze off without relying on instinct. I did it all in my head, which was satisfactory enough. She tumbled, a blur of feathers, and splashed behind the reeds. I let Sean go in to pick her up.

We walked a mile and a half of sage; there were no birds anywhere and it seemed just as well. Sean had his eye out for ringnecks, I could tell, though he knew they were impossible to flush without a bird dog. But he was very young, only twenty.

Finally we sprawled on the highest of the black dunes. Here you could see the whole length of the wasteway, its pools of sunlight, its matted rush, glistening down toward the Saddle Mountains.

"We're not getting the shots," Sean said, lying back with his hands behind his head. "I hate a slow day. I really do."

"It's good just being out," I reminded him.

"You know something? Pop hasn't fired a shot all day. You'd think he would've by now."

"He's shot his share over the years, Sean."

Sean pumped a shell loose and blew sand from it. "Still," he said. That was all.

"He'll get a shot before the day's out," I predicted. "We all will. At twilight."

Heading in we worked the margins of the wasteway together, cutting up the bracken quietly. I remembered what Pop said about the shallows on a busy day: because flight had proved itself too precarious, strays holed up and refused to bounce out unless you nearly stepped on their tail feathers. I figured if they flushed it would be with the wind under them, so we spread and beat the edges with the breeze in our faces. Sure enough a pair of pintails towered, and Sean took them both, a head-on and a going-over. They were good shots and he gave a shout when the birds fell, holding his twelve-gauge aloft.

We brought the three birds in and retrieved our two drifters from where the current had pinned them to the reeds. Sean thrust his pintails up for Pop to see, and Pop answered by raising his pipe above his head.

Gusts came up again in the late afternoon. I stood in with Pop to keep him ready, knowing he would sit on the bracken when he tired. "Where was it we got our Christmas goose?" he asked. "I believe it was down toward the reservoir from here. Just this side of those big bluffs."

"It was back that way. The twin ponds. Up underneath where the butte bulges."

The first of the blackbirds began to work now. Solitary pairings, gliding after insects, then clouds of them, wave after wave, undulant and synchronized, like schools of fish. They dropped steeply, then banked, spun in a whirlwind, exploded toward the twilight heavens. Mallards began to move in flurries. A pair circled, once, twice—their arcs enormous, elongated coils—then set from behind, so that we had to take them late, a drake and a hen dropping in from over the shoulder, two rough going-away shots in the end. I left the lead bird for Sean and told Pop to let fly, but he hesitated and Sean missed altogether; they banked and whirled on a fortunate draft and we had no birds to show for it.

"*Mark,*" Sean called out. "They're coming out of the woodwork now."

A lone mallard hen, skimming low, nearly set among our decoys before Sean fired at her—neatly and with the proper composure. It was a rare display of patience on his part, I thought, but he missed at any rate and she veered over the cattails, skimming still, before he dropped her cleanly with a long second shot. He was still reloading when a group of eight began to circle the upwind reeds, turned away as if to give it up, then coiled back again, suspicious, circling twice more and then angling in uncertainly, pulling up at thirty yards and stroking hard over our blinds; I fell back in the bracken and squeezed off at a going-over without giving her the proper lead time and the eight of them soon cleared gun range.

"Call them in!" Sean screamed. "*Mark!*"

I gave out with the feeding call, as anticipatory as any boy, for it seemed to me, with the coming darkness inevitable, that these would be the last birds of the day. They were green-winged teal, two dozen or more, listing to the right and approaching on a low slant, a tight flock swift in flight but apparent from far off, so that I had time to remind Pop to get shouldered and fire when I did. When they dropped precipitously against the wind I knew Sean would hold himself; then they were settling down on the water, then trailing up away from the still decoys with their wings bucking, breasts opened, then floundering in slow motion over little splash pockets on the pond, tails dripping quicksilver, and I stood in and fired with perfect ease. Sean put two birds down, firing too quickly in succession when he had time—missing on the second shot—but I took a triple with the kind of slow deliberation I have found myself in recent years capable of. I have no quick shot any longer.

"Nice shooting," Pop said, with his hand on my arm. "You did it just like I would have. Pretty as a picture shooting."

In the final light I hauled out our decoys and wrapped their anchors, and my son collected, on the drift, the six birds still on the water. I didn't ask my father why he hadn't shot, but Sean did, with the blind ease of youth. "I don't lead so well," Pop told him. "It's just opening day. I'm a tad ragged, I guess. I can't get onto them yet."

But we had plenty of birds, eleven for the day; things felt right and it had been a perfect hunt. I let Sean carry them strung and draped over his shoulders, and I knew—or rather, know—what illusory thing he felt wading. Pop sloshed along behind us with his burlap bag across his back and his pipe clutched between his front teeth. "Beginning to get cold," he said once.

The day reversed itself; it was dark again and, freed from our waders, guns emptied of shells, we sojourned back across the sage and black dunes. Sean explained to Pop how he'd come by his pintails, how with the head-on the barrel of his gun had temporarily obscured the bird from sight, how with the going-over he'd swiveled and planted to take him nearly on the going-away. Chains of geese reeled overhead. The blackbirds had settled in for the night. When the first stars came up a coyote began to cry; I stopped to listen, smelling the sage, and Sean left me in his boot tracks. He went off with all the birds over his shoulders and his flashlight broadcasting across the sagelands.

Pop limped up behind and we sat down. "Knee," he said. I gave him my canteen; we rested in silence. "Down in there," I said, pointing below us, "are the ponds where you got that good triple jumpshooting. It was the south pond. Nineteen sixty-five, I believe."

Pop, wiping his lips with the back of his hand, only nodded blankly and returned the canteen. But I could see that he remembered.

"It's kid's stuff to live for that sort of thing," I told him.

I had to pull him up because he didn't want to rise on his own. I stayed behind him now. I watched his back, the burlap sack, the way he picked his knee up gingerly and kept the weight from his left leg. We sat every so often. "Damn sage," Pop said. "It just sort of fills you up."

I didn't know what to say. So I said nothing. If anyone should have had words for him then it would have been me, but I couldn't think of any.

Near the end we were hardly moving. "We're at the coot ponds," I pointed out. "It's not more than two hundred yards to the fence." But we sat for a long time in the sand, saying nothing. I could see that my son had the headlights on. "Just a few more steps," I said to Pop. "Come on."

"You go on ahead," he answered. "I'll get there sooner or later."

"You sure?"

"I want to just sit here for a while."

I went ahead and waited with Sean. On the truck's hood, one by one, we laid the ducks out and looked them over. The teal had buffy under-tail coverts; one of the mallards had the tightest curl of tail feathers either of us had ever seen. "Not a bad opening day," Sean said. "Eleven birds. Count them."

He kept running his flashlight over them. "Meat for the table," he said. I wanted to tell him how wrong he was, how meat for the table was a boy's illusion, but I didn't because I knew that quite soon enough he would find it out for himself.

At last Pop was at the barbed wire. "All right," he said firmly. "Let's get out of here."

He slept as we drove back across the mountains, slept like a baby with his chin against his chest after dinner at a roadstop in Vantage. Sean slept too and I crossed Snoqualmie Pass on my own, alone with my thoughts. There was snow at twenty-five hundred feet but the semis had it cleared from one lane nicely and I followed their track over the summit with the wipers barreling and the defroster roaring in my ears. At North Bend Pop perked up and, pipe lit again, sat with his head against the side window.

"What is it?" I said.

"Nothing."

We crossed the floating bridge into Seattle. Sean woke up, wiped his eyes with his knuckles and looked around at the rainy streets. "We're back," he said. "Damn, Dad."

"You can't hunt every day," I told him.

Then when I pulled up in front of Pop's apartment building I began to understand his silence. I opened up the back of the camper and hauled out his burlap sack with its waders, thermos and field jacket inside. It smelled powerfully of sage, and when I looked in I found the sprigs of it he'd collected for his living room.

Everyone shook hands all around and a lot of things were left unsaid. My father didn't want to take any of the birds; didn't want to draw and pluck them, he said. I walked him down the corridor and got him inside; Pop limped away and started up the bathwater.

Settling in beside my son again, turning the key in the ignition, it came to me what Pop had left behind. The engine hadn't caught before Sean noticed it, too, and he turned to me for a resolution. "Pop's gun," he said. "He forgot it."

I put my hand on his forearm. "Go on and take it into him," I almost said, but I didn't, I stopped myself, and the two of us drove away from there. My son didn't say another word.

Here is as heartwarming a tale about kids and Christmas as one could hope to find. Nearly a century old, it lovingly depicts the values of country life. Economic hardships interfere with the hope for a special meal at Christmas, and two young boys set out hunting to put meat on the family table. Try to keep a dry eye when you read this one.

"Escohos"
THE HARLOWS' CHRISTMAS DINNER (1903)

REAKFAST IS READY, BOYS," said Mrs. Harlow. "Can you stop long enough to eat?"

It was Christmas morning and Danny and Jim were still gloating over a bright new jackknife and a box of water-color paints which their respective stockings had revealed. Each stocking had also contained a pair of thick, warm mittens which their mother had knit, and a package of homemade candy. That was all, but the boys were fully satisfied, for each had received what he most wanted.

Mrs. Harlow was rather quiet during the morning meal, serving the boys in silence while she listened to their merry talk. She was thinking how best to tell them something which was on her mind; for she was loath to spoil their holiday mood.

At length she said: "I am afraid your Christmas dinner will be a disappointment to you. You know we are very poor, and this year it seems as though money has come in more slowly than ever before. For some reason I have found less sewing to do at the village than usual. So it looks as though we would have to get along without any meat this Christmas, for I have no money to buy it with. But we have plenty of vegetables which you raised in the garden, and there are apples and nuts and canned berries. I will do my best with these, and perhaps we shall not have such a bad dinner after all."

The boys' faces fell at first, but before she had finished they had brightened again and Danny said, "Don't worry, mother. It will be a jolly good dinner I know."

"Of course it will," echoed little Jim, though he loved chicken dearly. Tears came into Mrs. Harlow's eyes as she said, "Whatever else I lack I have two of the best boys in the world."

Suddenly an idea came to Danny. "Mother," he said, "if you will let Jim and me take father's gun this morning, perhaps we can shoot a rabbit or a partridge. I am sure we can." His mother smiled at his enthusiasm, but shook her head. "You are too young to use it yet," said she. "I am afraid you would shoot yourselves."

"But Dick Purcell showed me how to load and shoot it last summer and I killed a woodchuck with it myself," protested Danny.

"Yes," said Jim. "I saw him." It was Jim's province to uphold Danny always. Young Dick Purcell was the Harlows' nearest neighbor. In summer he planted and cultivated their few acres of tillage land, taking half the resultant crops in payment for his labor. As a successful fisherman and mighty hunter he was the boys' ideal. Finally, after many entreaties and promises to "be careful every minute" from Danny and Jim, Mrs. Harlow consented to their taking the gun. "But you must be at home by ten o'clock," she admonished. "That will give you nearly three hours and I shall worry myself to death if you two boys are gone longer than that."

There was no dallying after this. The boys swallowed their breakfast almost at a single mouthful. Then Danny went to the closet and took down the old gun. It was a muzzle loader and of so long a pattern that when resting on the floor it stood much higher than his head. But fortunately the barrel was rolled very thin, so that the piece was really much lighter than it looked. Jim produced a shot pouch and powder horn, and Danny proudly proceeded to load the gun, as he had seen Dick do many times. There was but one size shot in the pouch, B.B.'s, and he put in a generous load of these, determined that whatever came in range should get no farther than the dinner table.

Donning their warmest clothes, including the new mittens, the youthful hunters set off. "Don't worry about us," Danny shouted to his mother, who stood in the doorway. "We shall be back soon with a fat bird." An odd picture they made as they crossed the yard toward the pasture and wood-lot beyond, and in spite of her misgivings Mrs. Harlow could not resist a smile as she watched them go. Danny was in the lead, the long gun shouldered and reaching far out behind, while Jim, who had insisted upon carrying something, brought up the rear bravely accoutered with shot pouch and powder horn.

Only a few inches of snow had fallen as yet and the boys found the walking quite easy. But the morning was a sharp one and their faces smarted with the cold as they crossed the open pasture. Their fingers, too, tingled in spite of the new mittens. Soon, however, they reached the woods and entered a thick copse of small evergreens, dotted here and there with trunks of maples and yellow birch. It was warmer here, and aching fingers were speedily forgotten in the search for game. They had started a large flock of partridges among these spruces the summer before and it seemed that some of them ought still to be about.

As they crept along Danny stopped quickly and pointed at the snow. "See," he said, "one is still here, at any rate." Jim looked down and saw the track made by a single bird walking in the snow. "Good!" he exclaimed. "I'll bet he's an old boomer, too. Those tracks are as big as a hen's." They moved stealthily onward, but had not taken three steps when there was a rustle near at hand and a big cock partridge ran out from behind an old log. Clucking excitedly, it started to cross a little opening just in front of them, its head erect, its tail at full spread, and its dark ruff distended. To the surprised boys it looked as large as a turkey.

Danny was so startled that for an instant he forgot to shoot. Then collecting himself, he raised the gun with trembling hand, took a quick aim and fired. "Boom!" The old piece went off with a prodigious roar, well-nigh knocking him off his feet. But it was not that which brought tears to his eyes a second later. They were tears of vexation and disappointment. For, mingled with the report of the gun, had sounded the whir-r-r-r of wings as the bird sailed away unhurt.

Slowly Danny turned and looked at Jim. Jim looked back at him. For a long minute neither said anything. It was not a time for words. Disappointment was too plainly written on their faces to need any other expression.

At last Danny spoke. "Oh, Jim!" he said, "how did I miss him?"

"I don't know," Jim answered. "I guess we wanted him too bad."

"But he was so big," said Danny. "I could have hit him with a stone." For once Jim had no consolation to offer. The bird had really looked big. He could not deny that.

After a while Danny reached for the powder horn and began half-heartedly to reload. "We may as well go home," he said. "I've had my only chance and thrown it away."

But Jim, who had missed nothing and was fast regaining his natural cheerfulness, encouraged him as best he could. "There must be other partridges here," he said. "Or perhaps we shall find that one again. We must get something," he added—"for mother."

Unwittingly the little fellow had touched the right chord. Danny said no more about returning, but set his teeth grimly and started on again. They slipped along as silently as wood sprites or brownies, peering with sharp eyes into the dark spaces beneath the evergreens and listening intently for the "*p-r-r-t, p-r-r-t*" of a frightened bird. Once a quick scratching and scurrying startled them and set their hearts beating wildly. But it was only a saucy red squirrel which ran up a nearby spruce and, perching upon a bough, barked its defiance at them, punctuating its remarks with angry flirts of its tail.

They reached the farther edge of the copse without seeing other game. Evidently the big cock was sole lord and tenant of this bit of woods, and for the time he had fled, panic-stricken, beyond its borders.

Leaving the evergreens Danny and Jim came out at the top of a long, sparsely wooded slope which stretched away to a big swamp below them. Here the sunshine on the snow seemed of dazzling brightness after the shadow of the spruces, and they could hardly keep their eyes open as they descended the slope.

A flock of grosbeaks feeding quietly among the sumacs on the hillside watched them with bright, round eyes as they passed—interested, but unafraid. And up from the swamp ahead floated the cheery *"chick-a-dee-dee-dee"* of winter's little gray-coated songster. Others were out in search of a Christmas dinner as well as they.

Down in the swamp bottom the growth was thicker. For the most part it consisted of alders and willows, with scattering cedars and tamaracks. But here and there were little bunches of spruces and fir balsams like those on the hill above, growing so thickly as to form an almost impenetrable screen from without.

"We ought to see a rabbit here," said Danny. "That would be better than nothing." They knew this to be a famous retreat for rabbits, for they had seen hunters from the village returning from the swamp well laden with dead bunnies. But they had always had hounds with them. "If we only had a dog," lamented Jim.

They saw tracks on every side, but not a single rabbit showed himself, though they walked as quietly as they could, stopping every little way to look carefully about them. Probably the little long-ears were snugly ensconced in their nests this frosty morning.

The boys were near the center of the swamp and were passing one of the thick evergreen clumps when a sound from within it brought them to a quick halt. Listening intently they heard it again. It was a slight crunching of the snow, as if some animal was walking stealthily about. Creeping to the edge of the spruces they crouched low and looked beneath the bottommost boughs. But just there the trees grew so thickly that they could see nothing.

A little to the right was a spot which looked more open and they started to crawl toward it on their hands and knees, Danny in front, dragging the gun after him. Suddenly he felt Jim clutch his ankle from behind. Turning he saw the little fellow, motionless as a statue, looking into the copse, his eyes big with wonder at something he saw there.

Danny was beside him in an instant. "Look," whispered Jim, without once taking his eyes from the object of his gaze, whatever it was. At first Danny saw nothing. Then through a narrow opening in the trees he suddenly made out the thing that Jim saw and almost cried out in his surprise. Standing in a little open space among the spruces and looking uncertainly at them was a deer, its handsome head and half its body in plain view.

Danny had never seen a live, wild deer before, and for an instant he watched it, fascinated. Then of a sudden he remembered the gun which lay beside him in the snow. As quickly as he dared he raised it, drew back the hammer and took aim at that dark red shoulder. Surely it was sighted right this time, he thought, and pulled the trigger.

When the smoke cleared away the deer had disappeared, but there was a loud thrashing and thumping among the evergreens. Was it the sound of the creature running away, Danny wondered, with sinking heart. Quickly he and Jim leaped to their feet and ran around the clump. Half way around Danny stopped. "See," he said, pointing downward, "it was wounded before." Sure enough there were the deer's tracks going in, and beside them a faint trail of blood.

No sound came from within, and looking ahead they could see no marks of the animal having left the copse. "I'll bet you finished him," Jim cried, and dived into the clump. Danny was close behind. An instant later they raised a shout that would have done credit to two grown men.

Inside the screen of spruces was a hard, blood-soaked place in the snow, showing where the deer had rested, and close beside it, still slightly quivering, but quite dead, lay the deer itself. It was a buck, and its fine head and great antlers would have delighted the eyes of older sportsmen than Danny and his little brother Jim.

"Isn't he a dandy?" said Danny, when their youthful exuberance had partially spent itself. "The old gun did the business that time," he added, pointing to where the heavy charge, acting like a single slug at that distance, had crushed in the creature's shoulder.

A small hole in its flank, evidently made by a bullet, explained the bloody trail and blood-soaked space beside them. Jim was the first to see this wound, and showed it to Danny. "Somebody else came pretty near having you," he said, patting the buck's head. "But I guess they didn't need you as bad as we do."

"Won't mother be glad!" cried Danny. At that they whooped anew.

This raised the question of getting the animal home. For a moment both looked blank.

"We'll have to drag him," said Danny, at last.

Immediately they set to work to get the body out of the copse. It was no small task, the trees were so thick, but at last by dint of much tugging and lifting they accomplished it. Once outside their task was easier, though even in the open swamp the big creature dragged hard. Soon, however, they came to an old logging road where the going was comparatively easy. Once, on their homeward way a rabbit hopped slowly across in front of them. Small heed they paid to him now. "Humph!" said Jim. "Who wants *you?*"

An hour later two small boys, tired but very much alive, and one large deer, very much dead, drew up before the Harlows' door. Mrs. Harlow's astonishment at the sight of the procession may well be imagined. At first she could hardly believe her eyes, but when the boys, both talking at once, had told the story, she accepted it as a fact that it was really their game. "Well," she laughed, "you have certainly brought back a fat bird."

Danny started at once to get Dick Purcell to dress the "bird," and by eleven o'clock Mrs. Harlow had a fat roast of venison in the big oven. The remainder of the meat, together with the skin, was hung up in the granary. Promising to come again next day and cut the meat into suitable pieces for freezing and packing, Dick went away, taking with him a liberal portion of venison for his own Christmas dinner. "I take a back seat to you youngsters," he had said; which remark, coming from him, had completed their happiness.

A few minutes after he went away, and while the boys were hovering about the kitchen watching their mother turn the roast and feasting their noses on the many alluring smells that filled the air, there sounded a knock at the door.

Danny answered it promptly and found there two hunters—city sportsmen they seemed to be, judging from their natty outfits.

"Hulloa," said one, the taller of the two. "Are you the young Nimrod who shot a big buck this morning?"

"Yes, sir," said Danny, rather doubtfully. He wondered what a Nimrod was. Perhaps it had something to do with a ramrod, he thought.

"We heard about it from your neighbor whom we met down the road," said the other sportsman, "and called to see the buck if we may."

"Certainly," said Danny, and ran to get his cap. Jim went along and they led the way to the granary.

"It has been dressed," Danny said as they went in. "But you can see the head and skin. There it is."

The tall sportsman lifted the buck's head, which Dick had left attached to the skin, and looked at it with admiration. "By George, he is a beauty," he said, running his hands over the fine antlers.

His companion was intently examining the skin. "Look here!" he exclaimed suddenly. "Here's your bullet mark as sure as fate." He was pointing to the hole in the flank.

"I guess you are right," said the tall one. "That looks like my mark."

"Yes, it's our buck fast enough," replied the other.

Danny felt a sudden chill of fear. So these were the hunters who had wounded it first. And it was "their buck." They had come to take it, of course. His own buck! His own precious buck! And after Jim and he had worked so hard to get it home! A big lump came into his throat and he had to wink fast to keep back the tears. He looked at Jim. The little fellow had understood, too, and his face was as woeful as Danny's own. Slipping close to Danny he whispered, "Don't tell them about the piece in the oven."

Both sportsmen were now inspecting the buck's head. Presently the tall one turned to Danny.

"Well, young man," he said, "you certainly did a good job that time, and I congratulate you. There seems to be no doubt that this is the buck

I wounded yesterday, and which we have been following since early this morning. He led us such a long chase that we gave him up and were returning to the village when we met your friend. Now I have a proposition to make to you. That is a grand head and I want it. What do you say to twenty-five dollars for it?"

Again Danny underwent a sudden revulsion of feeling. "B-but I don't understand," he stammered. "I thought it was your buck. You shot him first."

A light dawned upon the sportsman. "And you thought I had come to take him away from you," he said. "Not much! I shot him first, yes, but you shot last and best. Here is your money. Is it a trade?"

It was. Twenty-five dollars! Danny had never seen so much money at one time in all his life before. Ten minutes later, when the sportsmen had gone, taking the head with them, Mrs. Harlow was well-nigh run over by two breathless youngsters who burst in upon her like a small cyclone.

For the second time that day she received a surprise that brought joy to her heart and for a moment rendered her speechless. Twenty-five dollars was a large sum to her, and just now it meant a good deal. She could not restrain a few tears of thankfulness as she said, "God has given us a Merry Christmas indeed."

And what a Christmas dinner that was to which they sat down two hours later. First there was roast venison, stuffed, with mealy potatoes, and turnips and squash and highbush cranberry sauce. Then came raspberry pie and pumpkin pie and pudding. And last of all there were butternuts and candy. How the boys did justice to it after their morning's work!

At last little Jim pushed back his chair, clasped both hands over his stomach, and said with a satisfied air, "I don't feel very poor, *now*."

Montana is an apt setting for a hunting story. The teenage narrator goes hunting with his mother's boyfriend, a "Communist" who drives a motorcycle. Relationships and perceptions figure prominently in the story, featuring a climactic hunt for the magnificent snow goose. It was first published in Antaeus. *Richard Ford is an accomplished writer whose stories have also appeared in* Esquire, *the* New Yorker, *and* TriQuarterly. *Among his books are* The Sportswriter *(1986),* Rock Springs: Stories *(1987), and* Women with Men *(1997).*

Richard Ford
COMMUNIST
(1985)

MY MOTHER ONCE HAD A BOYFRIEND named Glen Baxter. This was in 1961. We—my mother and I—were living in the little house my father had left her up the Sun River, near Victory, Montana, west of Great Falls. My mother was thirty-two at the time. I was sixteen. Glen Baxter was somewhere in the middle, between us, though I cannot be exact about it.

We were living then off the proceeds of my father's life insurance policies, with my mother doing some part-time waitressing work up in Great Falls and going to the bars in the evenings, which I know is where she met Glen Baxter. Sometimes he would come back with her and stay in her room at night, or she would call up from town and explain that she was staying with him in his little place on Lewis Street by the GN yards. She gave me his number every time, but I never called it. I think she probably thought that what she was doing was terrible, but simply couldn't help herself. I thought it was all right, though. Regular life it seemed, and still does. She was young, and I knew that even then.

Glen Baxter was a Communist and liked hunting, which he talked about a lot. Pheasants. Ducks. Deer. He killed all of them, he said. He had been to Vietnam as far back as then, and when he was in our house he often talked about shooting the animals over there—monkeys and beautiful parrots—using military guns just for sport. We did not know what Vietnam was then, and Glen, when he talked about that, referred to it only as "the Far East." I think now he must've been in the CIA and been disillusioned by something he saw or found out about and been thrown out, but that kind of thing did not matter to us. He was a tall, dark-eyed man with short black hair, and was usually in a good humor. He had gone halfway through college in Peoria, Illinois, he said, where he grew up. But when he was around our life he worked wheat farms as a ditcher, and stayed out of work winters and in the bars drinking with women like my mother, who had work and some money. It is not an uncommon life to lead in Montana.

What I want to explain happened in November. We had not been seeing Glen Baxter for some time. Two months had gone by. My mother knew other men, but she came home most days from work and stayed inside watching television in her bedroom and drinking beers. I asked about Glen once, and she said only that she didn't know where he was, and I assumed they had had a fight and that he was gone off on a flyer back to Illinois or Massachusetts, where he said he had relatives. I'll admit that I liked him. He had something on his mind always. He was a labor man as well as a Communist, and liked to say that the country was poisoned by the rich, and strong men would need to bring it to life again, and I liked that because my father had been a labor man, which was why we had a house to live in and money coming through. It was also true that I'd had a few boxing bouts by then—just with town boys and one with an Indian from Choteau—and there were some girlfriends I knew from that. I did not like my mother being around the house so much at night, and I wished Glen Baxter would come back, or that another man would come along and entertain her somewhere else.

At two o'clock on a Saturday, Glen drove up into our yard in a car. He had had a big brown Harley-Davidson that he rode most of the year, in his black-and-red irrigators and a baseball cap turned backwards. But this time he had a car, a blue Nash Ambassador. My mother and I went out on the porch when he stopped inside the olive trees my father had planted as a shelter belt, and my mother had a look on her face of not much pleasure. It was starting to be cold in earnest by then. Snow was down already onto the Fairfield Bench, though on this day a chinook was blowing, and it could as easily have been spring, though the sky above the Divide was turning over in silver and blue clouds of winter.

"We haven't seen you in a long time, I guess," my mother said coldly.

"My little retarded sister died," Glen said, standing at the door of his old car. He was wearing his orange VFW jacket and canvas shoes we called wino shoes, something I had never seen him wear before. He seemed to be in a good humor. "We buried her in Florida near the home."

"That's a good place," my mother said in a voice that meant she was a wronged party in something.

"I want to take this boy hunting today, Aileen," Glen said. "There're snow geese down now. But we have to go right away, or they'll be gone to Idaho by tomorrow."

"He doesn't care to go," my mother said.

"Yes I do," I said, and looked at her.

My mother frowned at me. "Why do you?"

"Why does he need a reason?" Glen Baxter said and grinned.

"I want him to have one, that's why." She looked at me oddly. "I think Glen's drunk, Les."

"No, I'm not drinking," Glen said, which was hardly ever true. He looked at both of us, and my mother bit down on the side of her lower lip and stared at me in a way to make you think she thought something was being put over on her and she didn't like you for it. She was very pretty, though when she was mad her features were sharpened and less pretty by a long way. "All right, then I don't care," she said to no one in particular. "Hunt, kill, maim. Your father did that too." She turned to go back inside.

"Why don't you come with us, Aileen?" Glen was smiling still, pleased.

"To do what?" my mother said. She stopped and pulled a package of cigarettes out of her dress pocket and put one in her mouth.

"It's worth seeing."

"See dead animals?" my mother said.

"These geese are from Siberia, Aileen," Glen said. "They're not like a lot of geese. Maybe I'll buy us dinner later. What do you say?"

"But what with?" my mother said. To tell the truth, I didn't know why she was so mad at him. I would've thought she'd be glad to see him. But she just suddenly seemed to hate everything about him.

"I've got some money," Glen said. "Let me spend it on a pretty girl tonight."

"Find one of those and you're lucky," my mother said, turning away toward the front door.

"I already found one," Glen Baxter said. But the door slammed behind her, and he looked at me then with a look I think now was helplessness, though I could not see a way to change anything.

My mother sat in the backseat of Glen's Nash and looked out the window while we drove. My double gun was in the seat between us beside Glen's Belgian pump, which he kept loaded with five shells in case, he said, he saw something beside the road he wanted to shoot. I had hunted rabbits before, and had ground-sluiced pheasants and other birds, but I had never been on an actual hunt before, one where you drove out to some special place and did it formally. And I was excited. I had a feeling that something important was about to happen to me, and that this would be a day I would always remember.

My mother did not say anything for a long time, and neither did I. We drove up through Great Falls and out the other side toward Fort Benton, which was on the benchland where wheat was grown.

"Geese mate for life," my mother said, just out of the blue, as we were driving. "I hope you know that. They're special birds."

"I know that," Glen said in the front seat. "I have every respect for them."

"So where were you for three months?" she said. "I'm only curious."

"I was in the Big Hole for a while," Glen said, "and after that I went over to Douglas, Wyoming."

"What were you planning to do there?" my mother asked.

"I wanted to find a job, but it didn't work out."

"I'm going to college," she said suddenly, and this was something I had never heard about before. I turned to look at her, but she was staring out her window and wouldn't see me.

"I knew French once," Glen said, "*Rosé*'s pink. *Rouge*'s red." He glanced at me and smiled. "I think that's a wise idea, Aileen. When are you going to start?"

"I don't want Les to think he was raised by crazy people all his life," my mother said.

"Les ought to go himself," Glen said.

"After I go, he will."

"What do you say about that, Les?" Glen said, grinning.

"He says it's just fine," my mother said.

"It's just fine," I said.

Where Glen Baxter took us was out onto the high flat prairie that was disked for wheat and had high, high mountains out to the east, with lower heartbreak hills in between. It was, I remember, a day for blues in the sky, and down in the distance we could see the small town of Floweree, and the state highway running past it toward Fort Benton and the Hi-line. We drove out on top of the prairie on a muddy dirt road fenced on both sides, until we had gone about three miles, which is where Glen stopped.

"All right," he said, looking up in the rearview mirror at my mother. "You wouldn't think there was anything here, would you?"

"*We're* here," my mother said. "You brought us here."

"You'll be glad though," Glen said, and seemed confident to me. I had looked around myself but could not see anything. No water or trees, nothing that seemed like a good place to hunt anything. Just wasted land. "There's a big lake out there, Les," Glen said. "You can't see it now from here because it's low. But the geese are there. You'll see."

"It's like the moon out here, I recognize that," my mother said, "only it's worse." She was staring out at the flat wheatland as if she could actually see something in particular, and wanted to know more about it. "How'd you find this place?"

"I came once on the wheat push," Glen said.

"And I'm sure the owner told you just to come back and hunt anytime you like and bring anybody you wanted. Come one, come all. Is that it?"

"People shouldn't own land anyway," Glen said. "Anybody should be able to use it."

"Les, Glen's going to poach here," my mother said. "I just want you to know that, because that's a crime and the law will get you for it. If you're a man now, you're going to have to face the consequences."

"That's not true," Glen Baxter said, and looked gloomily out over the steering wheel down the muddy road toward the mountains. Though for myself I believed it was true, and didn't care. I didn't care about anything at that moment except seeing geese fly over me and shooting them down.

"Well, I'm certainly not going out there," my mother said. "I like towns better, and I already have enough trouble."

"That's okay," Glen said. "When the geese lift up you'll get to see them. That's all I wanted. Les and me'll go shoot them, won't we, Les?"

"Yes," I said, and I put my hand on my shotgun, which had been my father's and was heavy as rocks.

"Then we should go on," Glen said, "or we'll waste our light."

We got out of the car with our guns. Glen took off his canvas shoes and put on his pair of black irrigators out of the trunk. Then we crossed the barbed wire fence, and walked out into the high, tilled field toward nothing. I looked back at my mother when we were still not so far away, but I could only see the small, dark top of her head, low in the backseat of the Nash, staring out and thinking what I could not then begin to say.

On the walk toward the lake, Glen began talking to me. I had never been alone with him, and knew little about him except what my mother said—that he drank too much, or other times that he was the nicest man she had ever known in the world and that someday a woman would marry him, though she didn't think it would be her. Glen told me as we walked that he wished he had finished college, but that it was too late now, that his mind was too old. He said he had liked the Far East very much, and that people there knew how to treat each other, and that he would go back some day but couldn't go now. He said also that he would like to live in Russia for a while and mentioned the names of people who had gone there, names I didn't know. He said it would be hard at first, because it was so different, but that pretty soon anyone would learn to like it and wouldn't want to live anywhere else, and that Russians treated Americans who came to live there like kings. There were Communists everywhere now, he said. You didn't know them, but they were there. Montana had a large number, and he was in touch with all of them. He said that Communists were always in danger and that he had to protect himself all the time. And when he said that he pulled back his VFW jacket and showed me the butt of a pistol he had stuck under his shirt against his bare skin. "There are people who want to kill me right now," he said, "and I would kill a man myself if I thought I had to." And we kept walking. Though in a while he said, "I don't think I know much about you, Les. But I'd like to. What do you like to do?"

"I like to box," I said. "My father did it. It's a good thing to know."

"I suppose you have to protect yourself too," Glen said.

"I know how to," I said.

"Do you like to watch TV," Glen asked, and smiled.

"Not much."

"I love to," Glen said. "I could watch it instead of eating if I had one."

I looked out straight ahead over the green tops of sage that grew to the edge of the disked field, hoping to see the lake Glen said was there. There was an airishness and a sweet smell that I thought might be the place we were going, but I couldn't see it. "How will we hunt these geese?" I said.

"It won't be hard," Glen said. "Most hunting isn't even hunting. It's only shooting. And that's what this will be. In Illinois you would dig holes in the ground and hide and set out your decoys. Then the geese come to you, over and over again. But we don't have time for that here." He glanced at me. "You have to be sure the first time here."

"How do you know they're here now," I asked. And I looked toward the Highwood Mountains twenty miles away, half in snow and half dark blue at the bottom. I could see the little town of Floweree then, looking shabby and dimly lighted in the distance. A red bar sign shone. A car moved slowly away from the scattered buildings.

"They always come November first," Glen said.

"Are we going to poach them?"

"Does it make any difference to you," Glen asked.

"No, it doesn't."

"Well then, we aren't," he said.

We walked then for a while without talking. I looked back once to see the Nash far and small in the flat distance. I couldn't see my mother, and I thought that she must've turned on the radio and gone to sleep, which she always did, letting it play all night in her bedroom. Behind the car the sun was nearing the rounded mountains southwest of us, and I knew that when the sun was gone it would be cold. I wished my mother had decided to come along with us, and I thought for a moment of how little I really knew her at all.

Glen walked with me another quarter-mile, crossed another barbed wire fence where sage was growing, then went a hundred yards through wheatgrass and spurge until the ground went up and formed a kind of long hillock bunker built by a farmer against the wind. And I realized the lake was just beyond us. I could hear the sound of a car horn blowing and a dog barking all the way down in the town, then the wind seemed to move and all I could hear then and after then were geese. So many geese, from the sound of them, though I still could not see even one. I stood and listened to the high-pitched shouting sound, a sound I had never heard so close, a sound with size to it—though it was not loud. A sound that meant great numbers and that made your chest rise and your shoulders tighten with expectancy. It was a sound to make you feel separate from it and everything else, as if you were of no importance in the grand scheme of things.

"Do you hear them singing," Glen asked. He held his hand up to make me stand still. And we both listened. "How many do you think, Les, just hearing?"

"A hundred," I said. "More than a hundred."

"Five thousand," Glen said. "More than you can believe when you see them. Go see."

I put down my gun and on my hands and knees crawled up the earthwork through the wheatgrass and thistle, until I could see down to the lake and see the geese. And they were there, like a white bandage laid on the water, wide and long and continuous, a white expanse of snow geese, seventy yards from me, on the bank, but stretching far onto the lake, which was large itself—a half-mile across, with thick tules on the far side and wild plums farther and the blue mountain behind them.

"Do you see the big raft?" Glen said from below me, in a whisper.

"I see it," I said, still looking. It was such a thing to see, a view I had never seen and have not since.

"Are any on the land?" he said.

"Some are in the wheatgrass," I said, "but most are swimming."

"Good," Glen said. "They'll have to fly. But we can't wait for that now."

And I crawled backwards down the heel of land to where Glen was, and my gun. We were losing our light, and the air was purplish and cooling. I looked toward the car but couldn't see it, and I was no longer sure where it was below the lighted sky.

"Where do they fly to?" I said in a whisper, since I did not want anything to be ruined because of what I did or said. It was important to Glen to shoot the geese, and it was important to me.

"To the wheat," he said. "Or else they leave for good. I wish your mother had come, Les. Now she'll be sorry."

I could hear the geese quarreling and shouting on the lake surface. And I wondered if they knew we were here now. "She might be," I said with my heart pounding, but I didn't think she would be much.

It was a simple plan he had. I would stay behind the bunker, and he would crawl on his belly with his gun through the wheatgrass as near to the geese as he could. Then he would simply stand up and shoot all the ones he could close up, both in the air and on the ground. And when all the others flew up, with luck some would turn toward me as they came into the wind, and then I could shoot them and turn them back to him, and he would shoot them again. He could kill ten, he said, if he was lucky, and I might kill four. It didn't seem hard.

"Don't show them your face," Glen said. "Wait till you think you can touch them, then stand up and shoot. To hesitate is lost in this."

"All right," I said. "I'll try it."

"Shoot one in the head, and then shoot another one," Glen said. "It won't be hard." He patted me on the arm and smiled. Then he took off his VFW jacket and put it on the ground, climbed up the side of the bunker, cradling his shotgun in his arms, and slid on his belly into the dry stalks of yellow grass out of my sight.

Then, for the first time in that entire day, I was alone. And I didn't mind it. I sat squat down in the grass, loaded my double gun and took my other two shells out of my pocket to hold. I pushed the safety off and on to see that it was right. The wind rose a little, scuffed the grass and made me shiver. It was not the warm chinook now, but a wind out of the north, the one geese flew away from if they could.

Then I thought about my mother, in the car alone, and how much longer I would stay with her, and what it might mean to her for me to leave. And I wondered when Glen Baxter would die and if someone would kill him, or whether my mother would marry him and how I would feel about it. And though I didn't know why, it occurred to me that Glen Baxter and I would not be friends when all was said and done, since I didn't care if he ever married my mother or didn't.

Then I thought about boxing and what my father had taught me about it. To tighten your fists hard. To strike out straight from the shoulder and never punch backing up. How to cut a punch by snapping your fist inwards, how to carry your chin low, and to step toward a man when he is falling so you can hit him again. And most important, to keep your eyes open when you are hitting in the face and causing damage, because you need to see what you're doing to encourage yourself, and because it is when you close your eyes that you stop hitting and get hurt badly. "Fly all over your man, Les," my father said. "When you see your chance, fly on him and hit him till he falls." That, I thought, would always be my attitude in things.

And then I heard the geese again, their voices in unison, louder and shouting, as if the wind had changed again and put all new sounds in the cold air. And then a *boom*. And I knew Glen was in among them and had stood up to shoot. The noise of geese rose and grew worse, and my fingers burned where I held my gun too tight to the metal, and I put it down and opened my fist to make the burning stop so I could feel the trigger when the moment came. *Boom*, Glen shot again, and I heard him shuck a shell, and all the sounds out beyond the bunker seemed to be rising—the geese, the shots, the air itself going up. *Boom*, Glen shot another time, and I knew he was taking his careful time to make his shots good. And I held my gun and started to crawl up the bunker so as not to be surprised when the geese came over me and I could shoot.

From the top I saw Glen Baxter alone in the wheatgrass field, shooting at a white goose with black tips of wings that was on the ground not far from him, but trying to run and pull into the air. He shot it once more, and it fell over dead with its wings flapping.

Glen looked back at me and his face was distorted and strange. The air around him was full of white rising geese and he seemed to want them all. "Behind you, Les," he yelled at me and pointed. "They're all behind you now." I looked behind me, and there were geese in the air as far as I could see, more than I knew how many, moving so slowly, their wings wide out and working calmly and filling the air with noise, though their voices were not as loud or as shrill as I had thought they would be. And they were so close! Forty feet, some of them. The air around me vibrated and I could feel the wind from their wings and it seemed to me I could kill as many as the times I could shoot—a hundred or a thousand—and I raised my gun, put the muzzle on the head of a white goose, and fired. It shuddered in the air, its wide feet sank below its belly, its wings cradled out to hold back air, and it fell straight down and landed with an awful sound, a noise a human would make, a thick, soft, *hump* noise. I looked up again and shot another goose, could hear the pellets hit its chest, but it didn't fall or even break its pattern for flying. *Boom*, Glen shot again. And then again. "Hey," I heard him shout, "Hey, hey." And there were geese flying over me, flying in line after line. I broke my gun and reloaded, and thought to myself as I did: I need confidence here, I need to be sure with this. I pointed at another goose and shot it in the head, and it fell the way the first one had, wings out, its belly down, and with the same thick noise of hitting. Then I sat down in the grass on the bunker and let geese fly over me.

By now the whole raft was in the air, all of it moving in a slow swirl above me and the lake and everywhere, finding the wind and heading out south in long wavering lines that caught the last sun and turned to silver as they gained a distance. It was a thing to see, I will tell you now. Five thousand white geese all in the air around you, making a noise like you have never heard before. And I thought to myself then: this is something I will never see again. I will never forget this. And I was right.

Glen Baxter shot twice more. One he missed, but with the other he hit a goose flying away from him, and knocked it half falling and flying into the empty lake not far from shore, where it began to swim as though it was fine and make its noise.

Glen stood in the stubby grass, looked out at the goose, his gun lowered. "I didn't need to shoot that one, did I, Les?"

"I don't know," I said, sitting on the little knoll of land, looking at the goose swimming in the water.

"I don't know why I shoot 'em. They're so beautiful." He looked at me.

"I don't know either," I said.

Maybe there's nothing else to do with them." Glen stared at the goose again and shook his head. "Maybe this is exactly what they're put on earth for."

I did not know what to say because I did not know what he could mean by that, though what I felt was embarrassment at the great numbers of geese there were, and a dulled feeling like a hunger because the shooting had stopped and it was over for me now.

Glen began to pick up his geese, and I walked down to my two that had fallen close together and were dead. One had hit with such an impact that its stomach had split and some of its inward parts were knocked out. Though the other looked unhurt, its soft white belly turned up like a pillow, its head and jagged bill-teeth, its tiny black eyes looking as they would if they were alive.

"What's happened to the hunters out here?" I heard a voice speak. It was my mother, standing in her pink dress on the knoll above us, hugging her arms. She was smiling though she was cold. And I realized that I had lost all thought of her in the shooting. "Who did all this shooting? Is this your work, Les?"

"No," I said.

"Les is a hunter, though, Aileen," Glen said. "He takes his time." He was holding two white geese by their necks, one in each hand, and he was smiling. He and my mother seemed pleased.

"I see you didn't miss too many," my mother said and smiled. I could tell she admired Glen for his geese, and that she had done some thinking in the car alone. "It *was* wonderful, Glen," she said. "I've never seen anything like that. They were like snow."

"It's worth seeing once, isn't it?" Glen said. "I should've killed more, but I got excited."

My mother looked at me then. "Where's yours, Les?"

"Here," I said and pointed to my two geese on the ground beside me.

My mother nodded in a nice way, and I think she liked everything then and wanted the day to turn out right and for all of us to be happy. "Six, then. You've got six in all."

"One's still out there," I said, and motioned where the one goose was swimming in circles on the water.

"Okay," my mother said and put her hand over her eyes to look. "Where is it?"

Glen Baxter looked at me then with a strange smile, a smile that said he wished I had never mentioned anything about the other goose. And I wished I hadn't either. I looked up in the sky and could see the lines of geese by the thousands shining silver in the light, and I wished we could just leave and go home.

"That one's my mistake there," Glen Baxter said and grinned. "I shouldn't have shot that one, Aileen. I got too excited."

My mother looked out on the lake for a minute, then looked at Glen and back again. "Poor goose." She shook her head. "How will you get it, Glen?"

"I can't get that one now," Glen said.

My mother looked at him. "What do you mean?"

"I'm going to leave that one," Glen said.

"Well, no. You can't leave one," my mother said. "You shot it. You have to get it. Isn't that a rule?"

"No," Glen said.

And my mother looked from Glen to me. "Wade out and get it, Glen," she said in a sweet way, and my mother looked young then, like a young girl, in her flimsy short-sleeved waitress dress and her skinny, bare legs in the wheatgrass.

"No." Glen Baxter looked down at his gun and shook his head. And I didn't know why he wouldn't go, because it would've been easy. The lake was shallow. And you could tell that anyone could've walked out a long way before it got deep, and Glen had on his boots.

My mother looked at the white goose, which was not more than thirty yards from the shore, its head up, moving in slow circles, its wings settled and relaxed so you could see the black tips. "Wade out and get it, Glenny, won't you, please?" she said. "They're special things."

"You don't understand the world, Aileen," Glen said. "This can happen. It doesn't matter."

"But that's so cruel, Glen," she said, and a sweet smile came on her lips.

"Raise up your own arms, 'Leeny," Glen said. "I can't see any angel's wings, can you, Les?" He looked at me, but I looked away.

"Then you go on and get it, Les," my mother said. "You weren't raised by crazy people." I started to go, but Glen Baxter suddenly grabbed me by my shoulder and pulled me back hard, so hard his fingers made bruises in my skin that I saw later.

"Nobody's going," he said. "This is over with now."

And my mother gave Glen a cold look then. "You don't have a heart, Glen," she said. "There's nothing to love in you. You're just a son of a bitch, that's all."

And Glen Baxter nodded at my mother, then, as if he understood something he had not understood before, but something that he was willing to know. "Fine," he said, "that's fine." And he took his big pistol out from against his belly, the big blue revolver I had only seen part of before and that he said protected him, and he pointed it out at the goose on the water, his arm straight away from him, and shot and missed. And then he shot and missed again. The goose made its noise once. And then he hit it dead, because there was no splash. And then he shot it three times more until the gun was empty and the goose's head was down and it was floating toward the middle of the lake where it was empty and dark blue. "Now who has a heart?" Glen said. But my mother was not there when he turned around. She had already started back to the car and was almost lost from sight in the darkness. And Glen smiled at me then and his face had a wild look on it. "Okay, Les?" he said.

"Okay," I said.

"There're limits to everything, right?"

"I guess so," I said.

"Your mother's a beautiful woman, but she's not the only beautiful woman in Montana." And I did not say anything. And Glen Baxter suddenly said, "Here," and he held the pistol out at me. "Don't you want this? Don't you want to shoot me? Nobody thinks they'll die. But I'm ready for it right now." And I did not know what to do then. Though it is true that what I wanted to do was to hit him, hit him as hard in the face as I could, and see him on the ground bleeding and crying and pleading for me to stop. Only at that moment he looked scared to me, and I had never seen a grown man scared before—though I have seen one since—and I felt sorry for him, as though he was already a dead man. And I did not end up hitting him at all.

A light can go out in the heart. All of this happened years ago, but I still can feel now how sad and remote the world was to me. Glen Baxter, I think now, was not a bad man, only a man scared of something he'd never seen before—something soft in himself—his life going a way he didn't like. A woman with a son. Who could blame him there? I don't know what makes people do what they do, or call themselves what they call themselves, only that you have to live someone's life to be the expert.

My mother had tried to see the good side of things, tried to be hopeful in the situation she was handed, tried to look out for us both, and it hadn't worked. It was a strange time in her life then and after that, a time when she had to adjust to being an adult just when she was on the thin edge of things. Too much awareness too early in life was her problem, I think.

And what I felt was only that I had somehow been pushed out into the world, into the real life then, the one I hadn't lived yet. In a year I was gone to hard-rock mining and no-paycheck jobs and not to college. And I have thought more than once about my mother saying that I had not been raised by crazy people, and I don't know what that could mean or what difference it could make, unless it means that love is a reliable commodity, and even that is not always true, as I have found out.

Late on the night that all this took place I was in bed when I heard my mother say, "Come outside, Les. Come and hear this." And I went out onto the front porch barefoot and in my underwear, where it was warm like spring, and there was a spring mist in the air. I could see the lights of the Fairfield Coach in the distance, on its way up to Great Falls.

And I could hear geese, white birds in the sky, flying. They made their high-pitched sound like angry yells, and though I couldn't see them high up, it seemed to me they were everywhere. And my mother looked up and said, "Hear them?" I could smell her hair wet from the shower. "They leave with the moon," she said. "It's still half wild out here."

And I said, "I hear them," and I felt a chill come over my bare chest, and the hair stood up on my arms the way it does before a storm. And for a while we listened.

"When I first married your father, you know, we lived on a street called Bluebird Canyon, in California. And I thought that was the prettiest street and the prettiest name. I suppose no one brings you up like your first love. You don't mind if I say that, do you?" She looked at me hopefully.

"No," I said.

"We have to keep civilization alive somehow." And she pulled her little housecoat together because there was a cold vein in the air, a part of the cold that would be on us the next day. "I don't feel part of things tonight, I guess."

"It's all right," I said.

"Do you know where I'd like to go?"

"No," I said. And I suppose I knew she was angry then, angry with life, but did not want to show me that.

"To the Straits of Juan de Fuca. Wouldn't that be something? Would you like that?"

"I'd like it," I said. And my mother looked off for a minute, as if she could see the Straits of Juan de Fuca out against the line of mountains, see the lights of things alive and a whole new world.

"I know you liked him," she said after a moment. "You and I both suffer fools too well."

"I didn't like him too much," I said. "I really didn't care."

"He'll fall on his face. I'm sure of that," she said. And I didn't say anything because I didn't care about Glen Baxter anymore, and was happy not to talk about him. "Would you tell me something if I asked you? Would you tell me the truth?"

"Yes," I said.

And my mother did not look at me. "Just tell the truth," she said.

"All right," I said.

"Do you think I'm still very feminine? I'm thirty-two years old now. You don't know what that means. But do you think I am?"

And I stood at the edge of the porch, with the olive trees before me, looking straight up into the mist where I could not see geese but could still hear them flying, could almost feel the air move below their white wings. And I felt the way you feel when you are on a trestle all alone and the train is coming, and you know you have to decide. And I said, "Yes, I do." Because that was the truth. And I tried to think of something else then and did not hear what my mother said after that.

And how old was I then? Sixteen. Sixteen is young, but it can also be a grown man. I am forty-one years old now, and I think about that time without regret, though my mother and I never talked in that way again, and I have not heard her voice now in a long, long time.

Ernest Hemingway (1898–1961), one of the most celebrated authors of the twentieth century, has become an almost mythical figure in world literature. Born in Oak Park, Illinois, Hemingway volunteered as an ambulance driver on the Italian front in World War I and was severely wounded while serving with the infantry. After the war he settled in Paris, where his writing career really took off with the publication of The Sun Also Rises *(1926). This was followed by other classic novels such as* A Farewell to Arms *(1929),* For Whom the Bell Tolls *(1939), and* The Old Man and the Sea *(1952). Hemingway also wrote a definitive treatise on bullfighting,* Death in the Afternoon *(1932), and an account of big-game hunting called* Green Hills of Africa *(1935). He was awarded the Nobel Prize in 1954. Hemingway was one of the most important influences on the development of the short story in American fiction. Many observers think that the one below is his best.*

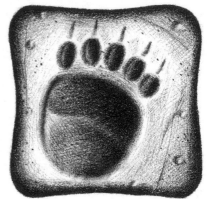

Ernest Hemingway
THE SHORT HAPPY LIFE OF FRANCIS MACOMBER (1936)

IT WAS NOW LUNCH TIME and they were all sitting under the double green fly of the dining tent pretending that nothing had happened.

"Will you have lime juice or lemon squash?" Macomber asked.

"I'll have a gimlet," Robert Wilson told him.

"I'll have a gimlet too. I need something," Macomber's wife said.

"I suppose it's the thing to do," Macomber agreed. "Tell him to make three gimlets."

The mess boy had started them already, lifting the bottles out of the canvas cooling bags that sweated wet in the wind that blew through the trees that shaded the tents.

"What had I ought to give them?" Macomber asked.

"A quid would be plenty," Wilson told him. "You don't want to spoil them."

"Will the headman distribute it?"

"Absolutely."

Francis Macomber had, half an hour before, been carried to his tent from the edge of the camp in triumph on the arms and shoulders of the cook, the personal boys, the skinner and the porters. The gun-bearers had taken no part in the demonstration. When the native boys put him down at the door of his tent, he had shaken all their hands, received their congratulations, and then gone into the tent and sat on the bed until his wife came in. She did not speak to him when she came in and he left the tent at once to wash his face and hands in the portable wash basin outside and go over to the dining tent to sit in a comfortable canvas chair in the breeze and the shade.

"You've got your lion," Robert Wilson said to him, "and a damned fine one too."

Mrs. Macomber looked at Wilson quickly. She was an extremely handsome and well-kept woman of the beauty and social position which had, five years before, commanded five thousand dollars as the price of endorsing, with photographs, a beauty product which she had never used. She had been married to Francis Macomber for eleven years.

"He is a good lion, isn't he?" Macomber said. His wife looked at him now. She looked at both these men as though she had never seen them before.

One, Wilson, the white hunter, she knew she had never truly seen before. He was about middle height with sandy hair, a stubby mustache, a very red face and extremely cold blue eyes with faint white wrinkles at the corners that grooved merrily when he smiled. He smiled at her now and she looked away from his face at the way his shoulders sloped in the loose tunic he wore with the four big cartridges held in loops where the left breast pocket should have been, at his big brown hands, his old slacks, his very dirty boots and back to his red face again. She noticed where the baked red of his face stopped in a white line that marked the circle left by his Stetson hat that hung now from one of the pegs of the tent pole.

"Well, here's to the lion," Robert Wilson said. He smiled at her again and, not smiling, she looked curiously at her husband.

Francis Macomber was very tall, very well built if you did not mind that length of bone, dark, his hair cropped like an oarsman, rather thin-lipped, and was considered handsome. He was dressed in the same sort of safari clothes that Wilson wore except that his were new, he was thirty-five years old, kept himself very fit, was good at court games, had a number of big-game fishing records, and had just shown himself, very publicly, to be a coward.

"Here's to the lion," he said. "I can't ever thank you for what you did."

Margaret, his wife, looked away from him and back to Wilson.

"Let's not talk about the lion," she said.

Wilson looked over at her without smiling and now she smiled at him.

"It's been a very strange day," she said. "Hadn't you ought to put your hat on even under the canvas at noon? You told me that, you know."

"Might put it on," said Wilson.

"You know you have a very red face, Mr. Wilson," she told him and smiled again.

"Drink," said Wilson.

"I don't think so," she said. "Francis drinks a great deal, but his face is never red."

"It's red today," Macomber tried a joke.

"No," said Margaret. "It's mine that's red today. But Mr. Wilson's is always red."

"Must be racial," said Wilson. "I say, you wouldn't like to drop my beauty as a topic, would you?"

"I've just started on it."

"Let's chuck it," said Wilson.

"Conversation is going to be so difficult," Margaret said.

"Don't be silly, Margot," her husband said.

"No difficulty," Wilson said. "Got a damn fine lion."

Margot looked at them both and they both saw that she was going to cry. Wilson had seen it coming for a long time and he dreaded it. Macomber was past dreading it.

"I wish it hadn't happened. Oh, I wish it hadn't happened," she said and started for her tent. She made no noise of crying but they could see that her shoulders were shaking under the rose-colored, sun-proofed shirt she wore.

"Women upset," said Wilson to the tall man. "Amounts to nothing. Strain on the nerves and one thing'n another."

"No," said Macomber. "I suppose that I rate that for the rest of my life now."

"Nonsense. Let's have a spot of the giant killer," said Wilson. "Forget the whole thing. Nothing to it anyway."

"We might try," said Macomber. "I won't forget what you did for me though."

"Nothing," said Wilson. "All nonsense."

So they sat there in the shade where the camp was pitched under some wide-topped acacia trees with a boulder-strewn cliff behind them, and a stretch of grass that ran to the bank of a boulder-filled stream in front with forest beyond it, and drank their just-cool lime drinks and avoided one another's eyes while the boys set the table for lunch. Wilson could tell that the boys all knew about it now and when he saw Macomber's personal boy looking curiously at his master while he was putting dishes on the table he snapped at him in Swahili. The boy turned away with his face blank.

"What were you telling him?" Macomber asked.

"Nothing. Told him to look alive or I'd see he got about fifteen of the best."

"What's that? Lashes?"

"It's quite illegal," Wilson said. "You're supposed to fine them."

"Do you still have them whipped?"

"Oh, yes. They could raise a row if they chose to complain. But they don't. They prefer it to the fines."

"How strange!" said Macomber.

"Not strange, really," Wilson said. "Which would you rather do? Take a good birching or lose your pay?"

Then he felt embarrassed at asking it and before Macomber could answer he went on, "We all take a beating every day, you know, one way or another."

This was no better. "Good God," he thought. "I am a diplomat, aren't I?"

"Yes, we take a beating," said Macomber, still not looking at him. "I'm awfully sorry about that lion business. It doesn't have to go any further, does it? I mean no one will hear about it, will they?"

"You mean will I tell it at the Mathaiga Club?" Wilson looked at him now coldly. He had not expected this. So he's a bloody four-letter man as well as a bloody coward, he thought. I rather liked him too until today. But how is one to know about an American?

"No," said Wilson. "I'm a professional hunter. We never talk about our clients. You can be quite easy on that. It's supposed to be bad form to ask us not to talk though."

He had decided now that to break would be much easier. He would eat, then, by himself and could read a book with his meals. They would eat by themselves. He would see them through the safari on a very formal basis—what was it the French called it? Distinguished consideration—and it would be a damn sight easier than having to go through this emotional trash. He'd insult him and make a good clean break. Then he could read a book with his meals and he'd still be drinking their whisky. That was the phrase for it when a safari went bad. You ran into another white hunter and you asked, "How is everything going?" and he answered, "Oh, I'm still drinking their whisky," and you knew everything had gone to pot.

"I'm sorry," Macomber said and looked at him with his American face that would stay adolescent until it became middle-aged, and Wilson noted his crew-cropped hair, fine eyes only faintly shifty, good nose, thin lips and handsome jaw. "I'm sorry I didn't realize that. There are lots of things I don't know."

So what could he do, Wilson thought. He was all ready to break it off quickly and neatly and here the beggar was apologizing after he had just insulted him. He made one more attempt. "Don't worry about me talking," he said. "I have a living to make. You know in Africa no woman ever misses her lion and no white man ever bolts."

"I bolted like a rabbit," Macomber said.

Now what in hell were you going to do about a man who talked like that, Wilson wondered.

Wilson looked at Macomber with his flat, blue, machine-gunner's eyes and the other smiled back at him. He had a pleasant smile if you did not notice how his eyes showed when he was hurt.

"Maybe I can fix it up on buffalo," he said. "We're after them next, aren't we?"

"In the morning if you like," Wilson told him. Perhaps he had been wrong. This was certainly the way to take it. You most certainly could not tell a damned thing about an American. He was all for Macomber again. If you could forget the morning. But, of course, you couldn't. The morning had been about as bad as they come.

"Here comes the Memsahib," he said. She was walking over from her tent looking refreshed and cheerful and quite lovely. She had a very perfect oval face, so perfect that you expected her to be stupid. But she wasn't stupid, Wilson thought, no, not stupid.

"How is the beautiful red-faced Mr. Wilson? Are you feeling better, Francis, my pearl?"

"Oh, much," said Macomber.

"I've dropped the whole thing," she said, sitting down at the table. "What importance is there to whether Francis is any good at killing lions? That's not his trade. That's Mr. Wilson's trade. Mr. Wilson is really very impressive killing anything. You do kill anything, don't you?"

"Oh, anything," said Wilson. "Simply anything." They are, he thought, the hardest in the world; the hardest, the cruelest, the most predatory and the most attractive and their men have softened or gone to pieces nervously as they have hardened. Or is it that they pick men they can handle? They can't know that much at the age they marry, he thought.

He was grateful that he had gone through his education on American women before now because this was a very attractive one.

"We're going after buff in the morning," he told her.

"I'm coming," she said.

"No, you're not."

"Oh, yes, I am. Mayn't I, Francis?"

"Why not stay in camp?"

"Not for anything," she said. "I wouldn't miss something like today for anything."

When she left, Wilson was thinking, when she went off to cry, she seemed a hell of a fine woman. She seemed to understand, to realize, to be hurt for him and for herself and to know how things really stood. She is away for twenty minutes and now she is back, simply enamelled in that American female cruelty. They are the damnedest women. Really the damnedest.

"We'll put on another show for you tomorrow," Francis Macomber said.

"You're not coming," Wilson said.

"You're very mistaken," she told him. "And I want *so* to see you perform again. You were lovely this morning. That is if blowing things' heads off is lovely."

"Here's the lunch," said Wilson. "You're very merry, aren't you?"

"Why not? I didn't come out here to be dull."

"Well, it hasn't been dull," Wilson said. He could see the boulders in the river and the high bank beyond with the trees and he remembered the morning.

"Oh, no," she said. "It's been charming. And tomorrow. You don't know how I look forward to tomorrow."

"That's eland he's offering you," Wilson said.

"They're the big cowy things that jump like hares, aren't they?"

"I suppose that describes them," Wilson said.

"It's very good meat," Macomber said.

"Did you shoot it, Francis?" she asked.

"Yes."

"They're not dangerous, are they?"

"Only if they fall on you," Wilson told her.

"I'm so glad."

"Why not let up on the bitchery just a little, Margot," Macomber said, cutting the eland steak and putting some mashed potato, gravy and carrot on the down-turned fork that tined through the piece of meat.

"I suppose I could," she said, "since you put it so prettily."

"Tonight we'll have champagne for the lion," Wilson said. "It's a bit too hot at noon."

"Oh, the lion," Margot said. "I'd forgotten the lion!"

So, Robert Wilson thought to himself, she *is* giving him a ride, isn't she? Or do you suppose that's her idea of putting up a good show? How should a woman act when she discovers her husband is a bloody coward? She's damn cruel but they're all cruel. They govern, of course, and to govern one has to be cruel sometimes. Still, I've seen enough of their damn terrorism.

"Have some more eland," he said to her politely.

That afternoon, late, Wilson and Macomber went out in the motor car with the native driver and the two gun-bearers. Mrs. Macomber stayed in the camp. It was too hot to go out, she said, and she was going with them in the early morning. As they drove off Wilson saw her standing under the big tree, looking pretty rather than beautiful in her faintly rosy khaki, her dark hair drawn back off her forehead and gathered in a knot low on her neck, her face as fresh, he thought, as though she were in England. She waved to them as the car went off through the swale of high grass and curved around through the trees into the small hills of orchard bush.

In the orchard bush they found a herd of impala, and leaving the car they stalked one old ram with long, wide-spread horns and Macomber killed it with a very creditable shot that knocked the buck down at a good two hundred yards and sent the herd off bounding wildly and leaping over one another's backs in long, leg-drawn-up leaps as unbelievable and as floating as those one makes sometimes in dreams.

"That was a good shot," Wilson said. "They're a small target."

"Is it a worth-while head?" Macomber asked.

"It's excellent," Wilson told him. "You shoot like that and you'll have no trouble."

"Do you think we'll find buffalo tomorrow?"

"There's a good chance of it. They feed out early in the morning and with luck we may catch them in the open.

"I'd like to clear away that lion business," Macomber said. "It's not very pleasant to have your wife see you do something like that."

I should think it would be even more unpleasant to do it, Wilson thought, wife or no wife, or to talk about it having done it. But he said, "I wouldn't think about that any more. Any one could be upset by his first lion. That's all over."

But that night after dinner and a whisky and soda by the fire before going to bed, as Francis Macomber lay on his cot with the mosquito bar over him and listened to the night noises it was not all over. It was neither all over nor was it beginning. It was there exactly as it happened with some parts of it indelibly emphasized and he was miserably ashamed at it. But more than shame he felt cold, hollow fear in him. The fear was still there like a cold slimy hollow in all the emptiness where once his confidence had been and it made him feel sick. It was still there with him now.

It had started the night before when he had wakened and heard the lion roaring somewhere up along the river. It was a deep sound and at the end there were sort of coughing grunts that made him seem just outside the tent, and when Francis Macomber woke in the night to hear it he was afraid. He could hear his wife breathing quietly, asleep. There was no one to tell he was afraid, nor to be afraid with him, and, lying alone, he did not know the Somali proverb that says a brave man is always frightened three times by a lion; when he first sees his track, when he first hears him roar and when he first confronts him. Then while they were eating breakfast by lantern light out in the dining tent, before the sun was up, the lion roared again and Francis thought he was just at the edge of camp.

"Sounds like an old-timer," Robert Wilson said, looking up from his kippers and coffee. "Listen to him cough."

"Is he very close?"

"A mile or so up the stream."

"Will we see him?"

"We'll have a look."

"Does his roaring carry that far? It sounds as though he were right in camp."

"Carries a hell of a long way," said Robert Wilson. "It's strange the way it carries. Hope he's a shootable cat. The boys said there was a very big one about here."

"If I get a shot, where should I hit him," Macomber asked, "to stop him?"

"In the shoulders," Wilson said. "In the neck if you can make it. Shoot for bone. Break him down."

"I hope I can place it properly," Macomber said.

"You shoot very well," Wilson told him. "Take your time. Make sure of him. The first one in is the one that counts."

"What range will it be?"

"Can't tell. Lion has something to say about that. Don't shoot unless it's close enough so you can make sure."

"At under a hundred yards?" Macomber asked.

Wilson looked at him quickly.

"Hundred's about right. Might have to take him a bit under. Shouldn't chance a shot at much over that. A hundred's a decent range. You can hit him wherever you want at that. Here comes the Memsahib."

"Good morning," she said. "Are we going after that lion?"

"As soon as you deal with your breakfast," Wilson said. "How are you feeling?"

"Marvellous," she said. "I'm very excited."

"I'll just go and see that everything is ready." Wilson went off. As he left the lion roared again.

"Noisy beggar," Wilson said. "We'll put a stop to that."

"What's the matter, Francis?" his wife asked him.

"Nothing," Macomber said.

"Yes, there is," she said. "What are you upset about?"

"Nothing," he said.

"Tell me," she looked at him. "Don't you feel well?"

"It's that damned roaring," he said. "It's been going on all night, you know."

"Why didn't you wake me," she said. "I'd love to have heard it."

"I've got to kill the damned thing," Macomber said, miserably.

"Well, that's what you're out here for, isn't it?"

"Yes. But I'm nervous. Hearing the thing roar gets on my nerves."

"Well then, as Wilson said, kill him and stop his roaring."

"Yes, darling," said Francis Macomber. "It sounds easy, doesn't it?"

"You're not afraid, are you?"

"Of course not. But I'm nervous from hearing him roar all night."

"You'll kill him marvellously," she said. "I know you will. I'm awfully anxious to see it."

"Finish your breakfast and we'll be starting."

"It's not light yet," she said. "This is a ridiculous hour."

Just then the lion roared in a deep-chested moaning, suddenly guttural, ascending vibration that seemed to shake the air and ended in a sigh and a heavy, deep-chested grunt.

"He sounds almost here," Macomber's wife said.

"My God," said Macomber. "I hate that damned noise."

"It's very impressive."

"Impressive. It's frightful."

Robert Wilson came up then carrying his short, ugly, shockingly big-bored .505 Gibbs and grinning.

"Come on," he said. "Your gun-bearer has your Springfield and the big gun. Everything's in the car. Have you solids?"

"Yes."

"I'm ready," Mrs. Macomber said.

"Must make him stop that racket," Wilson said. "You get in front. The Memsahib can sit back here with me."

They climbed into the motor car and, in the gray first daylight, moved off up the river through the trees. Macomber opened the breech of his rifle and saw he had metal-cased bullets, shut the bolt and put the rifle on safety. He saw his hand was trembling. He felt in his pocket for more cartridges and moved his fingers over the cartridges in the loops of his tunic front. He turned back to where Wilson sat in the rear seat of the doorless, box-bodied motor car beside his wife, them both grinning with excitement, and Wilson leaned forward and whispered.

"See the birds dropping. Means the old boy has left his kill."

On the far bank of the stream Macomber could see, above the trees, vultures circling and plummeting down.

"Chances are he'll come to drink along here," Wilson whispered. "Before he goes to lay up. Keep an eye out."

They were driving slowly along the high bank of the stream which here cut deeply to its boulder-filled bed, and they wound in and out through big trees as they drove. Macomber was watching the opposite bank when he felt Wilson take hold of his arm. The car stopped.

"There he is," he heard the whisper. "Ahead and to the right. Get out and take him. He's a marvellous lion."

Macomber saw the lion now. He was standing almost broadside, his great head up and turned toward them. The early morning breeze that blew toward them was just stirring his dark mane, and the lion looked huge, silhouetted on the rise of bank in the gray morning light, his shoulders heavy, his barrel of a body bulking smoothly.

"How far is he?" asked Macomber, raising his rifle.

"About seventy-five. Get out and take him."

"Why not shoot from where I am?"

"You don't shoot them from cars," he heard Wilson saying in his ear. "Get out. He's not going to stay there all day."

Macomber stepped out of the curved opening at the side of the front seat, onto the step and down onto the ground. The lion still stood looking majestically and coolly toward this object that his eyes only showed in silhouette, bulking like some super-rhino. There was no man smell carried toward him and he watched the object, moving his great head a little from side to side. Then watching the object, not afraid, but hesitating before going down the bank to drink with such a thing opposite him, he saw a man figure detach itself from it and he turned his heavy head and swung away toward the cover of the trees as he heard a cracking crash and felt the slam of a .30-06 220-grain solid bullet that bit his flank and ripped in sudden hot scalding nausea through his stomach. He trotted, heavy, big-footed, swinging wounded full-bellied, through the trees toward the tall grass and cover, and the crash came again to go past him ripping the air apart. Then it crashed again and he felt the blow as it hit his lower ribs and ripped on through, blood sudden hot and frothy in his mouth, and he galloped toward the high grass where he could crouch and not be seen and make them bring the crashing thing close enough so he could make a rush and get the man that held it.

Macomber had not thought how the lion felt as he got out of the car. He only knew his hands were shaking and as he walked away from the car it was almost impossible for him to make his legs move. They were stiff in the thighs, but he could feel the muscles fluttering. He raised the rifle, sighted on the junction of the lion's head and shoulders and pulled the trigger. Nothing happened though he pulled until he thought his finger would break. Then he knew he had the safety on and as he lowered the rifle to move the safety over he moved another frozen pace forward, and the lion seeing his silhouette flow clear of the silhouette of the car, turned and started off at a trot, and, as Macomber fired, he heard a whunk that meant that the bullet was home; but the lion kept on going. Macomber shot again and every one saw the bullet throw a spout of dirt beyond the trotting lion. He shot again, remembering to lower his aim, and they all heard the bullet hit, and the lion went into a gallop and was in the tall grass before he had the bolt pushed forward.

Macomber stood there feeling sick at his stomach, his hands that held the Springfield still cocked, shaking, and his wife and Robert Wilson were standing by him. Beside him too were the two gun-bearers chattering in Wakamba.

"I hit him," Macomber said. "I hit him twice."

"You gut-shot him and you hit him somewhere forward," Wilson said without enthusiasm. The gun-bearers looked very grave. They were silent now.

"You may have killed him," Wilson went on. "We'll have to wait a while before we go in to find out."

"What do you mean?"

"Let him get sick before we follow him up."

"Oh," said Macomber.

"He's a hell of a fine lion," Wilson said cheerfully. "He's gotten into a bad place though."

"Why is it bad?"

"Can't see him until you're on him."

"Oh," said Macomber.

"Come on," said Wilson. "The Memsahib can stay here in the car. We'll go to have a look at the blood spoor."

"Stay here, Margot," Macomber said to his wife. His mouth was very dry and it was hard for him to talk.

"Why?" she asked.

"Wilson says to."

"We're going to have a look," Wilson said. "You stay here. You can see even better from here."

"All right."

Wilson spoke in Swahili to the driver. He nodded and said, "Yes, Bwana."

Then they went down the steep bank and across the stream, climbing over and around the boulders and up the other bank, pulling up by some projecting roots, and along it until they found where the lion had been trotting when Macomber first shot. There was dark blood on the short grass that the gun-bearers pointed out with grass stems, and that ran away behind the river bank trees.

"What do we do?" asked Macomber.

"Not much choice," said Wilson. "We can't bring the car over. Bank's too steep. We'll let him stiffen up a bit and then you and I'll go in and have a look for him."

"Can't we set the grass on fire?" Macomber asked.

"Too green."

"Can't we send beaters?"

Wilson looked at him appraisingly. "Of course we can," he said. "But it's just a touch murderous. You see, we know the lion's wounded. You can drive an unwounded lion—he'll move on ahead of a noise—but a wounded lion's going to charge. You can't see him until you're right on him. He'll make himself perfectly flat in cover you wouldn't think would hide a hare. You can't very well send boys in there to that sort of a show. Somebody bound to get mauled."

"What about the gun-bearers?"

"Oh, they'll go with us. It's their *shauri*. You see, they signed on for it. They don't look too happy though, do they?"

"I don't want to go in there," said Macomber. It was out before he knew he'd said it.

"Neither do I," said Wilson very cheerily. "Really no choice though." Then, as an afterthought, he glanced at Macomber and saw suddenly how he was trembling and the pitiful look on his face.

"You don't have to go in, of course," he said. "That's what I'm hired for, you know. That's why I'm so expensive."

"You mean you'd go in by yourself? Why not leave him there?"

Robert Wilson, whose entire occupation had been with the lion and the problem he presented, and who had not been thinking about Macomber except to note that he was rather windy, suddenly felt as though he had opened the wrong door in a hotel and seen something shameful.

"What do you mean?"

"Why not just leave him?"

"You mean pretend to ourselves he hasn't been hit?"

"No. Just drop it."

"It isn't done."

"Why not?"

"For one thing, he's certain to be suffering. For another, some one else might run onto him."

"I see."

"But you don't have to have anything to do with it."

"I'd like to," Macomber said. "I'm just scared, you know."

"I'll go ahead when we go in," Wilson said, "with Kongoni tracking. You keep behind me and a little to one side. Chances are we'll hear him growl. If we see him we'll both shoot. Don't worry about anything. I'll keep you backed up. As a matter of fact, you know, perhaps you'd better not go. It might be much better. Why don't you go over and join the Memsahib while I just get it over with?"

"No, I want to go."

"All right," said Wilson. "But don't go in if you don't want to. This is my *shauri* now, you know."

"I want to go," said Macomber.

They sat under a tree and smoked.

"Want to go back and speak to the Memsahib while we're waiting?" Wilson asked.

"No."

"I'll just step back and tell her to be patient."

"Good," said Macomber. He sat there, sweating under his arms, his mouth dry, his stomach hollow feeling, wanting to find courage to tell Wilson to go on and finish off the lion without him. He could not know that Wilson was furious because he had not noticed the state he was in earlier and sent him back to his wife. While he sat there Wilson came up. "I have your big gun," he said. "Take it. We've given him time, I think. Come on."

Macomber took the big gun and Wilson said:

"Keep behind me and about five yards to the right and do exactly as I tell you." Then he spoke in Swahili to the two gun-bearers who looked the picture of gloom.

"Let's go," he said.

"Could I have a drink of water?" Macomber asked. Wilson spoke to the older gun-bearer, who wore a canteen on his belt, and the man unbuckled it, unscrewed the top and handed it to Macomber, who took it noticing how heavy it seemed and how hairy and shoddy the felt covering was in his hand. He raised it to drink and looked ahead at the high grass with the flat-topped trees behind it. A breeze was blowing toward them and the grass rippled gently in the wind. He looked at the gun-bearer and he could see the gun-bearer was suffering too with fear.

Thirty-five yards into the grass the big lion lay flattened out along the ground. His ears were back and his only movement was a slight twitching up and down of his long, black-tufted tail. He had turned at bay as soon as he had reached this cover and he was sick with the wound through his full belly, and weakening with the wound through his lungs that brought a thin foamy red to his mouth each time he breathed. His flanks were wet and hot and flies were on the little openings the solid bullets had made in his tawny hide, and his big yellow eyes, narrowed with hate, looked straight ahead, only blinking when the pain came as he breathed, and his claws dug in the soft baked earth. All of him, pain, sickness, hatred and all of his remaining strength, was tightening into an absolute concentration for a rush. He could hear the men talking and he waited, gathering all of himself into this preparation for a charge as soon as the men would come into the grass. As he heard their voices his tail stiffened to twitch up and down, and, as they came into the edge of the grass, he made a coughing grunt and charged.

Kongoni, the old gun-bearer, in the lead watching the blood spoor, Wilson watching the grass for any movement, his big gun ready, the second gun-bearer looking ahead and listening, Macomber close to Wilson, his rifle cocked, they had just moved into the grass when Macomber heard the blood-choked coughing grunt, and saw the swishing rush in the grass. The next thing he knew he was running; running wildly, in panic in the open, running toward the stream.

He heard the *ca-ra-wong!* of Wilson's big rifle, and again in a second crashing *carawong!* and turning saw the lion, horrible-looking now, with half his head seeming to be gone, crawling toward Wilson in the edge of the tall grass while the red-faced man worked the bolt on the short ugly rifle and aimed carefully as another blasting *carawong!* came from the muzzle, and the crawling, heavy, yellow bulk of the lion stiffened and the huge, mutilated head slid forward and Macomber, standing by himself in the clearing where he had run, holding a loaded rifle, while two black men and a white man looked back at him in contempt, knew the lion was dead. He came toward Wilson, his tallness all seeming a naked reproach, and Wilson looked at him and said:

"Want to take pictures?"

"No," he said.

That was all any one had said until they reached the motor car. Then Wilson had said:

"Hell of a fine lion. Boys will skin him out. We might as well stay here in the shade."

Macomber's wife had not looked at him nor he at her and he had sat by her in the back seat with Wilson sitting in the front seat. Once he had reached over and taken his wife's hand without looking at her and she had removed her hand from his. Looking across the stream to where the gun-bearers were skinning out the lion he could see that she had been able to see the whole thing. While they sat there his wife had reached forward and put her hand on Wilson's shoulder. He turned and she had leaned forward over the low seat and kissed him on the mouth.

"Oh, I say," said Wilson, going redder than his natural baked color.

"Mr. Robert Wilson," she said. "The beautiful red-faced Mr. Robert Wilson."

Then she sat down beside Macomber again and looked away across the stream to where the lion lay, with uplifted, white-muscled, tendon-marked naked forearms, and white bloating belly, as the black men fleshed away the skin. Finally the gun-bearers brought the skin over, wet and heavy, and climbed in behind with it, rolling it up before they got in, and the motor car started. No one had said anything more until they were back in camp.

That was the story of the lion. Macomber did not know how the lion had felt before he started his rush, nor during it when the unbelievable smash of the .505 with a muzzle velocity of two tons had hit him in the mouth, nor what kept him coming after that, when the second ripping crash had smashed his hind quarters and he had come crawling on toward the crashing, blasting thing that had destroyed him. Wilson knew something about it and only expressed it by saying, "Damned fine lion," but Macomber did not know how Wilson felt about things either. He did not know how this wife felt except that she was through with him.

His wife had been through with him before but it never lasted. He was very wealthy, and would be much wealthier, and he knew she would not leave him ever now. That was one of the few things that he really knew. He knew about that, about motor cycles—that was earliest—about motor cars, about duck-shooting, about fishing, trout, salmon and big-sea, about sex in books, many books, too many books, about all court games, about dogs, not much about horses, about hanging on to his money, about most of the other things his world dealt in, and about his wife not leaving him. His wife had been a great beauty and she was still a great beauty in Africa, but she was not a great enough beauty any more at home to be able to leave him and better herself and she knew it and he knew it. She had missed the chance to leave him and he knew it. If he had been better with women she would probably have started to worry about him getting another new, beautiful wife; but she knew too much about him to worry about him either. Also, he had always had a great tolerance which seemed the nicest thing about him if it were not the most sinister.

All in all they were known as a comparatively happily married couple, one of those whose disruption is often rumored but never occurs, and as the society columnist put it, they were adding more than a spice of *adventure* to their much envied and ever-enduring *Romance* by a *Safari* in what was known as *Darkest Africa* until the Martin Johnsons lighted it on so many silver screens where they were pursuing *Old Simba* the lion, the buffalo, *Tembo* the elephant and as well collecting specimens for the Museum of Natural History. This same columnist had reported them *on the verge* at least three times in the past and they had been. But they always made it up. They had a sound basis of union. Margot was too beautiful for Macomber to divorce her and Macomber had too much money for Margot ever to leave him.

It was now about three o'clock in the morning and Francis Macomber, who had been asleep a little while after he had stopped thinking about the lion, wakened and then slept again, woke suddenly, frightened in a dream of the bloody-headed lion standing over him, and listening while his heart pounded, he realized that his wife was not in the other cot in the tent. He lay awake with that knowledge for two hours.

At the end of that time his wife came into the tent, lifted her mosquito bar and crawled cozily into bed.

"Where have you been?" Macomber asked in the darkness.

"Hello," she said. "Are you awake?"

"Where have you been?"

"I just went out to get a breath of air."

"You did, like hell."

"What do you want me to say, darling?"

"Where have you been?"

"Out to get a breath of air."

"That's a new name for it. You *are* a bitch."

"Well, you're a coward."

"All right," he said. "What of it?"

"Nothing as far as I'm concerned. But please let's not talk, darling, because I'm very sleepy."

"You think that I'll take anything."

"I know you will, sweet."

"Well, I won't."

"Please, darling, let's not talk. I'm so very sleepy."

"There wasn't going to be any of that. You promised there wouldn't be."

"Well, there is now," she said sweetly.

"You said if we made this trip that there would be none of that. You promised."

"Yes, darling. That's the way I meant it to be. But the trip was spoiled yesterday. We don't have to talk about it, do we?"

"You don't wait long when you have an advantage, do you?"

"Please let's not talk. I'm so sleepy, darling."

"I'm going to talk."

"Don't mind me then, because I'm going to sleep." And she did.

At breakfast they were all three at the table before daylight and Francis Macomber found that, of all the many men that he had hated, he hated Robert Wilson the most.

"Sleep well?" Wilson asked in his throaty voice, filling a pipe.

"Did you?"

"Topping," the white hunter told him.

You bastard, thought Macomber, you insolent bastard.

So she woke him when she came in, Wilson thought, looking at them both with his flat, cold eyes. Well, why doesn't he keep his wife where she belongs? What does he think I am, a bloody plaster saint? Let him keep her where she belongs. It's his own fault.

"Do you think we'll find buffalo?" Margot asked, pushing away a dish of apricots.

"Chance of it," Wilson said and smiled at her. "Why don't you stay in camp?"

"Not for anything," she told him.

"Why not order her to stay in camp?" Wilson said to Macomber.

"You order her," said Macomber coldly.

"Let's not have any ordering, nor," turning to Macomber, "any silliness, Francis," Margot said quite pleasantly.

"Are you ready to start?" Macomber asked.

"Any time," Wilson told him. "Do you want the Memsahib to go?"

"Does it make any difference whether I do or not?"

The hell with it, thought Robert Wilson. The utter complete hell with it. So this is what it's going to be like. Well, this is what it's going to be like, then.

"Makes no difference," he said.

"You're sure you wouldn't like to stay in camp with her yourself and let me go out and hunt the buffalo?" Macomber asked.

"Can't do that," said Wilson. "Wouldn't talk rot if I were you."

"I'm not talking rot. I'm disgusted."

"Bad word, disgusted."

"Francis, will you please try to speak sensibly," his wife said.

"I speak too damned sensibly," Macomber said. "Did you ever eat such filthy food?"

"Something wrong with the food?" asked Wilson quietly.

"No more than with everything else."

"I'd pull yourself together, laddybuck," Wilson said very quietly. "There's a boy waits at table that understands a little English."

"The hell with him."

Wilson stood up and puffing on his pipe strolled away, speaking a few words in Swahili to one of the gun-bearers who was standing waiting for him. Macomber and his wife sat on at the table. He was staring at his coffee cup.

"If you make a scene I'll leave you, darling," Margot said quietly.

"No, you won't."

"You can try it and see."

"You won't leave me."

"No," she said. "I won't leave you and you'll behave your self."

"Behave myself? That's a way to talk. Behave myself."

"Yes. Behave yourself."

"Why don't *you* try behaving?"

"I've tried it so long. So very long."

"I hate that red-faced swine," Macomber said. "I loathe the sight of him."

"He's really *very* nice."

"Oh, *shut up*," Macomber almost shouted. Just then the car came up and stopped in front of the dining tent and the driver and the two gun-bearers got out. Wilson walked over and looked at the husband and wife sitting there at the table.

"Going shooting?" he asked.

"Yes," said Macomber, standing up. "Yes."

"Better bring a woolly. It will be cool in the car," Wilson said.

"I'll get my leather jacket," Margot said.

"The boy has it," Wilson told her. He climbed into the front with the driver and Francis Macomber and his wife sat, not speaking, in the back seat.

Hope the silly beggar doesn't take a notion to blow the back of my head off, Wilson thought to himself. Women *are* a nuisance on safari.

The car was grinding down to cross the river at a pebbly ford in the gray daylight and then climbed, angling up the steep bank, where Wilson had ordered a way shovelled out the day before so they could reach the parklike wooded rolling country on the far side.

It was a good morning, Wilson thought. There was a heavy dew and as the wheels went through the grass and low bushes he could smell the odor of the crushed fronds. It was an odor like verbena and he liked this early morning smell of the dew, the crushed bracken and the look of the tree trunks showing black through the early morning mist, as the car made its way through the untracked, parklike country. He had put the two in the back seat out of his mind now and was thinking about buffalo. The buffalo that he was after stayed in the daytime in a thick swamp where it was impossible to get a shot, but in the night they fed out into an open stretch of country and if he could come between them and their swamp with the car, Macomber would have a good chance at them in the open. He did not want to hunt buff with Macomber in thick cover. He did not want to hunt buff or anything else with Macomber at all, but he was a professional hunter and he had hunted with some rare ones in his time. If they got buff today there would only be rhino to come and the poor man would have gone through his dangerous game and things might pick up. He'd have nothing more to do with the woman and Macomber would get over that too. He must have gone through plenty of that before by the look of things. Poor beggar. He must have a way of getting over it. Well, it was the poor sod's own bloody fault.

He, Robert Wilson, carried a double size cot on safari to accommodate any windfalls he might receive. He had hunted for a certain clientele, the international, fast, sporting set, where the women did not feel they were getting their money's worth unless they had shared that cot with the white hunter. He despised them when he was away from them although he liked some of them well enough at the time, but he made his living by them; and their standards were his standards as long as they were hiring him.

They were his standards in all except the shooting. He had his own standards about the killing and they could live up to them or get some one else to hunt them. He knew, too, that they all respected him for this. This Macomber was an odd one though. Damned if he wasn't. Now the wife. Well, the wife. Yes, the wife. Hm, the wife. Well he'd dropped all that. He looked around at them. Macomber sat grim and furious. Margot smiled at him. She looked younger today, more innocent and fresher and not so professionally beautiful. What's in her heart God knows, Wilson thought. She hadn't talked much last night. At that it was a pleasure to see her.

The motor car climbed up a slight rise and went on through the trees and then out into a grassy prairie-like opening and kept in the shelter of the trees along the edge, the driver going slowly and Wilson looking carefully out across the prairie and all along its far side. He stopped the car and studied the opening with his field glasses. Then he motioned to the driver to go on and the car moved slowly along, the driver avoiding warthog holes and driving around the mud castles ants had built. Then, looking across the opening, Wilson suddenly turned and said,

"By God, there they are!"

And looking where he pointed, while the car jumped forward and Wilson spoke in rapid Swahili to the driver, Macomber saw three huge, black animals looking almost cylindrical in their long heaviness, like big black tank cars, moving at a gallop across the far edge of the open prairie. They moved at a stiff-necked, stiff-bodied gallop and he could see the upswept wide black horns on their heads as they galloped heads out; the heads not moving.

"They're three old bulls," Wilson said. "We'll cut them off before they get to the swamp."

The car was going a wild forty-five miles an hour across the open and as Macomber watched, the buffalo got bigger and bigger until he could see the gray, hairless, scabby look of one huge bull and how his neck was a part of his shoulders and the shiny black of his horns as he galloped a little behind the others that were strung out in that steady plunging gait; and then, the car swaying as though it had just jumped a road, they drew up close and he could see the plunging hugeness of the bull, and the dust in his sparsely haired hide, the wide boss of horn and his outstretched, wide-nostrilled muzzle, and he was raising his rifle when Wilson shouted, "Not from the car, you fool!" and he had no fear, only hatred of Wilson, while the brakes clamped on and the car skidded, plowing sideways to an almost stop and Wilson was out on one side and he on the other, stumbling as his feet hit the still speeding-by of the earth, and then he was shooting at the bull as he moved away, hearing the bullets whunk into him, emptying his rifle at him as he moved steadily away, finally re-membering to get his shots forward into the shoulder, and as he fumbled to re-load, he saw the bull was down. Down on his knees, his big head tossing, and seeing the other two still galloping he shot at the leader and hit him. He shot again and missed and he heard the *carawonging* roar as Wilson shot and saw the leading bull slide forward onto his nose.

"Get that other," Wilson said. "Now you're shooting!"

But the other bull was moving steadily at the same gallop and he missed, throwing a spout of dirt, and Wilson missed and the dust rose in a cloud and Wilson shouted, "Come on. He's too far!" and grabbed his arm and they were in the car again, Macomber and Wilson hanging on the sides and rocketing swayingly over the uneven ground, drawing up on the steady, plunging, heavy-necked, straight-moving gallop of the bull.

They were behind him and Macomber was filling his rifle, dropping shells onto the ground, jamming it, clearing the jam, then they were al-most up with the bull when Wilson yelled "Stop," and the car skidded so that it almost swung over and Macomber fell forward onto his feet, slammed his bolt forward and fired as far forward as he could aim into the galloping, rounded black back, aimed and shot again, then again, then again, and the bullets, all of them hitting, had no effect on the buf-falo that he could see. Then Wilson shot, the roar deafening him, and he could see the bull stagger. Macomber shot again, aiming carefully, and down he came, onto his knees.

"All right," Wilson said. "Nice work. That's the three."

Macomber felt a drunken elation.

"How many times did you shoot?" he asked.

"Just three," Wilson said. "You killed the first bull. The biggest one. I helped you finish the other two. Afraid they might have got into cover. You had them killed. I was just mopping up a little. You shot damn well."

"Let's go to the car," said Macomber. "I want a drink."

"Got to finish off that buff first," Wilson told him. The buffalo was on his knees and he jerked his head furiously and bellowed in pig-eyed, roaring rage as they came toward him.

"Watch he doesn't get up," Wilson said. Then, "Get a little broadside and take him in the neck just behind the ear."

Macomber aimed carefully at the center of the huge, jerking, rage-driven neck and shot. At the shot the head dropped forward.

"That does it," said Wilson. "Got the spine. They're a hell of a looking thing, aren't they?"

"Let's get the drink," said Macomber. In his life he had never felt so good.

In the car Macomber's wife sat very white-faced. "You were marvellous, darling," she said to Macomber. "What a ride."

"Was it rough?" Wilson said.

"It was frightful. I've never been more frightened in my life."

"Let's all have a drink," Macomber said.

"By all means," said Wilson. "Give it to the Memsahib." She drank the neat whisky from the flask and shuddered a little when she swallowed. She handed the flask to Macomber who handed it to Wilson.

"It was frightfully exciting," she said. "It's given me a dreadful headache. I didn't know you were allowed to shoot them from cars though."

"No one shot from cars," said Wilson coldly.

"I mean chase them from cars."

"Wouldn't ordinarily," Wilson said. "Seemed sporting enough to me though while we were doing it. Taking more chance driving that way across the plain full of holes and one thing and another than hunting on foot. Buffalo could have charged us each time we shot if he liked. Gave him every chance. Wouldn't mention it to any one though. It's illegal if that's what you mean."

"It seemed very unfair to me," Margot said, "chasing those big help-less things in a motor car."

"Did it?" said Wilson.

"What would happen if they heard about it in Nairobi?"

"I'd lose my licence for one thing. Other unpleasantnesses," Wilson said, taking a drink from the flask. "I'd be out of business."

"Really?"

"Yes, really."

"Well," said Macomber, and he smiled for the first time all day. "Now she has something on you."

"You have such a pretty way of putting things, Francis," Margot Macomber said. Wilson looked at them both. If a four-letter man marries a five-letter woman, he was thinking, what number of letters would their children be? What he said was, "We lost a gun-bearer. Did you notice it?"

"My God, no," Macomber said.

"Here he comes," Wilson said. "He's all right. He must have fallen off when we left the first bull."

Approaching them was the middle-aged gun-bearer, limping along in his knitted cap, khaki tunic, shorts and rubber sandals, gloomy-faced and disgusted looking. As he came up he called out to Wilson in Swahili and they all saw the change in the white hunter's face.

"What does he say?" asked Margot.

"He says the first bull got up and went into the bush," Wilson said with no expression in his voice.

"Oh," said Macomber blankly.

"Then it's going to be just like the lion," said Margot, full of anticipation.

"It's not going to be a damned bit like the lion," Wilson told her. "Did you want another drink, Macomber?"

"Thanks, yes," Macomber said. He expected the feeling he had had about the lion to come back but it did not. For the first time in his life he really felt wholly without fear. Instead of fear he had a feeling of def-inite elation.

"We'll go and have a look at the second bull," Wilson said. "I'll tell the driver to put the car in the shade."

"What are you going to do?" asked Margaret Macomber.

"Take a look at the buff," Wilson said.

"I'll come."

"Come along."

The three of them walked over to where the second buffalo bulked blackly in the open, head forward on the grass, the massive horns swung wide.

"He's a very good head," Wilson said. "That's close to a fifty-inch spread."

Macomber was looking at him with delight.

"He's hateful looking," said Margot. "Can't we go into the shade?"

"Of course," Wilson said. "Look," he said to Macomber, and pointed. "See that patch of bush?"

"Yes."

"That's where the first bull went in. The gun-bearer said when he fell off the bull was down. He was watching us helling along and the other two buff galloping. When he looked up there was the bull up and looking at him. Gun-bearer ran like hell and the bull went off slowly into that bush."

"Can we go in after him now?" asked Macomber eagerly.

Wilson looked at him appraisingly. Damned if this isn't a strange one, he thought. Yesterday he's scared sick and today he's a ruddy fire eater.

"No, we'll give him a while."

"Let's please go into the shade," Margot said. Her face was white and she looked ill.

They made their way to the car where it stood under a single, wide-spreading tree and all climbed in.

"Chances are he's dead in there," Wilson remarked. "After a little we'll have a look."

Macomber felt a wild unreasonable happiness that he had never known before.

"By God, that was a chase," he said. "I've never felt any such feeling. Wasn't it marvellous, Margot?"

"I hated it."

"Why?"

"I hated it," she said bitterly. "I loathed it."

"You know I don't think I'd ever be afraid of anything again," Macomber said to Wilson. "Something happened in me after we first saw the buff and started after him. Like a dam bursting. It was pure excitement."

"Cleans out your liver," said Wilson. "Damn funny things happen to people."

Macomber's face was shining. "You know something did happen to me," he said. "I feel absolutely different."

His wife said nothing and eyed him strangely. She was sitting far back in the seat and Macomber was sitting forward talking to Wilson who turned sideways talking over the back of the front seat.

"You know, I'd like to try another lion," Macomber said. "I'm really not afraid of them now. After all, what can they do to you?"

"That's it," said Wilson. "Worst one can do is kill you. How does it go? Shakespeare. Damned good. See if I can remember. Oh, damned good. Used to quote it to myself at one time. Let's see. 'By my troth, I care not; a man can die but once; we owe God a death and let it go which way it will, he that dies this year is quit for the next.' Damned fine, eh?"

He was very embarrassed, having brought out this thing he had lived by, but he had seen men come of age before and it always moved him. It was not a matter of their twenty-first birthday.

It had taken a strange chance of hunting, a sudden precipitation into action without opportunity for worrying beforehand, to bring this about with Macomber, but regardless of how it had happened it had most certainly happened. Look at the beggar now, Wilson thought. It's that some of them stay little boys so long, Wilson thought. Sometimes all their lives. Their figures stay boyish when they're fifty. The great American boy-men. Damned strange people. But he liked this Macomber now. Damned strange fellow. Probably meant the end of cuckoldry too. Well, that would be a damned good thing. Damned good thing. Beggar had probably been afraid all his life. Don't know what started it. But over now. Hadn't had time to be afraid with the buff. That and being angry too. Motor car too. Motor cars made it familiar. Be a damn fire eater now. He'd seen it in the war work the same way. More of a change than any loss of virginity. Fear gone like an operation. Something else grew in its place. Main thing a man had. Made him into a man. Women knew it too. No bloody fear.

From the far corner of the seat Margaret Macomber looked at the two of them. There was no change in Wilson. She saw Wilson as she had seen him the day before when she had first realized what his great talent was. But she saw the change in Francis Macomber now.

"Do you have that feeling of happiness about what's going to happen?" Macomber asked, still exploring his new wealth.

"You're not supposed to mention it," Wilson said, looking in the other's face. "Much more fashionable to say you're scared. Mind you, you'll be scared too, plenty of times."

"But you *have* a feeling of happiness about action to come?"

"Yes," said Wilson. "There's that. Doesn't do to talk too much about all this. Talk the whole thing away. No pleasure in anything if you mouth it up too much."

"You're both talking rot," said Margot. "Just because you've chased some helpless animals in a motor car you talk like heroes."

"Sorry," said Wilson. "I have been gassing too much." She's worried about it already, he thought.

"If you don't know what we're talking about why not keep out of it?" Macomber asked his wife.

"You've gotten awfully brave, awfully suddenly," his wife said contemptuously, but her contempt was not secure. She was very afraid of something.

Macomber laughed, a very natural hearty laugh. "You know I *have*," he said. "I really have."

"Isn't it sort of late?" Margot said bitterly. Because she had done the best she could for many years back and the way they were together now was no one person's fault.

"Not for me," said Macomber.

Margot said nothing but sat back in the corner of the seat.

"Do you think we've given him time enough?" Macomber asked Wilson cheerfully.

"We might have a look," Wilson said. "Have you any solids left?"

"The gun-bearer has some."

Wilson called in Swahili and the older gun-bearer, who was skinning out one of the heads, straightened up, pulled a box of solids out of his pocket and brought them over to Macomber, who filled his magazine and put the remaining shells in his pocket.

"You might as well shoot the Springfield," Wilson said. "You're used to it. We'll leave the Mannlicher in the car with the Memsahib. Your gun-bearer can carry your heavy gun. I've this damned cannon. Now let me tell you about them." He had saved this until the last because he did not want to worry Macomber. "When a buff comes he comes with his head high and thrust straight out. The boss of the horns covers any sort of a brain shot. The only shot is straight into the nose. The only other shot is into his chest or, if you're to one side, into the neck or the shoulders. After they've been hit once they take a hell of a lot of killing. Don't try anything fancy. Take the easiest shot there is. They've finished skinning out that head now. Should we get started?"

He called to the gun-bearers, who came up wiping their hands, and the older one got into the back.

"I'll only take Kongoni," Wilson said. "The other can watch to keep the birds away."

As the car moved slowly across the open space toward the island of brushy trees that ran in a tongue of foliage along a dry water course that cut the open swale, Macomber felt his heart pounding and his mouth was dry again, but it was excitement, not fear.

"Here's where he went in," Wilson said. Then to the gun-bearer in Swahili, "Take the blood spoor."

The car was parallel to the patch of bush. Macomber, Wilson and the gun-bearer got down. Macomber, looking back, saw his wife, with the rifle by her side, looking at him. He waved to her and she did not wave back.

The brush was very thick ahead and the ground was dry. The middle-aged gun-bearer was sweating heavily and Wilson had his hat down over his eyes and his red neck showed just ahead of Macomber. Suddenly the gun-bearer said something in Swahili to Wilson and ran forward.

"He's dead in there," Wilson said. "Good work," and he turned to grip Macomber's hand and as they shook hands, grinning at each other, the gun-bearer shouted wildly and they saw him coming out of the bush sideways, fast as a crab, and the bull coming, nose out, mouth tight closed, blood dripping, massive head straight out, coming in a charge, his little pig eyes bloodshot as he looked at them. Wilson, who was ahead, was kneeling shooting, and Macomber, as he fired, unhearing his shot in the roaring of Wilson's gun, saw fragments like slate burst from the huge boss of the horns, and the head jerked, he shot again at the wide nostrils and saw the horns jolt again and fragments fly, and he did not see Wilson now and, aiming carefully, shot again with the buffalo's huge bulk almost on him and his rifle almost level with the on-coming head, nose out, and he could see the little wicked eyes and the head started to lower and he felt a sudden white-hot, blinding flash explode inside his head and that was all he ever felt.

Wilson had ducked to one side to get in a shoulder shot. Macomber had stood solid and shot for the nose, shooting a touch high each time and hitting the heavy horns, splintering and chipping them like hitting a slate roof, and Mrs. Macomber, in the car, had shot at the buffalo with the 6.5 Mannlicher as it seemed about to gore Macomber and had hit her husband about two inches up and a little to one side of the base of his skull.

Francis Macomber lay now, face down, not two yards from where the buffalo lay on his side and his wife knelt over him with Wilson beside her.

"I wouldn't turn him over," Wilson said.

The woman was crying hysterically.

"I'd get back in the car," Wilson said. "Where's the rifle?"

She shook her head, her face contorted. The gun-bearer picked up the rifle.

"Leave it as it is," said Wilson. Then, "Go get Abdulla so that he may witness the manner of the accident."

He knelt down, took a handkerchief from his pocket, and spread it over Francis Macomber's crew-cropped head where it lay. The blood sank into the dry, loose earth.

Wilson stood up and saw the buffalo on his side, his legs out, his thinly-haired belly crawling with ticks. "Hell of a good bull," his brain registered automatically. "A good fifty inches, or better. Better." He called to the driver and told him to spread a blanket over the body and stay by it. Then he walked over to the motor car where the woman sat crying in the corner.

"That was a pretty thing to do," he said in a toneless voice. "He *would* have left you too."

"Stop it," she said.

"Of course it's an accident," he said. "I know that."

"Stop it," she said.

"Don't worry," he said. "There will be a certain amount of unpleasantness but I will have some photographs taken that will be very useful at the inquest. There's the testimony of the gun-bearers and the driver too. You're perfectly all right."

"Stop it," she said.

"There's a hell of a lot to be done," he said. "And I'll have to send a truck off to the lake to wireless for a plane to take the three of us into Nairobi. Why didn't you poison him? That's what they do in England."

"Stop it. Stop it. Stop it," the woman cried.

Wilson looked at her with his flat blue eyes.

"I'm through now," he said. "I was a little angry. I'd begun to like your husband."

"Oh, please stop it," she said. "Please stop it."

"That's better," Wilson said. "Please is much better. Now I'll stop."

Duck hunters are stoic characters with plenty of time to contemplate and reflect on life in the bone-chilling cold and loneliness of the duck blind. Author Ted Walker has this situation down pat and can spin a compelling yarn with the best of writers. He was a frequent contributor to the New Yorker, *for which this story was written, and he also wrote several books.*

Ted Walker

EASTERLY (1982)

THERE'S AN EVIL WIND that blows along the English Channel coast sometimes in winter. Scarcely a wind: rather, an intermittent current of air just strong enough to disturb the shoreline tamarisks and to trace veins of incipient ice on the water's skin. Farm laborers round here hate and fear it. "It can have a man laid up for months," they'll tell you.

"It's a wind you daren't turn your back on. Bad always comes of it." It plugs the nose, aches behind the eyes. Marauding all the way from the Urals, Poland, Germany, the dank Low Countries, it gathers to itself slow accretions of pernicious coldness. Then it slides off the sea, over damp sands, up and over slippery stones and slabs at the foreshore, through barbed-wire fences and between hard clods in the empty fields; it sidles into our yards, infiltrates the outhouses, finds a way past heavy doors into rooms where your fire won't draw in the hearth. Mornings, you can track its spoor. It leaves deposits of frost not on every surface but only along the thin edges of objects in its path. It deserves some name of its own—a word whose vowels and consonants would aptly evoke its nature, as "mistral," "sirocco," "simoom" evoke the particular qualities of those more celebrated winds. Yet perhaps plain "easterly" conveys well enough its hateful austerity. A silent and parsimonious wind without the bounty of snow, it numbs the bones.

Two months ago, my father and I faced into such an easterly. We slammed the car doors and climbed up and over the shingle bank and saw that the tide was out. It was dawn, bleakest February, the year's lowest ebb. We each carried a 12-bore shotgun, and about a dozen cartridges chinked loose in our anorak pockets. This was the first time in three years we'd been wildfowling together.

"Time I gave up this nonsense for good," he said. "A man my age ought to stay in the warm."

"Don't blame me. You wanted to come."

"Should've talked me out of it."

We covered the few hundred yards to the estuary, where the draining stones met the sand, in silence, in step. I supposed we were making for his favorite cover—the tangle of stunted oak and buckthorn colonizing the last, short promontory before the river empties itself into the sea. At low water the sport can be swift from this hide; it commands a wide arc of fire over a network of runnels where large skeins will settle and graze on the mud spits dividing passages of sea lavender. We were none too early arriving: already the first curlews were uttering their melancholy

calls somewhere upriver, and I saw a cormorant kick from its perch atop
a bell buoy and scud low along the fairway like a flung beer bottle.

"You bring your flask, then?" I asked my father as we entered the trees.

He propped his gun against a trunk, struggled through thicknesses of
clothes, and withdrew the flask. I took it from him and had a long pull.
It was rum, and I'd been expecting Scotch.

"You want whiskey," he said, observing my grimace, "you bring your
own."

"Smoke?"

"Listen." He wedged his flask in the cleft of the tree beside him and
cocked an ear. For several seconds we stood motionless, straining to detect the cries of approaching geese—those insane gabblings you'll hear
from far off, often long before the V formation is visible. But the air was
without sound, and the sky, matte gray, was utterly blank. We broke our
guns, loaded, laid them on the ground, and lit cigarettes.

"I could have sworn I heard something," he said.

We lay down by the guns, enjoying our smoke, staring over the water
and beyond the further bank. By now the true dawn was beginning.
Along miles and miles of the river inland, in flooded meadows and plow-
land, the birds would be disturbing the morning; they'd be lifting, forming, wheeling, flying fast and direct above the network of watercourses,
the streams and tributaries, heading south for the brackish pastures and
the saltings where we waited and watched for them.

"Might've been the pigs," I said.

"What you on about, pigs?"

"That old run-down dairy farm this side the church changed hands
since you came here last. All pigs now—hundreds and hundreds. They
run free-range in the fields. Lots of little metal shelters for them, dotted
about like a shantytown."

"Wasn't pigs I heard."

"I didn't hear a thing. I reckon you're cracking up."

I gave him a grin, but he didn't grin back. His face was taut as he turned
his gaze toward the line of wind-sculpted oaks whose exposed, crazily

twisted roots were sometimes dabbled by the highest spring tides. Behind them, concealed, was the pig farm.

"You often hear them," I said. "Something sets them off squealing—a fox, maybe, or a rogue dog. I've learned to ignore them. You know how it is. Just hear what you want to hear when you're out hunting."

A heron wafted down from one of the taller oaks, lazy as an open page of newsprint dropped from an upper window. It settled in a shallow pool, folded its wings, became an old stake post. My dad looked grim.

"It's *me* cracking up," I said. "Don't hear like I used to. Cheer up."

"That's not it," he said. "God damn it, why can't folks leave things be? Pigs!"

"Progress. Profit."

"Christ, I'm feeling the cold." He stood up and started to stamp his feet and slap his arms under the quiltings of his anorak.

Not twenty yards away there was a whirring, as of a clockwork mainspring suddenly released, as a cock partridge broke from our cover and darted, jinking, out toward the flats. I sprang to my feet and fired, and the bird fell soft as a cushion onto a tuft of marram grass.

"Me you've got to thank for that," he said. "Kicking up a racket. Nifty shot, though. I'll say that."

"Thanks."

"Going to pick up?"

"It can wait. Times like this, I miss old Grip." Grip—short for Agrippa—had been my dog for fifteen years, from a puppy. Just before Christmas I'd had to have him put down; he had a tumor on the brain. Not a pedigreed gundog, but there was a lot of curly-coated retriever in him. In my mind's eye I saw him now, slinking low-bellied by the most sensible route through the maze of islets, his velvet mouth lovingly tender round the warm feathers; I remembered how I would fondle his head briefly after accepting whatever he laid at my feet. Then I thought of the malignancy millimetres under my palm the last time he'd fetched for me, and I shuddered.

"You're feeling pinched, too," my father said. "It's what my father called a lazy wind. Goes through you, not round."

"I was thinking of poor old Grip. Never another one like him."

"You ought to look out for a decent pup."

"One of these days."

"I know what you mean. Takes getting used to, the notion of a new dog. Never the same. Things never stay the same. Though sometimes they go full circle, back the way they were years before. And that's often a damn sight worse still."

"How do you mean?"

He didn't answer. Instead, he lay on his side, cradling his gun, and he closed his eyes as he worked himself comfortably into the cluttered ground. There were the remnants of campfires around us, and spent cartridges, and in the twiggy underbrush there was a rusted tin can reduced to a delicate orange web. I reloaded, and a wisp of smoke escaped from the breech with a faint smell of hot oil. I knelt down and squinted into the strengthening light.

"How do you mean?" I said again, not turning my head.

"You *know.* Bad things happen. Your world's all changed. You take years breaking in the new one. Then history repeats itself, only worse than before."

"Such as?"

"Two world wars I've lived through. You're too young to remember the Depression in the thirties, the slump. I see it all happening again. Hydrogen bombs, dole queues."

"You want to stop reading the papers, Dad. Put it out of mind. Don't make yourself miserable."

"Maybe."

We heard a double detonation from perhaps a mile away. All I could see on the move was gulls and swans and a dinghy under sail emerging from the yacht marina. The tide was on the make. Soon there would be flocks of sandpipers browsing at the water's edge, delicately scampering back and forth as the tongues of froth advanced and receded up the flats. Then, in another half hour, the early risers from the village would be exercising their lapdogs at the very fringes of the hem of foam, directly in our line of fire.

"Be no good now," my father said. "Those two barrels upstream will send the birds shanking off-line or high. They'll not reach us here."

His eyes were still closed, and his lips were tight and blue. There was truth in what he said—the gun we'd heard was very likely indeed to send the birds off their normal course—but, time was, his zest and optimism would have made him doubly alert for whatever we might bag apart from geese or duck: another partridge, perhaps, from the fields, or the odd rabbit or pigeon. Instead, he lay there shivering. He'd been only a boy during the Kaiser's War, I thought. I wondered why he'd started talking about wars and hard times.

"Have a slug or two of rum and a smoke," I said. "You're probably right. No more sport for us today." And, as though to confirm this, five more shots rang out in quick succession, indicating that there must be at least three guns between us and the wildfowl.

"Tell you what," I went on. "We'll have ourselves a fire and thaw out. Then go home and have another breakfast. Find some tinder."

It's not often that I'll give him an order; but he looked so abject that he seemed, in that moment, not like my father but, rather, some old man, some perfect stranger I might be jollying along for his own good. Almost meekly, he stood up, emptied his gun, reached for his flask and unscrewed the top. It was an instant of embarrassment for both of us. I walked away toward the tidemark in search of driftwood.

When I returned with my third double armful of fuel, he'd got a brisk fire going. There was color, now, in his cheeks. We built a high pyramid, and soon the blaze was singeing the dome of interlocking branches above our heads.

"Feel better?" I asked him.

"Not bad," he said. "This damned wind. Once it's got that chill inside you, it's the very devil to get out again. Maybe you don't ever get it out. Like salt in leather. Keep polishing it away, still keeps showing through. A couple of years before you were born, I got cold like this. I still remember it pretty well every day that comes. Keep getting reminders."

"Hold on," I said. "I'd better go and pick up that bird before the tide gets at it. You keep thawing through."

Grip would have taken less than a minute to retrieve the partridge, but I found the going difficult. Again and again I sank up to the ankles in foul mud, and the water in the runnels was already too deep and wide to ford conveniently. But it suited me well to be apart from my father for a little while: I'd guessed that he'd been on the verge of recounting, yet again, the story of how his younger brother had died on this very beach.

That had been in the early forties; I'd have been about eight years old. It was a February evening, the wind in the east, the grudging fire in our living room scarcely visible. My mother was ironing in the kitchen, while my father and I sat in the dark, listening to the radio. There was a knock at the front door. My father answered it. A policeman told him that his brother had been blown up by a land mine on the beach; he'd been gathering firewood—the floorboards from a derelict bungalow. The policeman asked my father gently if he'd go and identify the remains. What shocked me most, as a little boy, was the sight of my father's tears. I'd never seen them before. Nor have I seen them since.

I picked up the bird. It was still, just, warm to the touch. A few underfeathers blew from my hand to the water swirling around me. I turned toward the promontory and saw that the flames were still licking high inside the trees. I could well imagine what my father's thoughts must have been. He'd watched me gathering the wood for the fire he was warming himself by, and he'd seen me picking a careful way to the spot where I now stood holding the dead partridge aloft. People have often remarked that we're much like brothers, he and I.

We shared the rest of the flask, kicked out the fire. There was thin sunshine by now, and the wind had almost dropped. The last remnants of smoke rose from the charred driftwood and were slow to disperse. I'd washed the mud from my boots, but they were dirty again with ashes. As I wiped them clean, I remembered what my father had been saying about salt in leather. "A couple of years before you were born," he'd said. And I'd been so convinced that he was going to talk about his brother that the words hadn't registered. Our broken guns under our arms, we came out of the trees.

"Pig farm, you said?"

"That's right."

"Think we might go and have a look?"

"If you like. Not much to see."

Shots were still being fired intermittently, though they hadn't disturbed the heron at its station. We were quite close to it before—as though lifted by some maverick gust of air—it rose and beat its ponderous wings away from us and up and over the shoreline oaks.

"It always used to be pig-farming country, this, back between the wars," my father said.

"Oh?"

"Ramshackle sties and pens everywhere, the ground all mashed up. Jerry-built chalets and bungalows, too—some of them so crude you wouldn't have bet on them housing pigs or humans. The Army took most of them down, end of '39. Tank traps, mines—You know all about that, though. No need to rake it over."

"Before that—before I was born—did you come here shooting with your father?"

"Good God, no! He never had a gun—good job, too. And even if he had he wouldn't have taken me with him. He'd come fishing, always on his own, sometimes for so long at a stretch our ma would get worried. One of us would have to come looking for him. A real solitary he was, like that old jack heron—in a sort of trance. You put me in mind of him when you fetched that bird just now."

We clambered up the bank, finding handholds in the crisscrossed roots. About ten yards behind the trees, there was a good, stout timber fence about four feet high and smelling of fresh creosote. Behind this, upward of two hundred pigs, brindled pink and black and all much of a size, were scattered about a broad meadow, with maybe fifty corrugated-iron shelters and zinc troughs set out in straight lines. We leaned on the fence, and my father tested its rigidity with approval.

"Not get out of this," he said. "Not like in the old days. They used to get out when they felt like it and go browsing down on the beach. Strange sight, that—like something in a dream. They eat anything, pigs. Go mad, hunt in a pack, heads down in the seaweed, tossing it in the air, rooting and snuffling, going berserk for whatever's to be found. These look placid enough, though. Queer."

"Why queer?"

"This wind. My father always reckoned it was this kind of wind put that lust in them for going on the rampage. Could've been the cold that made them extra hungry. Or maybe it's just that they got the scent of stuff washed up on the foreshore. I'd say it was that."

"Why?"

"Something my old man told me not long before he died. Like the Gadarene swine, he said. The wind turned round while he was fishing off the point, and suddenly there's a whole squealing bunch of them charging down to the inlet where that old Thames barge is. Biting each other, they were, as they ran. When they got to the edge of the water, there was mayhem. All clustered around something, jostling, savage as hyenas—horrible. He didn't dare go and look."

"Frightened of the pigs?"

"What they might have found, more like. It obsessed him. He told me about it so often it's almost as though I'd been there myself."

We climbed down the bank once more and strolled toward the promontory under the overhanging canopy of the oaks. A party of anglers had arrived and were setting up their beach casters on a spit of shingle.

"They'll do no good today," my father said. "Not with the wind in the east. Puts the fish off the feed—that's what the old fellow always said, and I know it's true. Wind in the east, he'd put his tackle away, sit in his garden shed, and mope all day long. Terrible melancholy man, your grandfather. Got worse and worse toward the end. My brother had to wrestle with him once to take a carving knife off him. God knows what he'd have done if he'd had a shotgun."

"Died of heart disease, didn't he?"

"That's what it said on the certificate. He just gave up. Every day sullen and moping, as though the wind was always from the east. You couldn't reach him; wouldn't hear you."

"These days he might have been cured."

"No knowing. I came down here after the funeral. A day like this it was. I was starved with the cold, but I had to get out of the house. Didn't stay long. Just poked about, wondering if I'd go the same way. Not long after that I met your mother. Tell you what—let's give it another twenty minutes. You never know."

The embers of our fire were still warm. He loaded both barrels, clicked the gun shut, and stood alert facing the open water, his thumb on the safety catch. I wasn't at all surprised when he gave me a nod and I saw the flight of duck heading for us; he has an uncanny sense for the propitious moment. He got his right and left of mallard, hitting both birds so that they'd fall quite close together on dry land.

I picked them up for him and laid them side by side at his feet, the way Grip would have done. "*Now* say I should've talked you out of coming," I said.

"Still true," he answered with a grin. "Man my age ought to stay in the warm."

This tale of fox hunting in the deep South was originally published in Outdoors. *Interestingly, it is told partly from the fox's perspective. "The
Dodger," as he is known, is a troublesome raider of chicken sheds, and the
farmers are determined to hunt him down with their dogs. Henry P. Davis
explained the character of dogs further in* The Modern Dog Encyclopedia
(*1949, 1958, 1970*).

Henry P. Davis

THE DODGER
(1947)

ABULLFROG BELLOWED A THROATY CHALLENGE, telegraphing to
The Dodger's subconscious mind and ever-alert ears the fact that evening
shades were falling. The sturdy gray fox uncoiled himself from his comfortable curl. He rose, stretched, searched the sharp, scented air of the autumn evening with his sensitive nose and gazed with wary eyes at the
valley below.

The peace and quietude of twilight promised an easy hunt for a juicy
meal. And The Dodger knew where it could be found. Meals presented
no great problem to him. Soon rabbits would be frolicking in the

moonlit spaces, fat frogs would be sending croaky serenades along the bayou's edge. Field mice and cotton rats could be garnered without too much trouble. Lush country and easy pickings!

Veteran of many a tilt with the hounds, wherein his fancy footwork had earned him the sobriquet "The Dodger," the big fox had grown a bit lazy of late. From his vantage point on the high hill he had watched the building of a new chicken house on Ellis Nelson's farm, had seen the fine young pullets become acclimated to their new surroundings and then be allowed the freedom of the Nelson acres. Easy pickings, indeed! It was a simple matter for him to sift down from his hillside lair, lie in wait along a hedgerow and pick off a plump pullet or fat hen returning home to roost.

He was smart enough not to confine his marauding to one farm, for he had felt the ire of many farmers in various forms—hounds, traps and guns. He had outwitted them all, except the one rifle bullet which had torn away the tip of one ear, and the confidence which comes with experience told him he could do it again. This evening he was hungry—and in the valley below a banquet table was laid. . . .

Young Tom Nelson was returning from the north forty with a load of corn. Lowering the bars of the home-lot, a snort from Nettie, the off-mare, brought him alert. Catching the line of the old mare's gaze, he saw it all. A loitering pullet; a flash of gray and red from the hedgerow; a smothered squawk—and The Dodger defiantly trotting toward the hills with his evening meal! Easy pickings, indeed.

"It was The Dodger! I know, dad," furious young Tommie informed his father. "He turned and practically laughed at me—then trotted away with that chicken as if the whole world belonged to him. I *know* it was The Dodger. I've seen him time and again. He's got a crop-ear."

"Unload your corn, son," replied Nelson. "I'm going to the store and 'phone The Judge. Maybe he'll bring his hounds out tonight."

"He'll never catch this old devil," grumbled Tommie.

No secrets could ever be hidden in a southern country store. Everything anyone says is heard by everyone else—and is a matter of general interest. News of the day, crop conditions, gossip of the community, are all subjects to be relayed, ofttimes shamelessly exaggerated. And when the store telephone is used there is an immediate hush. The user's end of the conversation becomes a personal matter to all sitters-around, who, naturally, strain their ears to hear what the party on the other end of the line has to say.

And so it was that those in Neal Harder's store that night knew that The Dodger, the crop-eared fox which denned on High Hill, had taken his tenth hen from Ellis Nelson's farm; that The Judge and Cap'n Zack had been planning to hunt Rough-top Ridge south of town that night; that, in prospect of a tilt with The Dodger, they had changed their plans and would show up at Nelson's farm along about "good moon-up."

Of course, this meant a brief stop at Harder's store. To give horses and dogs a breathing spell, to buy a few apples, probably some cheese and crackers, and, if Harder gave a certain wink, to repair to his back room where flasks might be filled with a certain potent fluid known as "mountain dew," which possessed the properties of warding off colds and accounted for some of the mighty fox-horn blasts which rang through the early morning air—recalling the hounds from their futile pursuit of The Dodger.

As the small cavalcade topped the hill near Harder's store, the musical clink of curb-chains blending with the timed beat of well-shod hoofs, all ears came to attention. At the head of the column rode The Judge and Cap'n Zack, bodies comfortably swaying to the gliding gait of the best "walking-horses" in the county. Behind, tails aloft and red tongues lolling, trotted eight couples of foxhounds, matched for speed, application and endurance—but of varied voice in order to round out a choral effect.

Behind them rode Esau, the colored kennel man, making sure that all went well with the hounds. And, at a short distance to the rear, a small group of lovers of the chase, each of which had joined the procession as it had passed his farmhouse, jogged along in keen anticipation of a good night's sport.

Respects paid, and refreshments enjoyed by both men and beast, the party repaired to Nelson's farm, where more saddled horses were hitched to the picket-fence.

"I don't know where we'll jump him," said Ellis Nelson to The Judge. "But his trail should not be too cold and Tommie knows exactly where you can pick it up."

"Are you sure it's The Dodger?" asked Cap'n Zack.

"Tommie saw him plain as day," replied Nelson. "He's the big 'un with the crop-ear. Sure hope you catch him, for it looks like I won't have any chickens left soon."

"The night is a good one, the hounds are keen and we'll do our best," replied The Judge. "If he hasn't left the country, we'll give him a run for his money. Tommie, where did you see him last?"

"He popped out of the hedgerow right by that wild cherry tree, grabbed the pullet, trotted up the path and went through the little gap by that bunch of sassafras. I *know* it was The Dodger. I saw the whole thing. But you'll never catch him. He's too smart for any pack of hounds," the youngster grumbled.

"We'll see, sonny," smiled The Judge.

Telling Esau to keep the eager hounds in hand, The Judge and Cap'n Zack drew off to one side for a consultation and a look at the lay of the land. Both were master strategists in the hunting of either the gray or red fox. An occasional catch was, of course, to the liking of both, particularly if it was necessary to "blood" young hounds, but both had long since learned that the taking of a brush meant that that fox would never run again. And a good race meant more than a kill to each of the veterans.

But here was a different matter. This fox was not living off the countryside's bounteous offer of natural prey. Rather, he was becoming a serious menace to a good citizen's property—and his brush was demanded by no less a person than the serious-minded young scion of the household. Tonight they were hunting for sport—and something more.

The Judge called Esau to him. "Esau," he asked, "if you were The Dodger and were jumped out of a good warm bed and had to run for your life, where would you head for?"

The old negro scratched his graying poll, grinned and said: "Jedge, Ah ben thinkin' 'bout 'at same thing mahse'f. They all tells us this hyeah's a smaht fox. He's had a big belly-full of fine fat chickens. Mos' likely he's had a nap by now and ef he ain't disturbed he'll prob'bly sleep in till mornin'. He's loaded heavy an' he doan want no race. So ef we jump him—and he's got as much sense as they say he is—he's gonna make for 'at big thicket down yonder, wind in an' aroun' through them briers, cross 'at creek a time or two and then, ef he cain't shake 'em, high tail it for dry groun' in them high hills—an' take his chances.

"He's a smaht fox but he's a *gray* fox. He ain't gonna run outa the country like a red fox might do. An' he ain't gonna git too far away frum that chicken roost. Ef he ain' a ghost an'll stay on the groun' we'll hang his hide on Mistuh Nelson's barn tonight, provided," the old negro smiled knowingly, "we can out-run him an' out-smaht him."

The Judge and Cap'n Zack exchanged understanding glances. Dignity must be maintained—and Esau understood.

The trio returned to the waiting group, Esau, as usual, three paces to the rear. "Gentlemen," The Judge said, "we are out to catch The Dodger tonight and to present his brush to Mr. Nelson. No hound has ever laid a tooth on him, but tonight we'll try to outwit him. Frankly, Cap'n Zack and I would like to see him live on and on—and match our hounds against him night after night. But he's proven himself to be an arrogant nuisance and we'll do our best to bring his career of thievery to an end. He has lived by his wits. Tonight we'll try tactics probably unfamiliar to him—and for which Cap'n Zack and I ask your pardon.

"Our consolation lies in the well-known fact," continued The Judge, "that a confirmed criminal must pay the penalty for his crimes."

Esau, in the background, gently rubbing the ear of a nervous young hound, mumbled under his breath. "Boss sho' makin' big talk tonight."

"We will work the hounds in relays tonight, putting in fresh hounds when the going gets too tough, and, if possible, taking up, for a rest, any tiring dog."

Reaching in his saddle-bags, The Judge produced a long leather leash and snapped it on the collar of a young hound coupled with white-black-and-tan Joe Wheeler, the veteran of the pack.

"Tommie," he said, "this young dog is your special charge for tonight. He's new to the pack, but he comes highly recommended and The Dodger will give him a test tonight. Stay close to Esau. He'll tell you what to do."

There was an audible gulp from Esau and he blurted out, "But, Jedge you ain' give me no instructions 'bout dis!"

"You'll get your instructions later," was the quiet reply.

"Gentlemen, we're going to try to pick up The Dodger's trail with three strike dogs, jump him and then point our tactics according to the turn of the tide. Tommie, look after that young dog. Esau, uncouple Joe Wheeler, Tip and Top. We'll await developments."

The three big hounds bounded away into the moonlit night. Presently the low rumbling roar of Joe Wheeler announced discovery of the trail. Tip and Top promptly chimed in. But there was a loss here and there. The entire pack was eager to go and difficult to restrain. But The Judge lifted his hand and said, "Let's wait until they jump him."

Black Esau whispered, "Jedge, 'at old fox done jumped hisself. Fust time Joe Wheeler opened he wuz on his way to duh thicket."

And Esau was right. The Dodger had enjoyed his chicken dinner. Had curled up and had a good nap, was settling down for the night when his crop-ear, always pointed up-wind, telegraphed "unusual noises in the valley below." The dog-fox lifted his head and listened. All was quiet. He licked his chops, curled up again and flicked his soft, bushy tail over his sensitive nose. Then the booming blare of Joe Wheeler's bass rang out—and The Dodger was on his way to the thicket.

Cap'n Zack and The Judge held another consultation. Then reached into their saddle-bags and withdrew a number of stout leashes.

"Gentlemen," said The Judge, "I'm sorry we can't give you a real race tonight, but we're out to *get* this fox—fair or foul. And it may be foul. With the help of some of you, Cap'n Zack will take part of the pack to the edge of the thicket, wait until you catch the line of the running dogs and try to pick up The Dodger's trail ahead of them. I will take the others and try to cut him off where Esau thinks he might pass. We'll get him *some way*."

When Cap'n Zack's party had passed out of hearing, The Judge turned to Esau and said, "Take Tommie and the young hound into the high country, wait till you hear the line of drive—then use your own judgment." To young Thomas Nelson, he said, "Son, you don't like The Dodger, do you?"

"No, sir," the boy replied, looking The Judge squarely in the eye. "He's an old devil—but I *do* like dogs. And this one's a dandy."

"Well, my boy," said The Judge, "if you like him you can have him—provided he catches The Dodger tonight. He's new in the pack and we haven't even given him a name yet. But I think he can show some of the old ones a thing or two. And, fair or foul, if he catches The Dodger tonight, he belongs to you."

"Geeee," breathed Tommie, and then, "C'mon, Esau."

The two rode away with the nameless young hound trotting along at the side of Tommie's mule.

The Dodger hit the thicket just according to Esau's prediction, and far ahead of schedule. But when the six hounds Cap'n Zack loosed picked up his trail there was no resting. He ducked and dodged through the heavy underbrush, but fresh hounds were right behind him all the time. He ripped through a favorite haunt of low-hanging grapevines, honeysuckle and blackberry bushes and brought his pursuers to a temporary loss, giving him a chance to race for the open country. But, foreseeing this, The Judge loosed his portion of the pack—and again there was no resting. It was hammer-and-tongs for an hour and a half, and The Dodger was confused. "Head for the ledge in the hills," was his reasoning and he streaked in that direction.

Esau and Tommie and the young nameless hound heard him pass. "Turn 'im loose, Mister Tommie, an' le's see what he's made of," said Esau. The plunging young hound couldn't miss the hot trail, far ahead of the pack. And Tommie and Esau rode like hellions over that rough country, without thought of life or limb.

"Come 'is way, Mister Tommie!" yelled Esau. "We'll see it all when we git on top!" And they did.

The Dodger, circling higher all the time, headed home with the young hound right behind him. Fagged out and tail drooping, the big dog-fox gave one frantic leap for his lair in the shadow of a cliff—and made it. The young dog tried to follow, but he couldn't scramble like a fox. On the third try he toppled back, to fall with a rib-cracking thump on a sharp rock. Painfully gaining his feet, he laboriously worked his way to the top of the cliff, and looked down. The hot scent of the exhausted fox smashed against his nostrils and he leaped into space—to land within three feet of The Dodger, done in but snarling. A brief struggle and it was all over.

Tommie and Esau watched it all—and Esau's struggle with Tommie was greater than the combat below. "He's caught him, and he belongs to me. The Judge told me so and I gotta get him!" yelled Tommie.

But the wise old negro would have none of it. Once he had calmed the trembling boy, he lifted his hunting horn and blew the notes which signalled the end of the hunt. Then carefully picked his way down the cliff to retrieve the body of The Dodger and the exhausted young hound.

In front of Ellis Nelson's fireplace, the young dog lay dozing. Tommie ran a caressing hand over a brier-torn ear. The Judge sipped a hot toddy, fortification against a long ride home.

"Tommie," he said, "we tricked The Dodger tonight and, frankly, I'm none too proud of it. But you won a good young dog and he proved his worth. We've never given him a name. What are you going to call him?"

The youngster's back straightened, and again he looked The Judge squarely in the eye. "If you don't mind, sir," he replied, "I'll name him The Dodger."

Two young men hunkered down in the cold gray dawn swap raunchy wisecracks and nostalgic asides on married life. The mallards eventually swoop in and the action is good. Despite the bantering dialogue, a touching vulnerability is revealed as one of the men struggles to cope with personal tragedy. Kim J. Zupan is a talented Montana writer who also works as a carpenter. His story came out in Epoch.

Kim J. Zupan

A LAST LOW PASS (1987)

ICLOSED THE DOOR CAREFULLY, easing it into its jamb, and stood out near the curb, and above me was a moon I didn't understand: clouds shifted and rolled, snow hissed down, writhed along the street and rattled the branches of the dead swaying elm, and through it all that moon burned like an imposter sun melting a hole in the storm. Five A.M. and its glare made a shadow beside me.

In a minute I saw the low-beams pushing up the street through the dark and I knew it was him, just by the steady way the lights came along up the middle of the road. He was sure of his traction and drove the centerline as though the whole world should stand aside.

"Hey, get in quick," he said. "Why're you standing on the street for?"

I moved my head back toward the house and smiled, putting a gloved finger to my lips. In the cab's dome light, Mike's smile turned, shadows bulged under knots of jaw muscle, and he scowled past me toward the house.

"I would've honked," he said. "Get in here before we freeze."

On the seat of the truck between us was a bottle of homemade port and a mickey of clear, rock-candy rye sent over by a dago relative from Wisconsin.

"What's with the sauce? This looks serious."

"We're going to get tight," he said.

"And here I thought we were going to get a bag full of greenheads."

"Well that, and we're going to get tight," he said. "It's been too long."

"Just the rye would do it."

"It would at that."

We drove out of town east, the sun still two hours on the other side of the world, and we didn't say anything. I always had the feeling of being in church when it was black out and storming, with only the snow sighing against the window and the heater fan buzzing low. It was like early Mass, when all you could hear was the priest saying Latin way down in his throat and the old Italian and Bohunk women breathing deep and rheumy from the back of the church. They followed the rite along in their missals, murmuring the prayers in the old-country tongues. The lights were dim, high up by the ceiling, and the painted saints in the windows showed no color for the dark outside. And when the priest wasn't talking the Latin, you could hear the old sad women sighing deep or coughing.

But Mike was no church goer and thought it comical—live people praying to long-dead people and statuary—so he wasn't probably thinking about any early Mass as we drove, but of the best places for ducks along the creek. And I finally did the same, running all the slow bends and warm-water stretches over in my mind.

A few window lights and purple yard lights were all that showed we were passing the string of washed-out coal towns in the dark, and in my head I rattled off the names in order, over and over like rosary prayers: Gerber, Number Nine, Tracy, Number Seven, Coal Car, Centerville, until we were up on the benchland and past old Finlayson's lonesome buildings, stuck out among the stubble strips and summerfallow with nothing at all to break the storm. After Finlayson's, it was all open country and his lights were the last. Overhead, as we jolted along, the near-full moon still shined through.

In our heads we planned and stalked the creek, as the cab warmed and the snow bumped the window in front of us. We thought the same things so in a way it was like conversation without words. But in the green and muggy dark, with this silent mental hunting going on, it was easy to fall asleep. When his eyelids sagged, Mike started in with his talking business.

"Could I ask you something?" This was how he got started.

"What?"

"Do you for Christ's sake ever get tired of doing that?"

"What?"

"That with your fingers. 'This is the church, this is the steeple.' How old are you anyway?"

"What, this?" I held up my fingers locked together, with my index fingers pointing straight up to make the steeple of the church. It was an automatic thing, and I didn't even realize my hands were doing it.

"Yes. That."

"Listen, would you do something for me?" I said.

"Oh, Jesus. What?"

"Do this—go crabbing with Ginny Blazevich." This was a half-sore high school thing referring to a drunken one-nighter and a condition Mike picked up.

"So that's how it's going to be, dredging up old rotten lies. Well, listen, do you remember that fall when it stayed so warm and there weren't any ducks down yet so we went up to the lake, and that warden—Schultz or some damn thing . . ."

"It was Schmudee."

"It wasn't any damn Schmudee."

"Schmudee."

"Well, whatever the hell it was, he caught us with all those planted rainbows and you said, no sir, you didn't have your license with you but you were sure I had mine and you knew goddamn good and well that I had no such thing."

"I had my bird license."

"Goddamn it."

"Well, we both got fined for Christ's sake," I said.

"Sure, but that's how it always is, you trying to lay it on me." He was enjoying it, ranting over the old story and playing mad.

"Now I see what you're trying to say," I said.

"Oh, you do?"

"Sure. You want to go fishing instead. That's obvious."

"Oh, Jesus."

"You're hinting at wanting to turn around and go try fishing the lake again, am I right?"

"Crockashit," Mike said.

"If you want to fish," I said, "just say so. That's perfectly fine."

"Listen," he said, "would you do something for *me*? I'll stop, you jump out and straddle that bobwire fence and run up and down awhile and see what that does for you."

"Well, I'll just say no thank you kindly."

And in the green gloom of the cab, Mike hunched over the wheel, smiling, driving with his forearms like he was bearhugging the feel of the engine trembling up through the column. He watched the snow blow in and above, the sky go pale, and I didn't remember him being this happy, this loose and easy in a long time.

"God, remember," I said, "that business at the lake was that fall right before I got married. God, Mary was pissed, screaming at me that my name in the paper for the poaching fine was just a *wuun*-derful wedding present, like she's getting hitched up to a con or something. Jesus, she's something when she gets mad. Remember that? Oh, Christ." And then

I was picturing it all, all the best time of my life rolling by fast-motion like the blizzardy windshield was a picture-house screen: the long, wild trips with Mike around this country for birds like a bachelor party that went on too long, blasting through boxes of shotgun shells and cases of beer at once, the whole, clattering mess of empties jittering around the bed of the truck; and then, finally, the day, the entire place decked out in flowers, Mary making her slow, swishing way up the aisle and Mike standing there straight-backed and giving me the jolly eyeball.

I looked at Mike across the cab. "You sure were a good-looking bastard in that tuxedo," I said. "And Mary walking up in all that silk, looking like a goddamned angel. Jesus, that was something."

But all I got from Mike was that jaw muscle jumping in the light and the profile of him peering hard at the road. I could see he was done talk- ing. He was funny like that, talking away, and then he was done, like all of a sudden the fun went out of it for him. But for me the remembering came racing back across the glass as the tire lugs droned on the asphalt. I remembered from early on the way she folded back the corner of the blanket before we went to sleep, and how on cold nights she would be curled with her back to me, nested in the covers with just the top of her head showing and light from the moon coming in the window. I would crawl in and curl in the same shape around her and feel the flannel of her old lady nightgown and her cold feet and say, "We just fit, don't we?" And she would reach and pull one of my hands over across her shoulder and hold it and go off to sleep.

In the cold months she made plans. The snow blew against the iced pane of our picture window and we stared out from the couch like the storm was a stage play, everything white but the grey columns of the elm trunks holding up the sky. She planned for the coming spring and sum- mer and years of springs and summers. Winter was her thinking season and she thought of spring then, just like when you remember the dead, you don't think of the white corpse but of them doing something when the blood ran in them. So in the dead season, she talked about the branches of those elms lolling under the weight of leaves and rubbing the window like a paw. She made strategy for the river, where we'd fish and the tackle we'd use. She discussed it like a person she missed, describing the woolly mullein and yarrow along the banks, the color of the water under those first spring skies as if I'd never in my whole life been there.

But I could see only the dark look of the river in the windshield, and the whole speeded-up movie of remembering stopped dead. In the cab of the truck it was like church again, the snow was all I saw in the glass, and this was another winter. Mike glared out at the flexings of the season. I hoped he felt spring was coming and that he and his wife made plans.

"Does she ever call you Honey?" I asked. "You wife?"

"Jesus, where in hell did that come from?"

"If you're embarrassed just say so."

"Christ," he said. "Sure, sometimes. I like it sometimes. She calls me Mikey and I don't like that. But Honey sometimes. There's nothing wrong there."

"No," I said. "That's good."

Mike looked away from me and eyed the white drifting shoulder, then eased the truck off the road. He stepped into the storm and scraped the ice from the windshield, the day so cold that the moaning defrost was losing ground. Inside, we poured coffee from the Thermos, adding just a perfect bite of the rye from the cough medicine bottle on the seat.

"You ever notice how the oldtimers 'take' coffee?" Mike asked. "They don't *have* coffee. They *take* coffee."

"Yeah, my Grandpa said it that way. He'd be splitting cottonwood in back of the house with old Zebio Cordini and I'd be sitting there watching and he'd tell Zebio, 'Let's take coffee.'"

"Sure," Mike said, "and I bet they put a little dago red or something in there for a kick." He lurched the truck onto the pavement and in half a mile we dropped down off the strip-farmed tableland and into the valley, and the moon finally went behind clouds, smouldering like a coal.

"Two old partners like us, spiking coffee," I said. "Now they're both dead."

"Here it is," Mike said, and I turned from Grandpa and his dead Italian crony in the windshield to the frosted side window, where I could see, finally, the lower end of the creek. First you see the steam rolling up, then when it loops back on itself, you see the open water and iced-over stretches in its black trench of summerfallow, coiling down the flat bottom of the valley and under the road through culverts and under bridges and the black criss-cross of trestles. On both sides of the creek the ground was worked, plowed fields with the dirt frozen hard, snow driven into the furrows, and above, in the moonlight and slow-coming sunlight, the sky was just a huge reflection of the rutted ground. The clouds were low and swollen to the tops of the hills. In this country it was all Bohunk and Finlander nesters, and one of them had worked the dirt with duck foot and discs and it was in deadwaiting for the spring.

With the snow blowing straight in and the steam from the warm water creek boiling up around us, the valley was just a grey tunnel upstream. The defroster groaned from its throat and the headlights went nowhere. Mike gripped his wheel and I leaned my head against the frosted side pane and thought about her, about Mary at home, stretched out on the couch with a satin pillow under her head, lying behind the iced glass of the picture window. The dog would have been there, asleep within her arm's reach, flopped out and breathing deep like a big dog has to, his side heaving up so slowly you think he'll never wake up. He was happiest to be next to her or to have her always in sight. With me he was independent, playing rough and showing his teeth like we were two dogs in a pack, but he stayed close to her whenever possible or kept a loving eye cocked, guarding dim-minded against a mean world.

And then there it is without warning, the dazzling picture of her out in the river in the low-angled August light, fishing downstream of me and lost to everything but the river. The sound is the water growling along the bank and the drone of a hatch in the air. She knows the bottom well, toe-feels her way out, casting for the fastest water. When she turns to wave at me, I see the rubber wader tops gape around her like the mouth of a toothless shark and the current slides by below her chest. Beyond her trout jump in the channel for the dying flies of the hatch. And always, the dog paces the rocky bank like a mother, whines and paces and bays until it all becomes too much and he swims out for her, thinking somehow he'll retrieve her from this dangerous foolishness. But the current tugs him downstream for all his churning paddling, and he turns back and swims to shore, where he sets in with his whining and shoreline pacing, crazy with his one love out of reach in the river.

My own line wags downstream as I watch the perfect arc of her line in the air. She lays the fly in natural among the raises. The frantic dog runs the bank as she edges out on the familiar bed. The water burns under the last strong rays of the sun, and with the river moving all around her, she glows from the reflected light like a heavenly vision. Overhead, two gulls scream and I watch them fight over the guts of fish cleaned upriver. They sail downstream, dipping and turning for position, tugging at the meal between them. I hear the screams again, hear the dog plunging in the water, his pitiful crying magnified a thousand times by the canyon walls, the whole sudden roar pounding around my head, the sick lap of the water, my own name sounding like a curse, the baying of a dog going mad.

And then just as quick the river is quiet and itself, moving along its bed like nothing could ever matter. The white entrails of the argument drop from between the birds and hit the water without a sound.

Outside the dawn sky was like bloated summerfallow and the frost was thick as a nickel across the side pane, despite the defrost grinding way on high speed. Mike stopped the truck by open-water stretches and half-hidden bends of the creek where we'd had luck for years of late-season hunts. Like a tank captain, binoculars around his neck, cap pulled low, he glassed through the steam for ducks.

"Well, we'll go to our spot. The hell with this candy-assing. I can't see in this shit, anyway."

We cranked the hubs into four-wheel and drove the five miles through the tunnel of weather and steam to where the creek took a lazy loop away from the road and shoved in against the hills. Mike eased the truck into the deep snow of the borrow ditch and the buried, high weeds rasped across the floorboards. Outside in the cold, as we jacked shells into the chambers of our guns, I watched the steam come up off the water hidden under the cutbank. Moving closer, plowing through knee-deep drifts in our waders, the frost-covered wild wheat and rosehip bushes on the bank looked like they were smouldering: steam huffed up from the creek the way smoke comes off a knot full of pitch.

"Let's have a hit of this rye," Mike said. "For a kick, like those old timers."

"Sure," I said, "and for luck." And standing in the middle of the white pasture we tipped up the mickey for a drink. Mike leaned his head back after a long burning gulp and grinned up at the snow and the bellied sky that seemed in arm's reach.

"It's really coming down now," he said.

"Mary'll be tickled," I said. "She loves this weather."

Mike looked away toward the creek where, this close, you could see the leafless tops of willows above the cutbank.

"Christ," he said. "The only thing this goddamn snow is good for is keeping the ducks down. Let's get the hell down there and get some dekes in the water."

We bulled our way across the pasture and stumbled down finally to the creek. Unseen from the road or even from the top of the rocky reef on the other side, this stretch of creek spilled from between the clay walls of the cutbanks onto a little flat and lost all discipline. The water spread against the reef wall, eddied careless and stagnant into a slough, and nuzzled in on the near side against a low bank. Even in this weather, the grass hung over and trailed loose in the water like a woman's hair, waggling in the current. To the grassy edge and all along the flat, willows grew close and tall. The water was flat and clear and almost noiseless. It was a hidden and comfortable place, the natural place for ducks to set down. It was our spot alone, kept secret, and when we hid in the snow in the tangled brush I felt we were part of the natural plan.

We uncoiled the anchor lines with their lead weights from around the bodies of the decoys, and pussy-footing along the slippery bottom, set the painted ducks facing into the current. Across the stream, reeds stuck up from the frozen slough. The only real sound was the lap of water panting against a thin plate of edge ice.

In the willow stand we tromped down the snow and squatted to wait. The wind blew straight from the east up the valley chute and snow piled up beside us as if we were tree trunks. I motioned down to the little drifts at our legs and at the hollows that formed on the lee side of us. Mostly, though, we were still and felt bad if we had to rub up our ears or faces, for fear the moving would spook any flyers. We held out against the cold as long as we could. Overhead the sun was rolling up somewhere behind the grey but it did no good.

"I don't think there's anything in the whole country flying," I said.

"Not yet," Mike said. "How're your feet?"

"What feet?"

"Are they bad?" he asked.

"No, not too bad. They'd warm up in a hell of a hurry if we brought in some quackers."

"Hit the call just once."

I worked the feeder call and we sat still, only rotating our eyeballs around under the brims of our caps and straining to hear: snow sighed into the creek and that was all.

Mike looked down at my feet and shook his head. He was a worrier. I liked him for that. A big Polack worrier with eyes set way back in his head and a neck like a rutting buck and a big dropping mustache that frosted white in the cold and made him look like one of those pipe-smoking, sad-looking immigrants you see leaning on the rails of ocean liners in the special edition *Life* magazines. He fretted on me a good deal, and fretted over my toes going blue at the bottom of my waders. But he was at ease himself around all this winter and he snuggled into the drifting brush-pile, smiling. He was at home in it.

The snow settled on the backs of the dekes and I watched the current slew them side to side, tugging against the anchor lines. I watched them weave slowly in the current, the painted heads bobbing up and down. The snow in the water made a breathing sound and I watched the sleepy, rolly moving of the dekes. Back and forth, up and down, lolling in the slow pull of the creek. And green tresses of moss waved under their bellies in the same rhythm.

Then I heard Mike suddenly move. He knocked against the brush, hissing as he jumped up, and the frost shaken from the branches flew in the air. He was braced and shooting and I saw them coming in, and then I was blasting through the steam at the group of Northern mallards that had slipped in under the fog and zeroed in on our decoys. They hovered in over the wooden ducks, committed themselves to set down and then it was too late.

When we fooled them they paid with dying. They sidled in and set their wings, and in that heart beat when we'd stand to shoot, the ducks suspended in that shutter pose second between landing and lifting off, between their feeling of security and the wild knowing that the whole thing is wrong, I always felt a kind of happiness, with something missing. Or with something more. I felt this way, too, hooking a big fish on a creek small as this one, knowing he had prowled the bottom for years living on eating his kind and by sheer wiliness. And walking the bank with him on my line, I had the same empty ache, like a door on the bottom of my belly had been sprung. He took the hook in his tough jaw, running down and down to his place and then finally slowly coming up for the last time ever because I had laid the fly in there just so and not left a shadow across the water. I set him up on the grass and the red and silver, that color I saw in the hole, never lasted long. He was just going white and stiff, drowning on air, an eye frozen fast on the sun. A mistake, a second of wrong thinking or not looking and like all those ducks, he paid. You always paid.

I watched the birds float downstream, bouncing along riffles and turning slowly in eddies. Some twitched from a nerve and the ones hit really good had their wings spread on the water in a final, dead glide. Mike chased after a cripple upstream around the bend and yelled back. "Wake up for Christ sake and grab the bastards." One fat drake was hung up on a decoy, curled around the false hen in the last embrace. I held him up and even in so dim a light, he was beautiful: the speculum blue of the wings and the head that changes a hundred shades of green. They were beautiful all right, and it was funny that next to them the females were so drab and plain-looking, when with us, with people, the woman is the beautiful one, the way they dress up so showy in colors like these mallard drakes or an old rooster pheasant, decked out and strutting, painted around the eye.

But that flashy green head was the right lead; it stood out and I always shot for it. Cradling the drake in my hands, I twisted his head to see the changing greens. Behind me I heard splashing and Mike came from around the corner of the creek, holding his pumpgun in the crook of his arm and lugging a long branch. His eyes burned from under the brim of his cap, and slogging through the steam in his waders, his mustache frosted, he made a great picture.

"What're you smiling about?" he said.

"Oh, I don't know."

"Well, goddamn it, she went under."

Disgusted, he threw his probing stick into the bank like a javelin. The cripple hen, the one he'd chased upstream, had gone under to die. We didn't generally shoot for the females, but sometimes in the frenzy of birds going everywhere for escape, we accidentally hit one. If you were unlucky it would happen, and the homely hen was usually the one to do it: they'd dive down, a hollow little wing bone broken or a bb up in the guts, hold onto a weed or branch sticking out from the bank and just drown there. That was her beauty, wanting to die alone and unhandled, her life-long mate probably one of the drakes whose neck I'd torqued and pitched on the bank. But it was awful to think of: you knew she was there somewhere, her yellow rolled-up eye glaring up at you through the roots or moss or fragile edge ice of the stream, staring up at you and dying slow as you stared down at her.

"Maybe she's just up under the bank," I said.

"I poked around all the way to the culvert," Mike said. "She's down dying."

"Well, she's *your* cripple."

"What the hell difference," Mike said. "She's dead anyway."

"Yeah, I guess she is soon."

Mike stared up at the clouds for a long time, and the creek sighed with the snow settling into it. We picked up the three drakes and set them under the cover of the willows. They bled from their mouths into the snow as we stomped down the drift and settled to wait. Our words and breath were sucked into the stream and the last downy breast feather was swept downstream. The dekes wobbled on their lines. And with the heavy snow blowing in, the water made one constant exhale, one steady drowsy breath in my ear. I remembered once when a nice bunch came sailing into our decoys and we were banging away, aiming for the drakes and that greenhead lead. And then as we gathered up the downed birds, the shots still throbbing loud in our ears and echoing between the hills, we suddenly heard the whistle of wings. Like a reflex we shouldered our guns and there, circling in low, a lone hen with an eye cocked down, taking a suicidal pass in search of her mate, longing to join him, confused to be alone, coming a determined pass one last time.

I listened for the hiss of wings coming low again. I heard Mike work the call that faked the sound of ducks safe and feeding.

"Does she really call you Honey?" I asked.

"I *told* you," he said.

"You know, Mary calls me Sweetheart," I said, "which I never thought I'd like but I do. It's one of those things you think sound stupid when somebody else says it, but when it's you, it's all right. Do you see what I mean?"

Mike stared at me long from under the bill of his cap. "Goddamn it, don't talk now. These ducks are moving."

"Well, anyway, my feet are okay now. They warmed right up with all the excitement."

"Fine," he said. "Now shut up and think ducks and keep your goddamn eyes open."

So I did that, eyeing up and down the creek, imagining against all other pictures mallards swinging in low and perfectly fooled. But the day all at once closed in around us: the steam, the low sky and the snow coming hard, all sagging steadily down on us like someone had closed tight a flue. Mike crouched in the willows with his shotgun held between his knees and his forehead pressed against the barrel, looking like one of those animals around the roof lines of old churches. His hat brim was bent over his eyes. He wasn't looking around at all.

"Mike, remember when the four of us drank our way out to Centerville that night and that harelip bartender pulls the .45 from under the bar when we wouldn't leave? You looked at him and made that crack about birdseed? Jesus, the wives were pissed off."

"Sure I remember," he said.

"Say birdseed the way you did."

"Just forget all that."

"Well, we'll have to make another appearance out there one of these days. Go out and razz that old shitter. The girls had fun that night, really, up to the pistol business. That was a good time. We ought to do that again."

Mike turned, slow-motion, and stared at me. I watched the snow angle down against the ice of the slough beyond the creek and heard it clatter in the reeds. And still Mike glared over, those close-set, mean dog-eyes coming at me.

After a long cold time he finally said, "Listen to me, open up your mind. She's gone, partner. Don't please think about it anymore. Put it back there in the past where all that bad shit belongs. There's nothing to do and it's been plenty long enough to turn it loose. You got me and your family, your nice house, and fifty seasons of ducks to be shot. And pretty soon, maybe not now, but soon you'll feel like fishing again, here or on the river. Believe me. We've talked and talked and talked. There's nothing you could do and you know it and it's time to get lined out and on with everything."

Mike's far away voice came from inside the storm. The snow sliced through the stand of willows on the wind that seemed all of a sudden angry at us there and made a roar I couldn't think in. I couldn't see the slough so close across the way, but the reeds rattled and the water, boiling with the snow blowing in, made a raspy breath like someone fighting for air. My eyes ached from gust after burning gust and the water overflowing lacquered my cheeks. There was only Mike and me in this icebox, and from the corner of my eye I could see he kept on watching me, those eyes from way under the brow and cap brim, two black barrel holes leveled at me through the storm.

"Yeah, Mike," I said, "I'm sorry as hell." He was always smart and I should believe him, I knew. But still I remembered that elm branch massaging the window some short way over west, over past Finlayson's strips and the dead coal towns, at home. I remembered her on the couch behind the glass, there under that elm, waiting under the moon.

Over the din of the snow in the creek and the wind through the reeds and brush, I could hear Mike settling in. He paid no mind at all to the noise and squinted through the steam for flyers. The day was tight around me and I couldn't feel anything for the cold.

The following is one of the most intriguing short stories ever written. It's a spine-tingling yarn about man hunting man. Crime is afoot here, in a unique form of "big-game" hunt. Anything goes in this classic tale of the macabre. Richard Connell (1893–1949) wrote several books, including Apes and Angels *(1924) and* Murder at Sea *(1929). His coauthored story, "Meet John Doe," was made into a popular movie produced and directed by Frank Capra in 1941.*

Richard Connell

THE MOST DANGEROUS GAME (1925)

"**O**FF THERE TO THE RIGHT—somewhere—is a large island," said Whitney. "It's rather a mystery—"

"What island is it?" Rainsford asked.

"The old charts call it 'Ship-Trap Island,'" Whitney replied. "A suggestive name, isn't it? Sailors have a curious dread of the place. I don't know why. Some superstition—"

"Can't see it," remarked Rainsford, trying to peer through the dank tropical night that was palpable as it pressed its thick warm blackness in upon the yacht.

"You've good eyes," said Whitney, with a laugh, "and I've seen you pick off a moose moving in the brown fall bush at four hundred yards, but even you can't see four miles or so through a moonless Caribbean night."

"Nor four yards," admitted Rainsford. "Ugh! It's like moist velvet."

"It will be light enough in Rio," promised Whitney. "We should make it in a few days. I hope the jaguar guns have come from Purdey's. We should have some good hunting up the Amazon. Great sport, hunting."

"The best sport in the world," agreed Rainsford.

"For the hunter," amended Whitney. "Not for the jaguar."

"Don't talk rot, Whitney," said Rainsford. "You're a big-game hunter, not a philosopher. Who cares how a jaguar feels?"

"Perhaps the jaguar does," observed Whitney.

"Bah! They've no understanding."

"Even so, I rather think they understand one thing at least—fear. The fear of pain and the fear of death."

"Nonsense," laughed Rainsford. "This hot weather is making you soft, Whitney. Be a realist. The world is made up of two classes—the hunters and the hunted. Luckily, you and I are hunters. Do you think we've passed that island yet?"

"I can't tell in the dark. I hope so."

"Why?" asked Rainsford.

"The place has a reputation—a bad one."

"Cannibals?" suggested Rainsford.

"Hardly. Even cannibals wouldn't live in such a God-forsaken place. But it's got into sailor lore, somehow. Didn't you notice that the crew's nerves seem a bit jumpy today?"

"They were a bit strange, now you mention it. Even Captain Nielsen—"

"Yes, even that tough-minded old Swede, who'd go up to the devil himself and ask him for a light. Those fishy blue eyes held a look I never saw there before. All I could get out of him was: 'This place has an evil name among seafaring men, sir.' Then he said to me, very gravely: 'Don't you feel anything?'—as if the air about us was actually poisonous. Now, you mustn't laugh when I tell you this—I did feel something like a sudden chill.

"There was no breeze. The sea was as flat as a plate-glass window. We were drawing near the island then. What I felt was a—a mental chill—a sort of sudden dread."

"Pure imagination," said Rainsford. "One superstitious sailor can taint the whole ship's company with his fear."

"Maybe. But sometimes I think sailors have an extra sense that tells them when they are in danger. Sometimes I think evil is a tangible thing—with wave lengths, just as sound and light have. An evil place can, so to speak, broadcast vibrations of evil. Anyhow, I'm glad we're getting out of this zone. Well, I think I'll turn in now, Rainsford."

"I'm not sleepy," said Rainsford. "I'm going to smoke another pipe up on the after deck."

"Good night, then, Rainsford. See you at breakfast."

"Right. Good night, Whitney."

There was no sound in the night as Rainsford sat there, but the muffled throb of the engine that drove the yacht swiftly through the darkness, and the swish and ripple of the wash of the propeller.

Rainsford, reclining in a steamer chair, indolently puffed on his favorite brier. The sensuous drowsiness of the night was on him. "It's so dark," he thought, "that I could sleep without closing my eyes; the night would be my eyelids—"

An abrupt sound startled him. Off to the right he heard it, and his ears, expert in such matters, could not be mistaken. Again he heard the sound, and again. Somewhere, off in the blackness, someone had fired a gun three times.

Rainsford sprang up and moved quickly to the rail, mystified. He strained his eyes in the direction from which the reports had come, but it was like trying to see through a blanket. He leaped upon the rail and balanced himself there, to get greater elevation; his pipe, striking a rope, was knocked from his mouth. He lunged for it; a short, hoarse cry came from his lips as he realized he had reached too far and had lost his balance. The cry was pinched off short as the blood-warm waters of the Caribbean Sea closed over his head.

He struggled up to the surface and tried to cry out, but the wash from the speeding yacht slapped him in the face and the salt water in his open mouth made him gag and strangle. Desperately he struck out with strong strokes after the receding lights of the yacht, but he stopped before he had swum fifty feet. A certain cool-headedness had come to him; it was not the first time he had been in a tight place. There was a chance that his cries could be heard by someone aboard the yacht, but that chance was slender, and grew more slender as the yacht raced on. He wrestled himself out of his clothes, and shouted with all his power. The lights of the yacht became faint and ever-vanishing fireflies; then they were blotted out entirely by the night.

Rainsford remembered the shots. They had come from the right, and doggedly he swam in that direction, swimming with slow, deliberate strokes, conserving his strength. For a seemingly endless time he fought the sea. He began to count his strokes desperately; he could do possibly a hundred more and then—

Rainsford heard a sound. It came out of the darkness, a high, screaming sound, the sound of an animal in an extremity of anguish and terror.

He did not recognize the animal that made the sound; he did not try to; with fresh vitality he swam toward the sound. He heard it again; then it was cut short by another noise, crisp, staccato.

"Pistol shot," muttered Rainsford, swimming on.

Ten minutes of determined effort brought another sound to his ears— the most welcome he had ever heard—the muttering and growling of the sea breaking on a rocky shore. He was almost on the rocks before he saw them; on a night less calm he would have been shattered against them. With his remaining strength he dragged himself from the swirling waters. Jagged crags appeared to jut up into the opaqueness; he forced himself upward, hand over hand. Gasping, his hands raw, he reached a flat place at the top. Dense jungle came down to the very edge of the cliffs. What perils that tangle of trees and underbrush might hold for him did not concern Rainsford just then. All he knew was that he was safe from his enemy, the sea, and that utter weariness was on him. He flung himself down at the jungle edge and tumbled headlong into the deepest sleep of his life.

When he opened his eyes he knew from the position of the sun that it was late in the afternoon. Sleep had given him new vigor; a sharp hunger was picking at him. He looked about him, almost cheerfully.

"Where there are pistol shots, there are men. Where there are men, there is food," he thought. But what kind of men, he wondered, in so forbidding a place? An unbroken front of snarled and jagged jungle fringed the shore.

He saw no sign of a trail through the closely knit web of weeds and trees; it was easier to go along the shore, and Rainsford floundered along by the water. Not far from where he had landed, he stopped.

Some wounded thing, by the evidence a large animal, had thrashed about in the underbrush; the jungle weeds were crushed down and the moss was lacerated; one patch of weeds was stained crimson. A small, glittering object not far away caught Rainsford's eye and he picked it up. It was an empty cartridge.

"A twenty-two," he remarked. "That's odd. It must have been a fairly large animal, too. The hunter had his nerve to tackle it with a light gun. It's clear that the brute put up a fight. I suppose the first three shots I heard was when the hunter flushed his quarry and wounded it. The last shot was when he trailed it here and finished it."

He examined the ground closely and found what he had hoped to find—the print of hunting boots. They pointed along the cliff in the direction he had been going. Eagerly he hurried along, now slipping on a rotten log or a loose stone, but making headway; night was beginning to settle down on the island.

Bleak darkness was blacking out the sea and jungle when Rainsford sighted the lights. He came upon them as he turned a crook in the coast line, and his first thought was that he had come upon a village, for there were many lights. But as he forged along he saw to his great astonishment that all the lights were in one enormous building—a lofty structure with pointed towers plunging upward into the gloom. His eyes made out the shadowy outlines of a palatial château; it was set on a high bluff, and on three sides of it cliffs dived down to where the sea licked greedy lips in the shadows.

"Mirage," thought Rainsford. But it was no mirage, he found, when he opened the tall spiked iron gate. The stone steps were real enough; the massive door with a leering gargoyle for a knocker was real enough; yet about it all hung an air of unreality.

He lifted the knocker, and it creaked up stiffly, as if it had never before been used. He let it fall, and it startled him with its booming loudness. He thought he heard footsteps within; the door remained closed. Again Rainsford lifted the heavy knocker, and let it fall. The door opened then, opened as suddenly as if it were on a spring, and Rainsford stood blinking in the river of glaring gold light that poured out. The first thing Rainsford's eyes discerned was the largest man Rainsford had ever seen—a gigantic creature, solidly made and black-bearded to the waist. In his hand the man held a long-barrel revolver, and he was pointing it straight at Rainsford's heart.

Out of the snarl of beard two small eyes regarded Rainsford.

"Don't be alarmed," said Rainsford, with a smile which he hoped was disarming. "I'm no robber. I fell off a yacht. My name is Sanger Rainsford of New York City."

The menacing look in the eyes did not change. The revolver pointed as rigidly as if the giant were a statue. He gave no sign that he understood Rainsford's words, or that he had even heard them. He was dressed in uniform, a black uniform trimmed with gray astrakhan.

"I'm Sanger Rainsford of New York," Rainsford began again. "I fell off a yacht. I am hungry."

The man's only answer was to raise with his thumb the hammer of his revolver. Then Rainsford saw the man's free hand go to his forehead in a military salute, and he saw him click his heels together and stand at attention. Another man was coming down the broad marble steps, an erect, slender man in evening clothes. He advanced to Rainsford and held out his hand.

In a cultivated voice marked by a slight accent that gave it added precision and deliberateness, he said: "It is a very great pleasure and honor to welcome Mr. Sanger Rainsford, the celebrated hunter, to my home."

Automatically Rainsford shook the man's hand.

"I've read your book about hunting snow leopards in Tibet, you see," explained the man. "I am General Zaroff."

Rainsford's first impression was that the man was singularly handsome; his second was that there was an original, almost bizarre quality about the general's face. He was a tall man past middle age, for his hair was a vivid white; but his thick eyebrows and pointed military mustache were as black as the night from which Rainsford had come. His eyes, too, were black and very bright. He had high cheek bones, a sharp-cut nose, a spare, dark face, the face of a man used to giving orders, the face of an aristocrat. Turning to the giant in uniform, the general made a sign. The giant put away his pistol, saluted, withdrew.

"Ivan is an incredibly strong fellow," remarked the general, "but he has the misfortune to be deaf and dumb. A simple fellow, but, I'm afraid, like all his race, a bit of a savage."

"Is he Russian?"

"He is a Cossack," said the general, and his smile showed red lips and pointed teeth. "So am I.

"Come," he said, "we shouldn't be chatting here. We can talk later. Now you want clothes, food, rest. You shall have them. This is a most restful spot."

Ivan had reappeared, and the general spoke to him with lips that moved but gave forth no sound.

"Follow Ivan, if you please, Mr. Rainsford," said the general. "I was about to have my dinner when you came. I'll wait for you. You'll find that my clothes will fit you, I think."

It was to a huge, beam-ceilinged bedroom with a canopied bed big enough for six men that Rainsford followed the silent giant. Ivan laid out an evening suit, and Rainsford, as he put it on, noticed that it came from a London tailor who ordinarily cut and sewed for none below the rank of duke.

The dining room to which Ivan conducted him was in many ways remarkable. There was a medieval magnificence about it; it suggested a baronial hall of feudal times with its oaken panels, its high ceiling, its vast refectory table where twoscore men could sit down to eat. About the hall were the mounted heads of many animals—lions, tigers, elephants, moose, bears; larger or more perfect specimens Rainsford had never seen. At the great table the general was sitting, alone.

"You'll have a cocktail, Mr. Rainsford," he suggested. The cocktail was surpassingly good; and, Rainsford noted, the table appointments were of the finest, the linen, the crystal, the silver, the china.

They were eating *borsch*, the rich, red soup with sour cream so dear to Russian palates. Half apologetically General Zaroff said: "We do our best to preserve the amenities of civilization here. Please forgive any lapses. We are well off the beaten track, you know. Do you think the champagne has suffered from its long ocean trip?"

"Not in the least," declared Rainsford. He was finding the general a most thoughtful and affable host, a true cosmopolite. But there was one small trait of the general's that made Rainsford uncomfortable. Whenever he looked up from his plate he found the general studying him, appraising him narrowly.

"Perhaps," said General Zaroff, "you were surprised that I recognized your name. You see, I read all books on hunting published in English, French, and Russian. I have but one passion in my life, Mr. Rainsford, and it is the hunt."

"You have some wonderful heads here," said Rainsford as he ate a particularly well cooked filet mignon. "That Cape buffalo is the largest I ever saw."

"Oh, that fellow. Yes, he was a monster."

"Did he charge you?"

"Hurled me against a tree," said the general. "Fractured my skull. But I got the brute."

"I've always thought," said Rainsford, "that the Cape buffalo is the most dangerous of all big game."

For a moment the general did not reply; he was smiling his curious red-lipped smile. Then he said slowly: "No. You are wrong, sir. The Cape buffalo is not the most dangerous big game." He sipped his wine. "Here in my preserve on this island," he said in the same slow tone, "I hunt more dangerous game."

Rainsford expressed his surprise. "Is there big game on this island?"

The general nodded. "The biggest."

"Really?"

"Oh, it isn't here naturally, of course. I have to stock the island."

"What have you imported, General?" Rainsford asked. "Tigers?"

The general smiled. "No," he said. "Hunting tigers ceased to interest me some years ago. I exhausted their possibilities, you see. No thrill left in tigers, no real danger. I live for danger, Mr. Rainsford."

The general took from his pocket a gold cigarette case and offered his guest a long black cigarette with a silver tip; it was perfumed and gave off a smell like incense.

"We will have some capital hunting, you and I," said the general. "I shall be most glad to have your society."

"But what game—" began Rainsford.

"I'll tell you," said the general. "You will be amused, I know. I think I may say, in all modesty, that I have done a rare thing. I have invented a new sensation. May I pour you another glass of port, Mr. Rainsford?"

"Thank you, General."

The general filled both glasses, and said: "God makes some men poets. Some He makes kings, some beggars. Me He made a hunter. My hand was made for the trigger, my father said. He was a very rich man with a quarter of a million acres in the Crimea, and he was an ardent sportsman. When I was only five years old he gave me a little gun, specially made in Moscow for me, to shoot sparrows with. When I shot some of his prize turkeys with it, he did not punish me; he complimented me on my marksmanship. I killed my first bear in the Caucasus when I was ten. My whole life has been one prolonged hunt. I went into the army—it was expected of noblemen's sons—and for a time commanded a division of Cossack cavalry, but my real interest was always the hunt. I have hunted every kind of game in every land. It would be impossible for me to tell you how many animals I have killed."

The general puffed at his cigarette.

"After the debacle in Russia I left the country, for it was imprudent for an officer of the Czar to stay there. Many noble Russians lost everything. I, luckily, had invested heavily in American securities, so I shall never have to open a tea room in Monte Carlo or drive a taxi in Paris. Naturally, I continued to hunt—grizzlies in your Rockies, crocodiles in the Ganges, rhinoceroses in East Africa. It was in Africa that the Cape buffalo hit me and laid me up for six months. As soon as I recovered I started for the Amazon to hunt jaguars, for I had heard they were unusually cunning. They weren't." The Cossack sighed. "They were no match at all for a hunter with his wits about him, and a high-powered rifle. I was bitterly disappointed. I was lying in my tent with a splitting headache one night when a terrible thought pushed its way into my mind. Hunting was beginning to bore me! And hunting, remember, had been my life. I have heard that in America business men often go to pieces when they give up the business that has been their life."

"Yes, that's so," said Rainsford.

The general smiled. "I had no wish to go to pieces," he said. "I must do something. Now, mine is an analytical mind, Mr. Rainsford. Doubtless that is why I enjoy the problems of the chase."

"No doubt, General Zaroff."

"So," continued the general, "I asked myself why the hunt no longer fascinated me. You are much younger than I am, Mr. Rainsford, and have not hunted as much, but you perhaps can guess the answer."

"What was it?"

"Simply this: hunting had ceased to be what you call 'a sporting proposition.' It had become too easy. I always got my quarry. Always. There is no greater bore than perfection."

The general lit a fresh cigarette.

"No animal had a chance with me any more. That is no boast; it is a mathematical certainty. The animal had nothing but his legs and his instinct. Instinct is no match for reason. When I thought of this it was a tragic moment for me, I can tell you."

Rainsford leaned across the table, absorbed in what his host was saying.

"It came to me as an inspiration what I must do," the general went on.

"And that was?"

The general smiled the quiet smile of one who has faced an obstacle and surmounted it with success. "I had to invent a new animal to hunt," he said.

"A new animal? You are joking."

"Not at all," said the general. "I never joke about hunting. I needed a new animal. I found one. So I bought this island, built this house, and here I do my hunting. The island is perfect for my purposes—there are jungles with a maze of trails in them, hills, swamps—"

"But the animal, General Zaroff?"

"Oh," said the general, "it supplies me with the most exciting hunting in the world. No other hunting compares with it for an instant. Every day I hunt, and I never grow bored now, for I have a quarry with which I can match my wits."

Rainsford's bewilderment showed in his face.

"I wanted the ideal animal to hunt," explained the general. "So I said: 'What are the attributes of an ideal quarry?' And the answer was, of course: 'It must have courage, cunning, and, above all, it must be able to reason.'"

"But no animal can reason," objected Rainsford.

"My dear fellow," said the general, "there is one that can."

"But you can't mean—" gasped Rainsford.

"And why not?"

"I can't believe you are serious, General Zaroff. This is a grisly joke."

"Why should I not be serious? I am speaking of hunting."

"Hunting? Good God, General Zaroff, what you speak of is murder."

The general laughed with entire good nature. He regarded Rainsford quizzically. "I refuse to believe that so modern and civilized a young man as you seem to be harbors romantic ideas about the value of human life. Surely your experiences in the war—" He stopped.

"Did not make me condone cold-blooded murder," finished Rainsford stiffly.

Laughter shook the general. "How extraordinarily droll you are!" he said. "One does not expect nowadays to find a young man of the educated class, even in America, with such a naïve, and, if I may say so, mid-Victorian point of view. It's like finding a snuffbox in a limousine. Ah, well, doubtless you had Puritan ancestors. So many Americans appear to have had. I'll wager you'll forget your notions when you go hunting with me. You've a genuine new thrill in store for you, Mr. Rainsford."

"Thank you, I'm a hunter, not a murderer."

"Dear me," said the general, quite unruffled, "again that unpleasant word. But I think I can show you that your scruples are quite ill founded."

"Yes?"

"Life is for the strong, to be lived by the strong, and, if needs be, taken by the strong. The weak of the world were put here to give the strong pleasure. I am strong. Why should I not use my gift? If I wish to hunt, why should I not? I hunt the scum of the earth—sailors from tramp ships—lascars, blacks, Chinese, whites, mongrels—a thoroughbred horse or hound is worth more than a score of them."

"But they are men," said Rainsford hotly.

"Precisely," said the general. "That is why I use them. It gives me pleasure. They can reason, after a fashion. So they are dangerous."

"But where do you get them?"

The general's left eyelid fluttered down in a wink. "This island is called Ship-Trap," he answered. "Sometimes an angry god of the high seas sends them to me. Sometimes, when Providence is not so kind, I help Providence a bit. Come to the window with me."

Rainsford went to the window and looked out toward the sea.

"Watch! Out there!" exclaimed the general, pointing into the night. Rainsford's eyes saw only blackness, and then, as the general pressed a button, far out to sea Rainsford saw the flash of lights.

The general chuckled. "They indicate a channel," he said, "where there's none: giant rocks with razor edges crouch like a sea monster with wide-open jaws. They can crush a ship as easily as I crush this nut." He dropped a walnut on the hardwood floor and brought his heel grinding down on it. "Oh, yes," he said casually, as if in answer to a question, "I have electricity. We try to be civilized here."

"Civilized? And you shoot down men?"

A trace of anger was in the general's black eyes, but it was there for but a second, and he said, in his most pleasant manner: "Dear me, what a righteous young man you are! I assure you I do not do the thing you suggest. That would be barbarous. I treat these visitors with every consideration. They get plenty of good food and exercise. They get into splendid physical condition. You shall see for yourself tomorrow."

"What do you mean?"

"We'll visit my training school," smiled the general. "It's in the cellar. I have about a dozen pupils down there now. They're from the Spanish bark *San Lucar* that had the bad luck to go on the rocks out there. A very inferior lot, I regret to say. Poor specimens and more accustomed to the deck than to the jungle."

He raised his hand, and Ivan, who served as waiter, brought thick Turkish coffee. Rainsford, with an effort, held his tongue in check.

"It's a game, you see," pursued the general blandly. "I suggest to one of them that we go hunting. I give him a supply of food and an excellent hunting knife. I give him three hours' start. I am to follow, armed only with a pistol of the smallest calibre and range. If my quarry eludes me for three whole days, he wins the game. If I find him"—the general smiled—"he loses."

"Suppose he refuses to be hunted."

"Oh," said the general, "I give him his option, of course. He need not play that game if he doesn't wish to. If he does not wish to hunt, I turn him over to Ivan. Ivan once had the honor of serving as official knouter to the Great White Czar, and he has his own ideas of sport. Invariably, Mr. Rainsford, invariably they chose the hunt."

"And if they win?"

The smile on the general's face widened. "To date I have not lost," he said.

Then he added, hastily: "I don't wish you to think me a braggart, Mr. Rainsford. Many of them afford only the most elementary sort of problem. Occasionally I strike a tartar. One almost did win. I eventually had to use the dogs."

"The dogs?"

"This way, please. I'll show you."

The general steered Rainsford to a window. The lights from the windows sent a flickering illumination that made grotesque patterns on the courtyard below, and Rainsford could see moving about there a dozen or so huge black shapes; as they turned toward him, their eyes glittered greenly.

"A rather good lot, I think," observed the general. "They are let out at seven every night. If anyone should try to get into my house—or out of it—something extremely regrettable would occur to him." He hummed a snatch of song from the Folies Bergère.

"And now," said the general, "I want to show you my new collection of heads. Will you come with me to the library?"

"I hope," said Rainsford, "that you will excuse me tonight, General Zaroff. I'm really not feeling at all well."

"Ah, indeed?" the general inquired solicitously. "Well, I suppose that's only natural, after your long swim. You need a good, restful night's sleep. Tomorrow you'll feel like a new man, I'll wager. Then we'll hunt, eh? I've one rather promising prospect—"

Rainsford was hurrying from the room.

"Sorry you can't go with me tonight," called the general. "I expect rather fair sport—a big, strong black. He looks resourceful—Well, good night, Mr. Rainsford; I hope that you have a good night's rest."

The bed was good and the pajamas of the softest silk, and he was tired in every fiber of his being, but nevertheless Rainsford could not quiet his brain with the opiate of sleep. He lay, eyes wide open. Once he thought he heard stealthy steps in the corridor outside his room. He sought to throw open the door; it would not open. He went to the window and looked out. His room was high up in one of the towers. The lights of the château were out now, and it was dark and silent, but there was a fragment of sallow moon, and by its wan light he could see, dimly, the courtyard; there, weaving in and out in the pattern of shadow, were black, noiseless forms; the hounds heard him at the window and looked up, expectantly, with their green eyes. Rainsford went back to the bed and lay down. By many methods he tried to put himself to sleep. He had achieved a doze when, just as morning began to come, he heard, far off in the jungle, the faint report of a pistol.

General Zaroff did not appear until luncheon. He was dressed faultlessly in the tweeds of a country squire. He was solicitous about the state of Rainsford's health.

"As for me," sighed the general, "I do not feel so well. I am worried, Mr. Rainsford. Last night I detected traces of my old complaint."

To Rainsford's questioning glance the general said: "Ennui. Boredom."

Then, taking a second helping of *Crêpes Suzette*, the general explained: "The hunting was not good last night. The fellow lost his head. He made a straight trail that offered no problems at all. That's the trouble with these sailors; they have dull brains to begin with, and they do not know how to get about in the woods. They do excessively stupid and obvious things. It's most annoying. Will you have another glass of Chablis, Mr. Rainsford?"

"General," said Rainsford firmly, "I wish to leave this island at once."

The general raised his thickets of eyebrows; he seemed hurt. "But, my dear fellow," the general protested, "you've only just come. You've had no hunting—"

"I wish to go today," said Rainsford. He saw the dead black eyes of the general on him, studying him. General Zaroff's face suddenly brightened.

He filled Rainsford's glass with venerable Chablis from a dusty bottle.

"Tonight," said the general, "we will hunt—you and I."

Rainsford shook his head. "No, General," he said. "I will not hunt."

The general shrugged his shoulders and delicately ate a hothouse grape. "As you wish, my friend," he said. "The choice rests entirely with you. But may I not venture to suggest that you will find my idea of sport more diverting than Ivan's?"

He nodded toward the corner to where the giant stood, scowling, his thick arms crossed on his hogshead of chest.

"You don't mean—" cried Rainsford.

"My dear fellow," said the general, "have I not told you I always mean what I say about hunting? This is really an inspiration. I drink to a foeman worthy of my steel—at last."

The general raised his glass, but Rainsford sat staring at him.

"You'll find this game worth playing," the general said enthusiastically. "Your brain against mine. Your woodcraft against mine. Your strength and stamina against mine. Outdoor chess! And the stake is not without value, eh?"

"And if I win—" began Rainsford huskily.

"I'll cheerfully acknowledge myself defeated if I do not find you by midnight of the third day," said General Zaroff. "My sloop will place you on the mainland near a town."

The general read what Rainsford was thinking.

"Oh, you can trust me," said the Cossack. "I will give you my word as a gentleman and a sportsman. Of course you, in turn, must agree to say nothing of your visit here."

"I'll agree to nothing of the kind," said Rainsford.

"Oh," said the general, "in that case—But why discuss it now? Three days hence we can discuss it over a bottle of Veuve Clicquot, unless—"

The general sipped his wine.

Then a businesslike air animated him. "Ivan," he said to Rainsford, "will supply you with hunting clothes, food, a knife. I suggest you wear moccasins; they leave a poorer trail. I suggest too that you avoid the big swamp in the southeast corner of the island. We call it Death Swamp. There's quicksand there. One foolish fellow tried it. The deplorable part of it was that Lazarus followed him. You can imagine my feelings, Mr. Rainsford. I loved Lazarus; he was the finest hound in my pack. Well, I must beg you to excuse me now. I always take a siesta after lunch. You'll hardly have time for a nap, I fear. You'll want to start, no doubt. I shall not follow till dusk. Hunting at night is so much more exciting than by day, don't you think? *Au revoir*, Mr. Rainsford, au revoir."

General Zaroff, with a deep, courtly bow, strolled from the room.

From another door came Ivan. Under one arm he carried khaki hunting clothes, a haversack of food, a leather sheath containing a long-bladed hunting knife; his right hand rested on a cocked revolver thrust in the crimson sash about his waist. . . .

Rainsford had fought his way through the bush for two hours. "I must keep my nerve. I must keep my nerve," he said through tight teeth.

He had not been entirely clear-headed when the château gates snapped shut behind him. His whole idea at first was to put distance between himself and General Zaroff, and, to this end, he had plunged along, spurred on by the sharp rowels of something very like panic. Now he had got a grip on himself, had stopped, and was taking stock of himself and the situation.

He saw that straight flight was futile; inevitably it would bring him face to face with the sea. He was in a picture with a frame of water, and his operations, clearly, must take place within that frame.

"I'll give him a trail to follow," muttered Rainsford, and he struck off from the rude path he had been following into the trackless wilderness. He executed a series of intricate loops; he doubled on his trail again and again, recalling all the lore of the fox hunt, and all the dodges of the fox. Night found him leg-weary, with hands and face lashed by the branches, on a thickly wooded ridge. He knew it would be insane to blunder on through the dark, even if he had the strength. His need for rest was imperative and he thought: "I have played the fox, now I must play the cat of the fable." A big tree with a thick trunk and outspread branches was near by, and, taking care to leave not the slightest mark, he climbed up into the crotch, and stretching out on one of the broad limbs, after a fashion, rested. Rest brought him new confidence and almost a feeling of security. Even so zealous a hunter as General Zaroff could not trace him there, he told himself; only the devil himself could follow that complicated trail through the jungle after dark. But, perhaps, the general was a devil—

An apprehensive night crawled slowly by like a wounded snake, and sleep did not visit Rainsford, although the silence of a dead world was on the jungle. Toward morning when a dingy gray was varnishing the sky, the cry of some startled bird focused Rainsford's attention in that direction. Something was coming through the bush, coming slowly, carefully, coming by the same winding way Rainsford had come. He flattened himself down on the limb, and through a screen of leaves almost as thick as tapestry, he watched. The thing that was approaching him was a man.

It was General Zaroff. He made his way along with his eyes fixed in utmost concentration on the ground before him. He paused, almost beneath the tree, dropped to his knees and studied the ground. Rainsford's impulse was to hurl himself down like a panther, but he saw that the general's right hand held something small and metallic—an automatic pistol.

The hunter shook his head several times, as if he were puzzled. Then he straightened up and took from his case one of his black cigarettes; its pungent incenselike smoke floated up to Rainsford's nostrils. Rainsford held his breath. The general's eyes had left the ground and were traveling inch by inch up the tree. Rainsford froze there, every muscle tensed for a spring. But the sharp eyes of the hunter stopped before they reached the limb where Rainsford lay; a smile spread over his brown face. Very deliberately he blew a smoke ring into the air; then he turned his back on the tree and walked carelessly away, back along the trail he had come. The swish of the underbrush against his hunting boots grew fainter and fainter.

The pent-up air burst hotly from Rainsford's lungs. His first thought made him feel sick and numb. The general could follow a trail through the woods at night; he could follow an extremely difficult trail; he must have uncanny powers; only by the merest chance had the Cossack failed to see his quarry.

Rainsford's second thought was even more terrible. It sent a shudder of cold horror through his whole being. Why had the general smiled? Why had he turned back?

Rainsford did not want to believe what his reason told him was true, but the truth was as evident as the sun that had by now pushed through the morning mists. The general was playing with him! The general was saving him for another day's sport! The Cossack was the cat; he was the mouse. Then it was that Rainsford knew the full meaning of terror.

"I will not lose my nerve. I will not."

He slid down from the tree, and struck off again into the woods. His face was set and he forced the machinery of his mind to function. Three hundred yards from his hiding place he stopped where a huge dead tree leaned precariously on a smaller, living one. Throwing off his sack of food, Rainsford took his knife from its sheath and began to work with all his energy.

The job was finished at last, and he threw himself down behind a fallen log a hundred feet away. He did not have to wait long. The cat was coming again to play with the mouse.

Following the trail with the sureness of a bloodhound came General Zaroff. Nothing escaped those searching black eyes, no crushed blade of grass, no bent twig, no mark, no matter how faint, in the moss. So intent was the Cossack on his stalking that he was upon the thing Rainsford had made before he saw it. His foot touched the protruding bough that was the trigger. Even as he touched it, the general sensed his danger and leaped back with the agility of an ape. But he was not quite quick enough; the dead tree, delicately adjusted to rest on the cut living one, crashed down and struck the general a glancing blow on the shoulder as it fell; but for his alertness, he must have been smashed beneath it. He staggered, but he did not fall; nor did he drop his revolver. He stood there, rubbing his injured shoulder, and Rainsford, with fear again gripping his heart, heard the general's mocking laugh ring through the jungle.

"Rainsford," called the general, "if you are within sound of my voice, as I suppose you are, let me congratulate you. Not many men know how to make a Malay man catcher. Luckily for me, I too have hunted in Malacca. You are proving interesting, Mr. Rainsford. I am going now to have my wound dressed; it's only a slight one. But I shall be back. I shall be back."

When the general, nursing his bruised shoulder, had gone, Rainsford took up his flight again. It was flight now, a desperate, hopeless flight, that carried him on for some hours. Dusk came, then darkness, and still he pressed on. The ground grew softer under his moccasins; the vegetation grew ranker, denser; insects bit him savagely. Then, as he stepped forward, his foot sank into the ooze. He tried to wrench it back, but the muck sucked viciously at his foot as if it were a giant leech. With a violent effort, he tore his foot loose. He knew where he was now. Death Swamp and its quicksand.

His hands were tight closed as if his nerve were something tangible that someone in the darkness was trying to tear from his grip. The softness of the earth had given him an idea. He stepped back from the quicksand a dozen feet or so and, like some huge prehistoric beaver, he began to dig.

Rainsford had dug himself in in France when a second's delay meant death. That had been a placid pastime compared to his digging now. The pit grew deeper; when it was above his shoulders, he climbed out and from some hard saplings cut stakes and sharpened them to a fine point. These stakes he planted in the bottom of the pit with the points sticking up. With flying fingers he wove a rough carpet of weeds and branches and with it he covered the mouth of the pit. Then, wet with sweat and aching with tiredness, he crouched behind the stump of a lightning-charred tree.

He knew his pursuer was coming; he heard the paddling sound of feet on the soft earth, and the night breeze brought him the perfume of the general's cigarette. It seemed to Rainsford that the general was coming with unusual swiftness; he was not feeling his way along, foot by foot. Rainsford, crouching there, could not see the general, nor could he see the pit. He lived a year in a minute. Then he felt an impulse to cry aloud with joy, for he heard the sharp crackle of the breaking branches as the cover of the pit gave way; he heard the sharp scream of pain as the pointed stakes found their mark. He leaped up from his place of concealment. Then he cowered back. Three feet from the pit a man was standing, with an electric torch in his hand.

"You've done well, Rainsford," the voice of the general called. "Your Burmese tiger pit has claimed one of my best dogs. Again you score. I think, Mr. Rainsford, I'll see what you can do against my whole pack. I'm going home for a rest now. Thank you for a most amusing evening."

At daybreak Rainsford, lying near the swamp, was awakened by a sound that made him know that he had new things to learn about fear. It was a distant sound, faint and wavering, but he knew it. It was the baying of a pack of hounds.

Rainsford knew he could do one of two things. He could stay where he was and wait. That was suicide. He could flee. That was postponing the inevitable. For a moment he stood there, thinking. An idea that held a wild chance came to him, and, tightening his belt, he headed away from the swamp.

The baying of the hounds drew nearer, then still nearer, nearer, ever nearer. On a ridge Rainsford climbed a tree. Down a watercourse, not a quarter of a mile away, he could see the bush moving. Straining his eyes, he saw the lean figure of General Zaroff; just ahead of him Rainsford made out another figure whose wide shoulders surged through the tall jungle weeds; it was the giant Ivan, and he seemed pulled forward by some unseen force; Rainsford knew that Ivan must be holding the pack in leash.

They would be on him any minute now. His mind worked frantically. He thought of a native trick he had learned in Uganda. He slid down the tree. He caught hold of a springy young sapling and to it he fastened his hunting knife, with the blade pointing down the trail; with a bit of wild grapevine he tied back the sapling. Then he ran for his life. The hounds raised their voices as they hit the fresh scent. Rainsford knew now how an animal at bay feels.

He had to stop to get his breath. The baying of the hounds stopped abruptly, and Rainsford's heart stopped too. They must have reached the knife.

He shinned excitedly up a tree and looked back. His pursuers had stopped. But the hope that was in Rainsford's brain when he climbed died, for he saw in the shallow valley that General Zaroff was still on his feet. But Ivan was not. The knife, driven by the recoil of the spring tree, had not wholly failed.

Rainsford had hardly tumbled to the ground when the pack took up the cry again.

"Nerve, nerve, nerve!" he panted, as he dashed along. A blue gap showed between the trees dead ahead. Ever nearer drew the hounds. Rainsford forced himself on toward the gap. He reached it. It was the shore of the sea. Across a cove he could see the gloomy gray stone of the château. Twenty feet below him the sea rumbled and hissed. Rainsford hesitated. He heard the hounds. Then he leaped far out into the sea. . . .

When the general and his pack reached the place by the sea, the Cossack stopped. For some minutes he stood regarding the blue-green expanse of water. He shrugged his shoulders. Then he sat down, took a drink of brandy from a silver flask, lit a perfumed cigarette, and hummed a bit from "Madame Butterfly."

General Zaroff had an exceedingly good dinner in his great paneled dining hall that evening. With it he had a bottle of Pol Roger and half a bottle of Chambertin. Two slight annoyances kept him from perfect enjoyment. One was the thought that it would be difficult to replace Ivan; the other was that his quarry had escaped him; of course, the American hadn't played the game—so thought the general as he tasted his after-dinner liqueur. In his library he read, to soothe himself, from the works of Marcus Aurelius. At ten he went up to his bedroom. He was deliciously tired, he said to himself, as he locked himself in. There was a little moonlight, so, before turning on his light, he went to the window and looked down at the courtyard. He could see the great hounds, and he called: "Better luck another time," to them. Then he switched on the light.

A man, who had been hiding in the curtains of the bed, was standing there.

"Rainsford!" screamed the general. "How in God's name did you get here?"

"Swam," said Rainsford. "I found it quicker than walking through the jungle."

The general sucked in his breath and smiled. "I congratulate you," he said. "You have won the game."

Rainsford did not smile. "I am still a beast at bay," he said, in a low, hoarse voice. "Get ready, General Zaroff."

The general made one of his deepest bows. "I see," he said. "Splendid! One of us is to furnish a repast for the hounds. The other will sleep in this very excellent bed. On guard, Rainsford." . . .

He had never slept in a better bed, Rainsford decided.

This sad but somehow uplifting story is of two boys' friendship sealed by tragedy and the thrill of hunting ducks. The location is northern Ohio in what appears to be the late 1950s. The story was initially published in Playboy *and was included in* The Best American Short Stories, 1986. *Author Thomas McGuane was educated at Michigan State University and the Yale School of Drama. He is well known for his short fiction and novels. Among McGuane's books are* The Bushwacked Piano (*1971*), Ninety-Two in the Shade (*1973*), *and* Keep the Change (*1989*).

Thomas McGuane

SPORTSMEN (1985)

WE KEPT THE PERCH IN a stone pool in front of the living room window. An elm shaded the pool, and when the heavy drapes of the living room were drawn, so that my mother could see the sheet music on the piano, the window reflected the barred shapes of the fish in the pool.

We caught them from the rocks on the edge of the lake, rocks that were submerged when the wakes of passing freighters hit the shore. From a distance, the freighters pushed a big swell in front of them without themselves seeming to move on the great flatness of the lake. My friend that year was a boy named Jimmy Meade and he was learning to identify the vessel stacks of the freighters. We liked the Bob-Lo Line, Cleveland Cliffs, and Wyandotte Transportation with the red Indian tall on the sides of the stacks. We looked for whalebacks and tankers and the laden ore ships and listened to the moaning signals from the horns as they carried over the water. The wakes of those freighters moved slowly toward the land along the unmoving surface of water. The wakes were the biggest feature out there, bigger than Canada behind them, which lay low and thin like the horizon itself.

Jimmy Meade and I were thirteen then. He had moved up from lower Ohio the previous winter and I was fascinated by his almost-southern accent. His father had an old pickup truck in a town which drove mostly sedans, and they had a big loose-limbed hound that seemed to stand for a distant, unpopulated place.

Hoods were beginning to appear in the school, beginning to grow drastic haircuts, wear Flagg Flyer shoes and sing Gene Vincent songs. They hung inside their cars from the wind vanes and stared at the girls I had grown up with, revealing an aspect of violence I had not known. They wolf-whistled. They laughed with their mouths wide open and their eyes glittering, and when they got into fights, they used their feet. They spent their weekends at the drags in Flat Rock. Jimmy and I loved the water, but when the hoods came near it, all they saw were the rubbers. We were downright afraid of the hoods, of how they acted, of the steel taps on their shoes, of the way they saw things, making us feel we would be crazy to ever cross them. We were sportsmen.

But then, we were lost in our plans. We wanted to refurbish a Civil War rifle Jimmy's father owned. We were going to make an ice boat, a duck blind, and a fishing shanty. We were going to dig up an Indian mound, sell the artifacts, and buy a racing hydroplane that would throw a rooster tail five times its own length. But above all, we wanted to be duck hunters.

That August we were diving off the pilings near the entrance to the Thoroughfare Canal. We were talking about salvaging boats from the Black Friday storm of 1916 when the Bob-Lo steamer passed. The wash came in and sucked the water down around the pilings. Jimmy dove from the tallest one, arcing down the length of the creosoted spar into the green, clear water. And then he didn't come up. Not to begin with. When he did, the first thing that surfaced was the curve of his back, white and Ohio-looking in its oval of lake water. It was a back that was never to widen with a muscle or stoop with worry because Jimmy had just then broken his neck. I remember getting him out on the gravel shore. He was wide awake and his eyes poured tears. His body shuddered continuously and I recall his fingers fluttered on the stones with a kind of purpose. I had never heard sounds like that from his mouth in the thousands of hours we had talked. I learned from a neighbor that my screams brought help and, similarly, I can't imagine what I would sound like screaming. Perhaps no one can.

My father decided that month that I was a worthless boy who blamed his troubles on outside events. He had quite a long theory about all of this, and hanging around on the lake or in the flat woods hunting rabbits with our .22s substantiated that theory. I forget how.

He found me a job over in Burr Oak cleaning die-cast aluminum molds with acid and a wire brush. That was the first time I had been around the country people who work in small factories across the nation. Once you get the gist of their ways, you can get along anyplace you go, because they are everywhere and they are good people.

When I tried to call Jimmy Meade from Burr Oak, his father said that he was unable to speak on the telephone. He said Jimmy was out of the hospital and he would always be paralyzed. In his father's voice, with its almost-southern Ohio accent, I could feel myself being made to know that though I had not done this to Jimmy, I had been there, and that there was villainly, somehow, in my escape.

I really don't think I could have gotten out of the factory job without crossing my own father worse than I then dared. But it's true, I missed the early hospitalization of Jimmy and of course I had missed having that accident happen to me in the first place. I still couldn't picture Jimmy not being able to move anything, being kind of frozen where we left off.

I finished up in August and stayed in Sturgis for a couple of days, in a boardinghouse run by an old woman and her sixty-year-old spinster daughter. I was so comfortable with them that I found myself sitting in the front hall watching the street for prospective customers. I told them I was just a duck hunter. Like the factory people, they had once had a farm. After that, I went home to see Jimmy.

He lived in a small house on Macomb Street about a half mile from the hardware. There was a layout duck boat in the yard and quite a few cars parked around, hot rods mostly. What could have explained this attendance? Was it popularity? A strange feeling shot through me.

I went in the screen door at the side of the house, propped ajar with a brick. There were eight or ten people inside, boys and girls our own age. My first feeling, that I had come back from a factory job in another town with tales to tell, vanished and I was suddenly afraid of the people in the room, who were faster, tougher kids than Jimmy and I had known. There were open beer bottles on the table and the radio played hits.

Jimmy was in the corner where the light came through the screens from two directions. He was in a wheelchair and his arms and legs had been neatly folded within the sides of the contraption. He had a duck-tail haircut and a girl held a beer to his lips, then replaced it with a Camel in a fake pearl-and-ebony cigarette holder. His weight had halved and there were copper-colored shadows under his eyes. He looked like a modernized station of the cross.

When he began to talk, his Ohio accent was gone. How did that happen? Insurance was going to buy him a flathead Ford. "I'm going to chop and channel it," he said, "kick the frame, french the headlights, bullnose the hood, and lead the trunk." He stopped and twisted his face to draw on the cigarette. "There's this hillbilly in Taylor Township who can roll and pleat the interior."

I didn't get the feeling he was particularly glad to see me. But what I did was just sit there and tough it out until the room got tense and people just began to pick up and go. That took no time at all: The boys crumpled beer cans in their fists conclusively. The girls smiled with their mouths open and snapped their eyes. Everyone knew something was fishy. They hadn't seen me around since the accident, and the question was: What was I doing there now?

"I seen a bunch of ducks moving," Jimmy said.

"I did too."

"Seen them from the house." Jimmy sucked on his cigarette. "Remember how old Minnow Milton used to shoot out of his boathouse when there was ducks?" Minnow Milton had lived in a floating house that had a trap attached to it from which he sold shiners for bait. The floating house was at the foot of Jimmy's road.

"I remember him."

"Well, Minnow's no longer with us. And the old boat is just setting there doing nothing."

The next morning before daybreak, Jimmy and I were in Minnow Milton's living room with the lake slapping underneath and the sash thrown up. There were still old photographs of the Milton family on the walls. Minnow was a bachelor and no one had come for them. I had my father's 12-gauge pump gun propped on the windowsill and I could see the blocks, the old Mason decoys, all canvasbacks, that I had set out beneath the window, thirty of them bobbing, wooden beaks to the wind, like steamboats seen from a mile up. I really couldn't see Jimmy. I had wheeled him in terror down the gangplank and into the dark. I set the blocks in the dark, and when I lit his cigarette, he stared down the length of the holder, intently, so I couldn't tell what he was thinking. I said, "What fun is there if you can't shoot?"

"Shoot," he said.

"I'm gonna shoot. I was just asking."

"You ain't got no ducks anyways."

To my relief, that was true. But it didn't last. A cold wind came with daylight. A slight snow spit across the dark gray water, touching and scattering down into the whitecaps. I saw a flight of mallards rocket over and disappear behind us. Then they reappeared and did the same thing again right across the roof over our heads. When they came the third time, they set their wings and reached their feet through hundreds of feet of cold air toward the decoys. I killed two and let the wind blow them up against the floating house. Jimmy grinned from ear to ear.

I built a fire in Minnow Milton's old stove and cooked those ducks on a stick. I had to feed Jimmy off the point of my Barlow knife, but we ate two big ducks for breakfast and lunch at once. I stood the pump gun in the corner.

Tall columns of snow advanced toward us across the lake, and among them, right in among them, were ducks, some of everything, including the big canvasbacks that stirred us like old music. Buffleheads raced along the surface.

"Fork me some of that there duck meat," said Jimmy Meade in his Ohio voice.

We stare down from our house window as our decoys fill with ducks. The weather gets so bad the ducks swim among the decoys without caring. After half a day we don't know which is real and which is not. I wrap Jimmy's blanket up under his chin.

"I hope those ducks keep on coming," he says. And they do. We are in a vast raft of ducks. We don't leave until the earth has turned clean around and it is dark again.

A nine-year-old girl goes deer hunting with her father and his friend with a young son. The setting is Pennsylvania, one of the most popular states for deer hunting. The girl's name is Andy and the story is largely told through her eyes. This was David Michael Kaplan's first published story, from the Atlantic Monthly. *Among his books are* Comfort (*1987*) *and* Skating in the Dark (*1991*).

David Michael Kaplan

DOE SEASON
(1985)

THEY WERE ALWAYS THE SAME woods, she thought sleepily as they drove through the early-morning darkness—deep and immense, covered with yesterday's snowfall, which had frozen overnight. They were the same woods that lay behind her house, *and they stretch all the way to here,* she thought, *for miles and miles, longer than I could walk in a day, or a week even, but they are still the same woods.* The thought made her feel good: it was like thinking of God; it was like thinking of the space between here and the moon; it was like thinking of all the foreign countries from her geography book where even now, Andy knew, people were going to bed, while they—she and her father and Charlie Spoon and Mac, Charlie's eleven-year-old son—were driving deeper into the Pennsylvania countryside, to go hunting.

They had risen long before dawn. Her mother, yawning and not trying to hide her sleepiness, cooked them eggs and French toast. Her father smoked a cigarette and flicked ashes into his saucer while Andy listened, wondering *Why doesn't he come?* and *Won't he ever come?,* until at last a car pulled into the graveled drive and honked. "That will be Charlie Spoon," her father said; he always said "Charlie Spoon," even though his real name was Spreun, because Charlie was, in a sense, shaped like a spoon, with a large head and a narrow waist and chest.

Andy's mother kissed her and her father and said, "Well, have a good time" and "Be careful." Soon they were outside in the bitter dark, loading gear by the back-porch light, their breath steaming. The woods behind the house were then only a black streak against the wash of night.

Andy dozed in the car and woke to find that it was half-light. Mac— also sleeping—had slid against her. She pushed him away and looked out the window. Her breath clouded the glass, and she was cold; the car's heater didn't work right. They were riding over gentle hills, the woods on both sides now—the same woods, she knew, because she had been watching the whole way, even while she slept. They had been in her dreams, and she had never lost sight of them.

Charlie Spoon was driving. "I don't understand why she's coming," he said to her father. "How old is she anyway—eight?"

"Nine," her father replied. "She's small for her age."

"So—nine. What's the difference? She'll just add to the noise and get tired besides."

"No, she won't," her father said. "She can walk me to death. And she'll bring good luck, you'll see. Animals—I don't know how she does it, but they come right up to her. We go walking in the woods, and we'll spot more raccoons and possums and such than I ever see when I'm alone."

Charlie grunted.

"Besides, she's not a bad little shot, even if she doesn't hunt yet. She shoots the .22 real good."

"Popgun," Charlie said, and snorted. "And target shooting ain't deer hunting."

"Well, she's not gonna be shooting anyway, Charlie," her father said. "Don't worry. She'll be no bother."

"I still don't know why she's coming," Charlie said.

"Because she wants to, and I want her to. Just like you and Mac. No difference."

Charlie turned onto a side road and after a mile or so slowed down. "That's it!" he cried. He stopped, backed up, and entered a narrow dirt road almost hidden by trees. Five hundred yards down, the road ran parallel to a fenced-in field. Charlie parked in a cleared area deeply rutted by frozen tractor tracks. The gate was locked. *In the spring,* Andy thought, *there will be cows here, and a dog that chases them,* but now the field was unmarked and bare.

"This is it," Charlie Spoon declared. "Me and Mac was up here just two weeks ago, scouting it out, and there's deer. Mac saw the tracks."

"That's right," Mac said.

"Well, we'll just see about that," her father said, putting on his gloves. He turned to Andy. "How you doing, honeybun?"

"Just fine," she said.

Andy shivered and stamped as they unloaded: first the rifles, which they unsheathed and checked, sliding the bolts, sighting through scopes, adjusting the slings; then the gear, their food and tents and sleeping bags and stove stored in four backpacks—three big ones for Charlie Spoon and her father and Mac, and a day pack for her.

"That's about your size," Mac said, to tease her.

She reddened and said, "Mac, I can carry a pack big as yours any day." He laughed and pressed his knee against the back of hers, so that her leg buckled. "Cut it out," she said. She wanted to make an iceball and throw it at him, but she knew that her father and Charlie were anxious to get going, and she didn't want to displease them.

Mac slid under the gate, and they handed the packs over to him. Then they slid under and began walking across the field toward the same woods that ran all the way back to her home, where even now her mother was probably rising again to wash their breakfast dishes and make herself a fresh pot of coffee. *She is there, and we are here:* the thought satisfied Andy. There was no place else she would rather be.

Mac came up beside her. "Over there's Canada," he said, nodding toward the woods.

"Huh!" she said. "Not likely."

"I don't mean *right* over there. I mean farther up north. You think I'm dumb?"

Dumb as your father, she thought.

"Look at that," Mac said, pointing to a piece of cow dung lying on a spot scraped bare of snow. "A frozen meadow muffin." He picked it up and sailed it at her. "Catch!"

"Mac!" she yelled. His laugh was as gawky as he was. She walked faster. He seemed different today somehow, bundled in his yellow-and-black-checkered coat, a rifle in hand, his silly floppy hat not quite covering his ears. They all seemed different as she watched them trudge through the snow—Mac and her father and Charlie Spoon—bigger, maybe, as if the cold landscape enlarged rather than diminished them, so that they, the only figures in that landscape, took on size and meaning just by being there. If they weren't there, everything would be quieter, and the woods would be the same as before. *But they are here,* Andy thought, looking behind her at the boot points in the snow, *and I am too, and so it's all different.*

"We'll go down to the cut where we found those deer tracks," Charlie said as they entered the woods. "Maybe we'll get lucky and get a late one coming through."

The woods descended into a gully. The snow was softer and deeper here, so that often Andy sank to her knees. Charlie and Mac worked the top of the gully while she and her father walked along the base some thirty yards behind them. "If they miss the first shot, we'll get the second," her father said, and she nodded as if she had known this all the time. She listened to the crunch of their boots, their breathing, and the drumming of a distant woodpecker. And the crackling. In winter the woods crackled as if everything were straining, ready to snap like dried chicken bones.

We are hunting, Andy thought. The cold air burned her nostrils.

They stopped to make lunch by a rock outcropping that protected them from the wind. Her father heated the bean soup her mother had made for them, and they ate it with bread already stiff from the cold. He and Charlie took a few pulls from a flask of Jim Beam while she scoured the plates with snow and repacked them. Then they all had coffee with sugar and powdered milk, and her father poured her a cup too. "We won't tell your momma," he said, and Mac laughed. Andy held the cup the way her father did, not by the handle but around the rim. The coffee tasted smoky. She felt a little queasy, but she drank it all.

Charlie Spoon picked his teeth with a fingernail. "Now, you might've noticed one thing," he said.

"What's that?" her father asked.

"You might've noticed you don't hear no rifles. That's because there ain't no other hunters here. We've got the whole damn woods to ourselves. Now, I ask you–do I know how to find 'em?"

"We haven't seen deer yet, neither."

"Oh, we will," Charlie said, "but not for a while now." He leaned back against the rock. "Deer're sleeping, resting up for the evening feed."

"I seen a deer behind our house once, and it was afternoon," Andy said.

"Yeah, honey, but that was *before* deer season," Charlie said, grinning. "They know something now. They're smart that way."

"That's right," Mac said.

Andy looked at her father–had she said something stupid?

"Well, Charlie," he said, "if they know so much, how come so many get themselves shot?"

"Them's the ones that don't *believe* what they know," Charlie replied. The men laughed. Andy hesitated, and then laughed with them.

They moved on, as much to keep warm as to find a deer. The wind became even stronger. Blowing through the treetops, it sounded like the ocean, and once Andy thought she could smell salt air. But that was impossible; the ocean was *hundreds* of miles away, further than Canada even. She and her parents had gone last summer to stay for a week at a motel on the New Jersey shore. That was the first time she'd seen the ocean, and it frightened her. It was huge and empty, yet always moving. Everything lay hidden. If you walked in it, you couldn't see how deep it was or what might be below; if you swam, something could pull you under and you'd never be seen again. Its musky, rank smell made her think of things dying. Her mother had floated beyond the breakers, calling to her to come in, but Andy wouldn't go farther than a few feet into the surf. Her mother swam and splashed with animal-like delight while her father, smiling shyly, held his white arms above the waist-deep water as if afraid to get them wet. Once a comber rolled over and sent them both tossing, and when her mother tried to stand up, the surf receding behind, Andy saw that her mother's swimsuit top had come off, so that her breasts swayed free, her nipples like two dark eyes. Embarrassed, Andy looked around: except for two women under a yellow umbrella farther up, the beach was empty. Her mother stood up unsteadily, regained her footing. Taking what seemed the longest time, she calmly refixed her top. Andy lay on the beach towel and closed her eyes. The sound of the surf made her head ache.

And now it was winter; the sky was already dimming, not just with the absence of light but with a mist that clung to the hunters' faces like cobwebs. They made camp early. Andy was chilled. When she stood still, she kept wiggling her toes to make sure they were there. Her father rubbed her arms and held her to him briefly, and that felt better. She unpacked the food while the others put up the tents.

"How about rounding us up some firewood, Mac?" Charlie asked.

"I'll do it," Andy said. Charlie looked at her thoughtfully and then handed her the canvas carrier.

There wasn't much wood on the ground, so it took her a while to get a good load. She was about a hundred yards from camp, near a cluster of high, lichen-covered boulders, when she saw through a crack in the rock a buck and two does walking gingerly, almost daintily, through the alder trees. She tried to hush her breathing as they passed not more than twenty yards away. There was nothing she could do. If she yelled, they'd be gone; by the time she got back to camp, they'd be gone. The buck stopped, nostrils quivering, tail up and alert. He looked directly at her. Still she didn't move, not one muscle. He was a beautiful buck, the color of late-turned maple leaves. Unafraid, he lowered his tail, and he and his does silently merged into the trees. Andy walked back to camp and dropped the firewood.

"I saw three deer," she said. "A buck and two does."

"Where?" Charlie Spoon cried, looking behind her as if they might have followed her into camp.

"In the woods yonder. They're gone now."

"Well, hell!" Charlie banged his coffee cup against his knee.

"Didn't I say she could find animals?" her father said, grinning.

"Too late to go after them," Charlie muttered. "It'll be dark in a quarter hour. Damn!"

"Damn," Mac echoed.

"They just walk right up to her," her father said.

"Well, leastwise this proves there's deer here." Charlie began snapping long branches into shorter ones. "You know, I think I'll stick with you," he told Andy, "since you're so good at finding deer and all. How'd that be?"

"Okay, I guess," Andy murmured. She hoped he was kidding: no way did she want to hunt with Charlie Spoon. Still, she was pleased he had said it.

Her father and Charlie took one tent, she and Mac the other. When they were in their sleeping bags, Mac said in the darkness, "I bet you really didn't see no deer, did you?"

She sighed. "I did, Mac. Why would I lie?"

"How big was the buck?"

"Four point. I counted."

Mac snorted.

"You just believe what you want, Mac," she said testily.

"Too bad it ain't buck season," he said. "Well, I got to go pee."

"So pee."

She heard him turn in his bag. "You ever see it?" he asked.

"It? What's it?"

"It. A pecker."

"Sure," she lied.

"Whose? Your father's?"

She was uncomfortable. "No," she said.

"Well, whose then?"

"Oh, I don't know! Leave me be, why don't you?"

"Didn't see a deer, didn't see a pecker," Mac said teasingly.

She didn't answer right away. Then she said, "My cousin Lewis. I saw his."

"Well, how old's he?"

"One and a half."

"Ha! A baby! A baby's is like a little worm. It ain't a real one at all."

If he says he'll show me his, she thought, *I'll kick him. I'll just get out of my bag and kick him.*

"I went hunting with my daddy and Versh and Danny Simmons last year in buck season," Mac said, "and we got ourselves one. And we hog-dressed the thing. You know what that is, don't you?"

"No," she said. She was confused. What was he talking about now?

"That's when you cut him open and take out all his guts, so the meat don't spoil. Makes him lighter to pack out, too."

She tried to imagine what the deer's guts might look like, pulled from the gaping hole. "What do you do with them?" she asked. "The guts?"

"Oh, just leave 'em for the bears."

She ran her finger like a knife blade along her belly.

"When we left them on the ground," Mac said, "they smoked. Like they were cooking."

"Huh," she said.

"They cut off the deer's pecker, too, you know."

Andy imagined Lewis's pecker and shuddered. "Mac, you're disgusting."

He laughed. "Well, I gotta go pee." She heard him rustle out of his bag. "Broo!" he cried, flapping his arms. "It's cold!"

He makes so much noise, she thought, *just noise and more noise.*

Her father woke them before first light. He warned them to talk softly and said that they were going to the place where Andy had seen the deer, to try to cut them off on their way back from their night feeding. Andy couldn't shake off her sleep. Stuffing her sleeping bag into its sack seemed to take an hour, and tying her boots was the strangest thing she'd ever done. Charlie Spoon made hot chocolate and oatmeal with raisins. Andy closed her eyes and, between beats of her heart, listened to the breathing of the forest. *When I open my eyes, it will be lighter,* she decided. But when she did, it was still just as dark, except for the swaths of their flashlights and the hissing blue flame of the stove. *There has to be just one moment when it all changes from dark to light,* Andy thought. She had missed it yesterday, in the car; today she would watch more closely.

But when she remembered again, it was already first light and they had moved to the rocks by the deer trail and had set up shooting positions—Mac and Charlie Spoon on the up-trail side, she and her father behind them, some six feet up on a ledge. The day became brighter, the sun piercing the tall pines, raking the hunters, yet providing little warmth. Andy now smelled alder and pine and the slightly rotten odor of rock lichen. She rubbed her hand over the stone and considered that it must be very old, had probably been here before the giant pines, *before anyone was in these woods at all.* A chipmunk sniffed on a nearby branch. She aimed an imaginary rifle and pressed the trigger. The chipmunk froze, then scurried away. Her legs were cramping on the narrow ledge. Her father seemed to doze, one hand in his parka, the other cupped lightly around the rifle. She could smell his scent of old wool and leather. His checks were speckled with gray-black whiskers, and he worked his jaws slightly, as if chewing a small piece of gum.

Please let us get a deer, she prayed.

A branch snapped on the other side of the rock face. Her father's hand stiffened on the rifle, startling her—*He hasn't been sleeping at all,* she marveled—and then his jaw relaxed, as did the lines around his eyes, and she heard Charlie Spoon call, "Yo, don't shoot, it's us." He and Mac appeared from around the rock. They stopped beneath the ledge. Charlie solemnly crossed his arms.

"I don't believe we're gonna get any deer here," he said drily.

Andy's father lowered his rifle to Charlie and jumped down from the ledge. Then he reached up for Andy. She dropped into his arms and he set her gently on the ground.

Mac sidled up to her. "I knew you didn't see no deer," he said.

"Just because they don't come when you want 'em to don't mean she didn't see them, her father said.

Still, she felt bad. Her telling about the deer had caused them to spend the morning there, cold and expectant, with nothing to show for it.

They tramped through the woods for another two hours, not caring much about noise. Mac found some deer tracks, and they argued about how old they were. They split up for a while and then rejoined at an old logging road that deer might use, and followed it. The road crossed a stream, which had mostly frozen over but in a few spots still caught leaves and twigs in an icy swirl. They forded it by jumping from rock to rock. The road narrowed after that, and the woods thickened.

They stopped for lunch, heating up Charlie's wife's corn chowder. Andy's father cut squares of applesauce cake with his hunting knife and handed them to her and Mac, who ate his almost daintily. Andy could faintly taste knife oil on the cake. She was tired. She stretched her leg; the muscle that had cramped on the rock still ached.

"Might as well relax," her father said, as if reading her thoughts. "We won't find deer till suppertime."

Charlie Spoon leaned back against his pack and folded his hands across his stomach. "Well, even if we don't get a deer," he said expansively, "it's still great to be out here, breathe some fresh air, clomp around a bit. Get away from the house and the old lady." He winked at Mac, who looked away.

"That's what the woods are all about, anyway," Charlie said. "It's where the women don't want to go." He bowed his head toward Andy. "With your exception, of course, little lady." He helped himself to another piece of applesauce cake.

"She ain't a woman," Mac said.

"Well, she damn well's gonna be," Charlie said. He grinned at her. "Or will you? You're half a boy anyway. You go by a boy's name. What's your real name? Andrea, ain't it?"

"That's right," she said. She hoped that if she didn't look at him, Charlie would stop.

"Well, which do you like? Andy or Andrea?"

"Don't matter," she mumbled. "Either."

"She's always been Andy to me," her father said.

Charlie Spoon was still grinning. "So what are you gonna be, Andrea? A boy or a girl?"

"I'm a girl," she said.

"But you want to go hunting and fishing and everything, huh?"

"She can do whatever she likes," her father said.

"Hell, you might as well have just had a boy and be done with it!" Charlie exclaimed.

"That's funny," her father said, and chuckled. "That's just what her momma tells me."

They were looking at her, and she wanted to get away from them all, even from her father, who chose to joke with them.

"I'm going to walk a bit," she said.

She heard them laughing as she walked down the logging trail. She flapped her arms; she whistled. *I don't care how much noise I make,* she thought. Two grouse flew from the underbrush, startling her. A little farther down, the trail ended in a clearing that enlarged into a frozen meadow; beyond it the woods began again. A few moldering posts were all that was left of a fence that had once enclosed the field. The low afternoon sunlight reflected brightly off the snow, so that Andy's eyes hurt. She squinted hard. A gust of wind blew across the field, stinging her face. And then, as if it had been waiting for her, the doe emerged from the trees opposite and stepped cautiously into the field. Andy watched: it stopped and stood quietly for what seemed a long time and then ambled across. It stopped again about seventy yards away and began to browse in a patch of sugar grass uncovered by the wind. Carefully, slowly, never taking her eyes from the doe, Andy walked backward, trying to step into the boot prints she'd already made. When she was far enough back into the woods, she turned and walked faster, her heart racing. *Please let it stay,* she prayed.

"There's a doe in the field yonder," she told them.

They got their rifles and hurried down the trail.

"No use," her father said. "We're making too much noise any way you look at it."

"At least we got us the wind in our favor," Charlie Spoon said, breathing heavily.

But the doe was still there, grazing.

"Good Lord," Charlie whispered. He looked at her father. "Well, whose shot?"

"Andy spotted it," her father said in a low voice. "Let her shoot it."

"What!" Charlie's eyes widened.

Andy couldn't believe what her father had just said. She'd only shot tin cans and targets; she'd never even fired her father's .30–.30, and she'd never killed anything.

"I can't," she whispered.

"That's right, she can't," Charlie Spoon insisted. "She's not old enough and she don't have a license even if she was!"

"Well, who's to tell?" her father said in a low voice. "Nobody's going to know but us." He looked at her. "Do you want to shoot it, punkin?"

Why doesn't it hear us? she wondered. *Why doesn't it run away?* "I don't know," she said.

"Well, I'm sure as hell gonna shoot it," Charlie said. Her father grasped Charlie's rifle barrel and held it. His voice was steady.

"Andy's a good shot. It's her deer. She found it, not you. You'd still be sitting on your ass back in camp." He turned to her again. "Now–do you want to shoot it, Andy? Yes or no."

He was looking at her; they were all looking at her. Suddenly she was angry at the deer, who refused to hear them, who wouldn't run away even when it could. "I'll shoot it," she said. Charlie turned away in disgust.

She lay on the ground and pressed the rifle stock against her shoulder bone. The snow was cold through her parka; she smelled oil and wax and damp earth. She pulled off one glove with her teeth. "It sights just like the .22," her father said gently. "Cartridge's already chambered." As she had done so many times before, she sighted down the scope; now the doe was in the reticle. She moved the barrel until the cross hairs lined up. Her father was breathing beside her.

"Aim where the chest and legs meet, or a little above, punkin," he was saying calmly. "That's the killing shot."

But now, seeing it in the scope, Andy was hesitant. Her finger weakened on the trigger. Still, she nodded at what her father said and sighted again, the cross hairs lining up in exactly the same spot—the doe had hardly moved, its brownish-gray body outlined starkly against the blue-backed snow. *It doesn't know*, Andy thought. *It just doesn't know.* And as she looked, deer and snow and faraway trees flattened within the circular frame to become like a picture on a calendar, not real, and she felt calm, as if she had been dreaming everything—the day, the deer, the hunt itself. And she, finger on trigger, was only a part of that dream.

"Shoot!" Charlie hissed.

Through the scope she saw the deer look up, ears high and straining.

Charlie groaned, and just as he did, and just at the moment when Andy knew—*knew*—the doe would bound away, as if she could feel its haunches tensing and gathering power, she pulled the trigger. Later she would think, *I felt the recoil, I smelled the smoke, but I don't remember pulling the trigger.* Through the scope the deer seemed to shrink into itself, and then slowly knelt, hind legs first, head raised as if to cry out. It trembled, still straining to keep its head high, as if that alone would save it; failing, it collapsed, shuddered, and lay still.

"Whoee!" Mac cried.

"One shot! One shot!" her father yelled, clapping her on the back. Charlie Spoon was shaking his head and smiling dumbly.

"I told you she was a great little shot!" her father said. "I told you!" Mac danced and clapped his hands. She was dazed, not quite understanding what had happened. And then they were crossing the field toward the fallen doe, she walking dreamlike, the men laughing and joking, released now from the tension of silence and anticipation. Suddenly Mac pointed and cried out, "Look at that!"

The doe was rising, legs unsteady. They stared at it, unable to comprehend, and in that moment the doe regained its feet and looked at them, as if it too were trying to understand. Her father whistled softly. Charlie Spoon unslung his rifle and raised it to his shoulder, but the doe was already bounding away. His hurried shot missed, and the deer disappeared into the woods.

"Damn, damn, damn," he moaned.

"I don't believe it," her father said. "That deer was dead."

"Dead, hell!" Charlie yelled. "It was gutshot, that's all. Stunned and gutshot. Clean shot, my ass!"

What have I done? Andy thought.

Her father slung his rifle over his shoulder. "Well, let's go. It can't get too far."

"Hell, I've seen deer run ten miles gutshot," Charlie said. He waved his arms. "We may never find her!"

As they crossed the field, Mac came up to her and said in a low voice, "Gutshoot a deer, you'll go to hell."

"Shut up, Mac," she said, her voice cracking. It was a terrible thing she had done, she knew. She couldn't bear to think of the doe in pain and frightened. *Please let it die,* she prayed.

But though they searched all the last hour of daylight, so that they had to recross the field and go up the logging trail in a twilight made even deeper by thick, smoky clouds, they didn't find the doe. They lost its trail almost immediately in the dense stands of alderberry and larch.

"I am cold, and I am tired," Charlie Spoon declared. "And if you ask me, that deer's in another county already."

"No one's asking you, Charlie," her father said.

They had a supper of hard salami and ham, bread, and the rest of the applesauce cake. It seemed a bother to heat the coffee, so they had cold chocolate instead. Everyone turned in early.

"We'll find it in the morning, honeybun," her father said, as she went to her tent.

"I don't like to think of it suffering." She was almost in tears.

"It's dead already, punkin. Don't even think about it." He kissed her, his breath sour and his beard rough against her cheek.

Andy was sure she wouldn't get to sleep; the image of the doe falling, falling, then rising again, repeated itself whenever she closed her eyes. Then she heard an owl hoot and realized that it had awakened her, so she must have been asleep after all. She hoped the owl would hush, but instead it hooted louder. She wished her father or Charlie Spoon would wake up and do something about it, but no one moved in the other tent, and suddenly she was afraid that they had all decamped, wanting nothing more to do with her. She whispered, "Mac, Mac," to the sleeping bag where he should be, but no one answered. She tried to find the flashlight she always kept by her side, but couldn't, and she cried in panic, "Mac, are you there?" He mumbled something, and immediately she felt foolish and hoped he wouldn't reply.

When she awoke again, everything had changed. The owl was gone, the woods were still, and she sensed light, blue and pale, light where before there had been none. *The moon must have come out,* she thought. And it was warm, too, warmer than it should have been. She got out of her sleeping bag and took off her parka—it was that warm. Mac was asleep, wheezing like an old man. She unzipped the tent and stepped outside.

The woods were more beautiful than she had ever seen them. The moon made everything ice-rimmed glimmer with a crystallized, immanent light, while underneath that ice the branches of trees were as stark as skeletons. She heard a crunching in the snow, the one sound in all that silence, and there, walking down the logging trail into their camp, was the doe. Its body, like everything around her, was silvered with frost and moonlight. It walked past the tent where her father and Charlie Spoon were sleeping and stopped no more than six feet from her. Andy saw that she had shot it, yes, had shot it cleanly, just where she thought she had, the wound a jagged, bloody hole in the doe's chest.

A heart shot, she thought.

The doe stepped closer, so that Andy, if she wished, could have reached out and touched it. It looked at her as if expecting her to do this, and so she did, running her hand, slowly at first, along the rough, matted fur, then down to the edge of the wound, where she stopped. The doe stood still. Hesitantly, Andy felt the edge of the wound. The torn flesh was sticky and warm. The wound parted under her touch. And then, almost without her knowing it, her fingers were within, probing, yet still the doe didn't move. Andy pressed deeper, through flesh and muscle and sinew, until her whole hand and more was inside the wound and she had found the doe's heart warm and beating. She cupped it gently in her hand. *Alive,* she marveled. *Alive.*

The heart quickened under her touch, becoming warmer and warmer until it was hot enough to burn. In pain, Andy tried to remove her hand, but the wound closed about it and held her fast. Her hand was burning. She cried out in agony, sure they would all hear and come help, but they didn't. And then her hand pulled free, followed by a steaming rush of blood, more blood than she ever could have imagined—it covered her hand and arm, and she saw to her horror that her hand was steaming. She moaned and fell to her knees and plunged her hand into the snow. The doe looked at her gently and then turned and walked back up the trail.

In the morning, when she woke, Andy could still smell the blood, but she felt no pain. She looked at her hand. Even though it appeared un-scathed, it felt weak and withered. She couldn't move it freely and was afraid the others would notice. *I will hide it in my jacket pocket,* she decided, *so nobody can see.* She ate the oatmeal that her father cooked and stayed apart from them all. No one spoke to her, and that suited her. A light snow began to fall. It was the last day of their hunting trip. She wanted to be home.

Her father dumped the dregs of his coffee. "Well, let's go look for her," he said.

Again they crossed the field. Andy lagged behind. She averted her eyes from the spot where the doe had fallen, already filling up with snow. Mac and Charlie entered the woods first, followed by her father. Andy re-mained in the field and considered the smear of gray sky, the nearby flock of crows pecking at unyielding stubble. *I will stay here,* she thought, *and not move for a long while.* But now someone—Mac—was yelling. Her fa-ther appeared at the woods' edge and waved for her to come. She ran and pushed through a brake of alderberry and larch. The thick underbrush scratched her face. For a moment she felt lost and looked wildly about. Then, where the brush thinned, she saw them standing quietly in the falling snow. They were staring down at the dead doe. A film covered its upturned eye, and its body was lightly dusted with snow.

"I told you she wouldn't get too far," Andy's father said triumphantly. "We must've just missed her yesterday. Too blind to see."

"We're just damn lucky no animal got to her last night," Charlie muttered.

Her father lifted the doe's foreleg. The wound was blood-clotted, brown, and caked like frozen mud. "Clean shot," he said to Charlie. He grinned. "My little girl."

Then he pulled out his knife, the blade gray as the morning. Mac whispered to Andy, "Now watch this," while Charlie Spoon lifted the doe from behind by its forelegs so that its head rested between his knees, its underside exposed. Her father's knife sliced thickly from chest to belly to crotch, and Andy was running from them, back to the field and across, scattering the crows who cawed and circled angrily. And now they were all calling to her–Charlie Spoon and Mac and her father–crying *Andy, Andy* (but that wasn't her name, she would no longer be called that); yet louder than any of them was the wind blowing through the treetops, like the ocean where her mother floated in green water, also calling *Come in, come in,* while all around her roared the mocking of the terrible, now inevitable, sea.

Initially published in Harper's Magazine, *this story may seem to be more about the complex relationship between a father and son than it is about duck hunting. But the hunting and eating of the ducks affects the relationship in subtle and important ways. Wallace Stegner is one of the most distinguished names in American literature. Born in 1909 in Lake Mills, Iowa, he received his Ph.D. from the University of Iowa. He taught at such universities as Wisconsin, Harvard, and Stanford, where he was head of the creative writing center. The prestigious Stegner Fellowship at Stanford is named in his honor. Among Stegner's best-known books are* Angle of Repose (1972), *which won the Pulitzer Prize, and* The Spectator Bird (1976), *which won the National Book Award. "The Blue-Winged Teal" won first prize in the O. Henry Awards and appears in* The Collected Stories of Wallace Stegner (1990).

Wallace Stegner

THE BLUE-WINGED TEAL (1950)

S TILL IN WADERS, WITH THE string of ducks across his shoulder, he stood hesitating on the sidewalk in the cold November wind. His knees were stiff from being cramped up all day in the blind, and his feet were cold. Today, all day, he had been alive; now he was back ready to be dead again.

Lights were on all up and down the street, and there was a rush of traffic and a hurrying of people past and around him, yet the town was not his town, the people passing were strangers, the sounds of evening in this place were no sounds that carried warmth or familiarity. Though he had spent most of his twenty years in the town, knew hundreds of its people, could draw maps of its streets from memory, he wanted to admit familiarity with none of it. He had shut himself off.

Then what was he doing here, in front of this poolhall, loaded down with nine dead ducks? What had possessed him in the first place to borrow gun and waders and car from his father and go hunting? If he had wanted to breathe freely for a change, why hadn't he kept right on going? What was there in this place to draw him back? A hunter had to have a lodge to bring his meat to and people who would be glad of his skill. He had this poolhall and his father, John Lederer, Prop.

He stepped out of a woman's path and leaned against the door. Downstairs, in addition to his father, he would find old Max Schmeckebier, who ran a cheap blackjack game in the room under the sidewalk. He would find Giuseppe Sciutti, the Sicilian barber, closing his shop or tidying up the rack of *Artists and Models* and *The Nudist* with which he lured trade. He would probably find Billy Hammond, the night clerk from the Windsor Hotel, having his sandwich and beer and pie, or moving alone around a pool table, whistling abstractedly, practicing shots. If the afternoon blackjack game had broken up, there would be Navy Edwards, dealer and bouncer for Schmeckebier. At this time of evening there might be a few counter customers and a cop collecting his tribute of a beer or that other tribute that Schmeckebier paid to keep the cardroom open.

And he would find sour contrast with the bright sky and the wind of the tule marshes, the cavelike room with its back corners in darkness, would smell that smell compounded of steam heat and cue-chalk dust, of sodden butts in cuspidors, of coffee and meat and beer smells from the counter, of cigarette smoke so unaired that it darkened the walls. From anywhere back of the middle tables there would be the pervasive reek of toilet disinfectant. Back of the lunch counter his father would be presiding, throwing the poolhall light switch to save a few cents when the place was empty, flipping it on to give an air of brilliant and successful use when feet came down the stairs past Sciutti's shop.

The hunter moved his shoulder under the weight of the ducks, his mind full for a moment with the image of his father's face, darkly pale, fallen in on its bones, and the pouched, restless, suspicious eyes that seemed always looking for someone. Over that image came the face of his mother, dead now and six weeks buried. His teeth clicked at the thought of how she had held the old man up for thirty years, kept him at a respectable job, kept him from slipping back into the poolroom Johnny he had been when she married him. Within ten days of her death he had hunted up this old failure of a poolhall.

In anger the hunter turned, thinking of the hotel room he shared with his father. But he had to eat. Broke as he was, a student yanked from his studies, he had no choice but to eat on the old man. Besides, there were the ducks. He felt somehow that the thing would be incomplete unless he brought his game back for his father to see.

His knees unwilling in the stiff waders, he went down the steps, descending into the light shining through Joe Sciutti's door, and into the momentary layer of clean bay-rum smell, talcum smell, hair-tonic smell, that rose past the still revolving barber pole in the angle of the stairs.

Joe Scuitti was sweeping wads of hair from his tile floor, and hunched over the counter beyond, their backs to the door, were Schmeckebier, Navy Edwards, Billy Hammond, and an unknown customer. John Lederer was behind the counter, mopping alertly with a rag. The poolroom lights were up bright, but when Lederer saw who was coming he flipped the switch and dropped the big room back into dusk.

As the hunter came to the end of the counter their heads turned toward him. "Well I'm a son of a bee," Navy Edwards said, and scrambled off his stool. Next to him Billy Hammond half stood up so that his pale yellow hair took a halo from the backbar lights. "Say!" Max Schmeckebier said. "Say, dot's goot, dot's pooty goot, Henry!"

But Henry was watching his father so intently he did not turn to them. He slid the string of ducks off his shoulder and swung them up onto the wide walnut bar. They landed solidly—offering or tribute or ransom or whatever they were. For a moment it was as if this little act were private between the two of them. He felt queerly moved, his stomach tightened in suspense or triumph. Then the old man's pouchy eyes slipped from his and the old man came quickly forward along the counter and laid hands on the ducks.

He handled them as if he were petting kittens, his big white hands stringing the heads one by one from the wire.

"Two spoonbill," he said, more to himself than to the others crowding around. "Shovel ducks. Don't see many of those any more. And two, no, three, hen mallards and one drake. Those make good eating."

Schmeckebier jutted his enormous lower lip. Knowing him for a stingy, crooked, suspicious little man, Henry almost laughed at the air he could put on, the air of a man of probity about to make an honest judgment in a dispute between neighbors. "I take a budderball," he said thickly. "A liddle budderball, dot is vot eats goot."

An arm fell across Henry's shoulders, and he turned his head to see the hand with red hairs rising from its pores, the wristband of a gray silk shirt with four pearl buttons. Navy Edwards' red face was close to his. "Come clean now," Navy said. "You shot 'em all sitting, didn't you, Henry?"

"I just waited till they stuck their heads out of their holes and let them have it," Henry said.

Navy walloped him on the back and convulsed himself laughing. Then his face got serious again, and he bore down on Henry's shoulder. "By God, you could've fooled me," he said. "If I'd been makin' book on what you'd bring in I'd've lost my shirt."

"Such a pretty shirt, too," Billy Hammond said.

Across the counter John Lederer cradled a little drab duck in his hand. Its neck, stretched from the carrier, hung far down, but its body was neat and plump and its feet were waxy. Watching the sallow face of his father, Henry thought it looked oddly soft.

"Ain't that a beauty, though?" the old man said. "There ain't a prettier duck made than a blue-winged teal. You can have all your wood ducks and redheads, all the flashy ones." He spread a wing until the hidden band of bright blue showed. "Pretty?" he said, and shook his head and laughed suddenly, as if he had not expected to. When he laid the duck down beside the others his eyes were bright with sentimental moisture.

So now, Henry thought, you're right in your element. You always did want to be one of the boys from the poolroom pouring out to see the elk on somebody's running board, or leaning on a bar with a schooner of beer talking baseball or telling the boys about the big German Brown somebody brought in in a cake of ice. We haven't any elk or German Browns right now, but we've got some nice ducks, a fine display along five feet of counter. And who brought them in? The student, the alien son. It must gravel you.

He drew himself a beer. Several other men had come in, and he saw three more stooping to look in the door beyond Sciutti's. Then they too came in. Three tables were going; his father had started to hustle, filling orders. After a few minutes Schmeckebier and Navy went into the card-room with four men. The poolroom lights were up bright again, there was an ivory click of balls, a rumble of talk. The smoke-filled air was full of movement.

Still more people dropped in, kids in high school athletic sweaters and bums from the fringes of skid road. They all stopped to look at the ducks, and Henry saw glances at his waders, heard questions and an-swers. John Lederer's boy. Some of them spoke to him, deriving impor-tance from contact with him. A fellowship was promoted by the ducks strung out along the counter. Henry felt it himself. He was so mellowed by the way they spoke to him that when the players at the first table thumped with their cues, he got off his stool to rack them up and col-lect their nickels. It occurred to him that he ought to go to the room and get into a bath, but he didn't want to leave yet. Instead he came back to the counter and slid the nickels toward his father and drew him-self another beer.

"Pretty good night tonight," he said. The old man nodded and slapped his rag on the counter, his eyes already past Henry and fixed on two youths coming in, his mouth fixing itself for the greeting and the "Well, boys, what'll it be?"

Billy Hammond wandered by, stopped beside Henry a moment. "Well, time for my nightly wrestle with temptation," he said.

"I was just going to challenge you to a game of call-shot."

"Maybe tomorrow," Billy said, and let himself out carefully as if afraid a noise would disturb someone—a mild, gentle, golden-haired boy who looked as if he ought to be in some prep school learning to say "Sir" to grownups instead of clerking in a girlie hotel. He was the only one of the poolroom crowd that Henry half liked. He thought he understood Billy Hammond a little.

He turned back to the counter to hear his father talking with Max Schmeckebier. "I don't see how we could on this rig. That's the hell of it, we need a regular oven."

"In my room in back," Schmeckebier said. "Dot old electric range."

"Does it work?"

"Sure. Vy not? I tink so."

"By God," John Lederer said. "Nine ducks, that ought to give us a real old-fashioned feed." He mopped the counter, refilled a coffee cup, came back to the end and pinched the breast of a duck, pulled out a wing and looked at the band of blue hidden among the drab feathers. "Just like old times, for a change," he said, and his eyes touched Henry's in a look that might have meant anything from a challenge to an apology.

Henry had no desire to ease the strain that had been between them for months. He did not forgive his father the poolhall, or forget the way the old man had sprung back into the old pattern, as if his wife had been a jailer and he was now released. He neither forgot nor forgave the red-haired woman who sometimes came to the poolhall late at night and waited on a bar stool while the old man closed up. Yet now when his father remarked that the ducks ought to be drawn and plucked right away, Henry stood up.

"I could do ten while you were doing one," his father said.

The blood spread hotter in Henry's face, but he bit off what he might have said. "All right," he said. "You do them and I'll take over the counter for you."

So here he was, in the poolhall he had passionately sworn he would never do a lick of work in, dispensing Mrs. Morrison's meat pies and tamales smothered in chile, clumping behind the counter in the waders which had been the sign of his temporary freedom. Leaning back between orders, watching the Saturday night activity of the place, he half understood why he had gone hunting, and why it had seemed to him essential that he bring his trophies back here.

That somewhat disconcerted understanding was still troubling him when his father came back. The old man had put on a clean apron and brushed his hair. His pouched eyes, brighter and less houndlike than usual, darted along the bar, counting, and darted across the bright tables, counting again. His eyes met Henry's, and both half smiled. Both of them, Henry thought, were a little astonished.

Later, propped in bed in the hotel room, he put down the magazine he had been reading and stared at the drawn blinds, the sleazy drapes, and asked himself why he was here. The story he had told others, and himself, that his mother's death had interrupted his school term and he was waiting for the new term before going back, he knew to be an evasion. He was staying because he couldn't get away, or wouldn't. He hated his father, hated the poolhall, hated the people he was thrown with. He made no move to hobnob with them, or hadn't until tonight, and yet he deliberately avoided seeing any of the people who had been his friends for years. Why?

He could force his mind to the barrier, but not across it. Within a half minute he found himself reading again, diving deep, and when he made himself look up from the page he stared for a long time at his father's bed, his father's shoes under the bed, his father's soiled shirts hanging in the open closet. All the home he had any more was this little room. He could not pretend that as long as he stayed here the fragments of his home and family were held together. He couldn't fool himself that he had any function in his father's life any more, or his father in his, unless his own hatred and his father's uneasy suspicion were functions. He ought to get out and get a job until he could go back to school. But he didn't.

Thinking made him sleepy, and he knew what that was, too. Sleep was another evasion, like the torpor and monotony of his life. But he let drowsiness drift over him, and drowsily he thought of his father behind the counter tonight, vigorous and jovial, Mine Host, and he saw that the usual fretful petulance had gone from his face.

He snapped off the bed light and dropped the magazine on the floor. Then he heard the rain, the swish and hiss of traffic in the wet street. He felt sad and alone, and he disliked the coldness of his own isolation. Again he thought of his father, of the failing body that had once been tireless and bull-strong, of the face before it had sagged and grown dewlaps of flesh on the square jaws. He thought of the many failures, the jobs that never quite worked out, the schemes that never quite paid off, and of the eyes that could not quite meet, not quite hold, the eyes of his cold son.

Thinking of this, and remembering when they had been a family and when his mother had been alive to hold them together, he felt pity, and he cried.

His father's entrance awakened him. He heard the fumbling at the door, the creak, the quiet click, the footsteps that groped in darkness, the body that bumped into something and halted, getting its bearings. He heard the sighing weight of his father's body on the other bed, his father's sighing breath as he bent to untie his shoes. Feigning sleep, he lay unmoving, breathing deeply and steadily, but an anguish of fury had leaped in him as sharp and sudden as a sudden fear, for he smelled the smells his father brought with him: wet wool, stale tobacco, liquor; and above all, more penetrating than any, spreading through the room and polluting everything there, the echo of cheap musky perfume.

The control Henry imposed upon his body was like an ecstasy. He raged at himself for the weak sympathy that had troubled him all evening. One good night, he said to himself now, staring furiously upward. One lively Saturday night in the joint and he can't contain himself, he has to go top off the evening with his girl friend. And how? A drink in her room? A walk over to some illegal afterhours bar on Rum Alley? Maybe just a trip to bed, blunt and immediate?

His jaws ached from the tight clamping of his teeth, but his orderly breathing went in and out, in and out, while the old man sighed into bed and creaked a little, rolling over, and lay still. The taint of perfume seemed even stronger now. The sow must slop it on by the cupful. And so cuddly. Such a sugar baby. How's my old sweetie tonight? It's been too long since you came to see your baby. I should be real mad at you. The cheek against the lapel, the unreal hair against the collar, the perfume like some gaseous poison tainting the clothes it touched.

The picture of his mother's bureau drawers came to him, the careless simple collection of handkerchiefs and gloves and lace collars and cuffs, and he saw the dusty blue sachet packets and smelled the faint fragrance. That was all the scent she had ever used.

My God, he said, how can he stand himself?

After a time his father began to breath heavily, then to snore. In the little prison of the room his breathing was obscene—loose and bubbling, undisciplined, animal. Henry with an effort relaxed his tense arms and legs, let himself sink. He tried to concentrate on his own breathing, but the other dominated him, burst out and died and whiffled and sighed again. By now he had a resolution in him like an iron bar. Tomorrow, for sure, for good, he would break out of his self-imposed isolation and see Frank, see Welby. They would lend him enough to get to the coast. Not another day in this hateful relationship. Not another night in this room.

He yawned. It must be late, two or three o'clock. He ought to get to sleep. But he lay uneasily, his mind tainted with hatred as the room was tainted with perfume. He tried cunningly to elude his mind, to get to sleep before it could notice, but no matter how he composed himself for blankness and shut his eyes and breathed deeply, his mind was out again in a half minute, bright-eyed, lively as a weasel, and he was helplessly hunted again from hiding place to hiding place.

Eventually he fell back upon his old device.

He went into a big dark room in his mind, a room shadowy with great half-seen tables. He groped and found a string above him and pulled, and light fell suddenly in a bright cone from the darker cone of the shade. Below the light lay an expanse of dark green cloth, and this was the only lighted thing in all that darkness. Carefully he gathered bright balls into a wooden triangle, pushing them forward until the apex lay over a round spot on the cloth. Quietly and thoroughly he chalked a cue: the inlaid handle and the smoother taper of the shaft were very real to his eyes and hands. He lined up the cue ball, aimed, drew the cue back and forth in smooth motions over the bridge of his left hand. He saw the balls run from the spinning shock of the break, and carom, and come to rest, and he hunted up the yellow 1-ball and got a shot at it between two others. He had to cut it very fine, but he saw the shot go true, the 1 angle off cleanly into the side pocket. He saw the cue ball rebound and kiss and stop, and he shot the 2 in a straight shot for the left corner pocket, putting drawers on the cue ball to get shape for the 3.

Yellow and blue and red, spotted and striped, he shot pool balls into pockets as deep and black and silent as the cellars of his consciousness. He was not now quarry that his mind chased, but an actor, a willer, a doer, a man in command. By an act of will or of flight he focused his whole awareness on the game he played. His mind undertook it with intent concentration. He took pride in little two-cushion banks, little triumphs of accuracy, small successes of foresight. When he had finished one game and the green cloth was bare he dug the balls from the bin under the end of the table and racked them and began another.

Eventually, he knew, nothing would remain in his mind but the clean green cloth traced with running color and bounced by simple problems, and sometime in the middle of an intricately planned combination shot he would pale off into sleep.

At noon, after the rain, the sun seemed very bright. It poured down from a clearing sky, glittered on wet roofs, gleamed in reflection from pavements and sidewalks. On the peaks beyond the city there was a purity of snow.

Coming down the hill, Henry noticed the excessive brightness and could not tell whether it was really as it seemed, or whether his plunge out of the dark and isolated hole of his life had restored a lost capacity to see. A slavery, or a paralysis, was ended; he had been for three hours in the company of a friend; he had been eyed with concern; he had been warmed by solicitude and generosity. In his pocket he had fifty dollars, enough to get him to the coast and let him renew his life. It seemed to him incredible that he had alternated between dismal hotel and dismal poolroom so long. He could not understand why he had not before this moved his legs in the direction of the hill. He perceived that he had been sullen and morbid, and he concluded with some surprise that even Schmeckebier and Edwards and the rest might have found him a difficult companion.

His father too. The fury of the night before had passed, but he knew he would not bend again toward companionship. That antipathy was too deep. He would never think of his father again without getting the whiff of that perfume. Let him have it; it was what he wanted, let him have it. They could part without an open quarrel, maybe, but they would part without love. They could part right now, within an hour.

Two grimy stairways led down into the cellar from the alley he turned into. One went to the furnace room, the other to the poolhall. The iron rail was blockaded with filled ashcans. Descent into Avernus, he said to himself, and went down the left-hand stair.

The door was locked. He knocked, and after some time knocked again. Finally someone pulled on the door from inside. It stuck, and was yanked irritably inward. His father stood there in his shirt sleeves, a cigar in his mouth.

"Oh," he said. "I was wondering what had become of you."

The basement air was foul and heavy, dense with the reek from the toilets. Henry saw as he stepped inside that at the far end only the night light behind the bar was on, but that light was coming from Schmeckebier's door at this end too, the two weak illuminations diffusing in the shadowy poolroom, leaving the middle in almost absolute dark. It was the appropriate time, the appropriate place, the stink of his prison appropriately concentrated. He drew his lungs full of it with a kind of passion, and he said, "I just came down to . . ."

"Who is dot?" Schmeckebier called out. He came to his door, wrapped to the armpits in a bar apron, with a spoon in his hand, and he bent, peering out into the dusk like a disturbed dwarf in an underhill cave. "John? Who? Oh, Henry. Shust in time, shust in time. It is not long now." His lower lip waggled, and he pulled it up, apparently with an effort.

Henry said, "What's not long?"

"Vot?" Schmeckebier said, and thrust his big head far out. "You forgot about it?"

"I must have," Henry said.

"The duck feed," his father said impatiently.

They stood staring at one another in the dusk. The right moment was gone. With a little twitch of the shoulder Henry let it go. He would wait awhile, pick his time. When Schmeckebier went back to his cooking, Henry saw through the doorway the lumpy bed, the big chair with a blanket folded over it, the rolltop desk littered with pots and pans, the green and white enamel of the range. A rich smell of roasting came out and mingled oddly with the chemical stink of toilet disinfectant.

"Are we going to eat in here?" he asked.

His father snorted. "How could we eat in there? Old Maxie lived in the ghetto too damn long. By God, I never saw such a boar's nest."

"Vot's duh matter? Vot's duh matter?" Schmeckebier said. His big lip thrust out, he stooped to look into the oven, and John Lederer went shaking his head up between the tables to the counter. Henry followed him, intending to make the break when he got the old man alone. But he saw the three plates set up on the bar, the three glasses of tomato juice, the platter of olives and celery, and he hesitated. His father reached with a salt shaker and shook a little salt into each glass of tomato juice.

"All the fixings," he said. "Soon as Max gets those birds out of the oven we can take her on."

Now it was easy to say, "As soon as the feed's over I'll be shoving off." Henry opened his mouth to say it, but was interrupted this time by a light tapping at the glass door beyond Sciutti's shop. He swung around angrily and saw duskily beyond the glass the smooth blond hair, the even smile.

"It's Billy," he said. "Shall I let him in?"

"Sure," the old man said. "Tell him to come in and have a duck with us."

But Billy Hammond shook his head when Henry asked him. He was shaking his head almost as he came through the door. "No thanks, I just ate. I'm full of chow mein. This is a family dinner anyway. You go on ahead."

"Got plenty," John Lederer said, and made a motion as if to set a fourth place at the counter.

"Who is dot?" Schmeckebier bawled from the back. "Who come in? Is dot Billy Hammond? Set him up a blate."

"By God, his nose sticks as far into things as his lip," Lederer said. Still holding the plate, he roared back, "Catch up with the parade, for Christ sake, or else tend to your cooking." He looked at Henry and Billy and chuckled.

Schmeckebier had disappeared, but now his squat figure blotted the lighted doorway again. "Vot? Vot you say?"

"Vot?" John Lederer said. "Vot, vot, vot? Vot does it matter vot I said? Get the hell back to your kitchen."

He was, Henry saw, in a high humor. The effect of last night was still with him. He was still playing Mine Host. He looked at the two of them and laughed so naturally that Henry almost joined him. "I think old Maxie's head is full of duck dressing," he said, and leaned on the counter. "I ever tell you about the time we came back from Reno together? We stopped off in the desert to look at a mine, and got lost on a little dirt road so we had to camp. I was trying to figure out where we were, and started looking for stars, but it was clouded over, hard to locate anything. So I ask old Maxie if he can see the Big Dipper anywhere. He thinks about that maybe ten minutes with his lip stuck out and then he says, 'I t'ink it's in duh water bucket.'"

He did the grating gutturals of Schmeckebier's speech so accurately that Henry smiled in spite of himself. His old man made another motion with the plate at Billy Hammond. "Better let me set you up a place."

"Thanks," Billy said. His voice was as polite and soft as his face, and his eyes had the ingenuous liquid softness of a girl's. "Thanks, I really just ate. You go on, I'll shoot a little pool if it's all right."

Now came Schmeckebier with a big platter held in both hands. He bore it smoking through the gloom of the poolhall and up the steps to the counter, and John Lederer took it from him there and with a flourish speared one after another three tight-skinned brown ducks and slid them onto the plates set side by side for the feast. The one frugal light from the backbar shone on them as they sat down. Henry looked over his shoulder to see Billy Hammond pull the cord and flood a table with a sharp-edged cone of brilliance. Deliberately, already absorbed, he chalked a cue. His lips pursed, and he whistled, and whistling, bent to take aim.

Lined up in a row, they were not placed for conversation, but John Lederer kept attempting it, leaning forward over his plate to see Schmeckebier or Henry. He filled his mouth with duck and dressing and chewed, shaking his head with pleasure, and snapped off a bit of celery with a crack like a breaking stick. When his mouth was clear he leaned and said to Schmeckebier, "Ah, das schmeckt gut, hey, Maxie?"

"Ja," Schmeckebier said, and sucked grease off his lip and only then turned in surprise. "Say, you speak German?"

"Sure I speak German," Lederer said. "I worked three weeks once with an old squarehead brick mason that taught me the whole language. He taught me about sehr gut and nicht wahr and besser I bleiben right hier, and he always had his frau make me up a lunch full of kalter aufschnitt and gemixte pickeln. I know all about German."

Schmeckebier stared a moment, grunted, and went back to his eating. He had already stripped the meat from the bones and was gnawing the carcass.

"Anyway," John Lederer said, "es schmecht God damn good." He got up and went around the counter and drew a mug of coffee from the urn. "Coffee?" he said to Henry.

"Please."

His father drew another mug and set it before him. "Maxie?"

Schmeckebier shook his head, his mouth too full for talk. For a minute, after he had set out two little jugs of cream, Lederer stood as if thinking. He was watching Billy Hammond move quietly around the one lighted table, whistling. "Look at that sucker," Lederer said. "I bet he doesn't even know where he is."

By the time he got around to his stool he was back at the German. "Schmeckebier," he said. "What's that mean?"

"Uh?"

"What's your name mean? Tastes beer? Likes beer?"

Schmeckebier rolled his shoulders. The sounds he made eating were like sounds from a sty. Henry was half sickened, sitting next to him, and he wished the old man would let the conversation drop. But apparently it had to be a feast, and a feast called for chatter.

"That's a hell of a name, you know it?" Lederer said, and already he was up again and around the end of the counter. "You couldn't get into any church with a name like that." His eyes fastened on the big drooping greasy lip, and he grinned.

"Schmeckeduck, that ought to be your name," he said. "What's German for duck? Vogel? Old Max Schmeckevogel. How about number two?"

Schmeckebier pushed his plate forward and Lederer forked a duck out of the steam table. Henry did not take a second.

"You ought to have one," his father told him. "You don't get grub like this every day."

"One's my limit," Henry said.

For a while they worked at their plates. Back of him Henry heard the clack of balls hitting, and a moment later the rumble as a ball rolled down the chute from a pocket. The thin, abstracted whistling of Billy Hammond broke off, became words:

"Now Annie doesn't live here any more.
So you're the guy that she's been waiting for?
She told me that I'd know you by the blue of your eyes . . ."

"Talk about one being your limit," his father said. "When we lived in Nebraska we used to put on some feeds. You remember anything about Nebraska at all?"

"A little," Henry said. He was irritated at being dragged into reminiscences, and he did not want to hear how many ducks the town hog could eat at a sitting.

"We'd go out, a whole bunch of us," John Lederer said. "The sloughs were black with ducks in those days. We'd come back with a buggyful, and the womenfolks'd really put us on a feed. Fifteen, twenty, thirty people. Take a hundred ducks to fill 'em up." He was silent a moment, staring across the counter, chewing. Henry noticed that he had tacked two wings of a teal up on the frame of the backbar mirror, small, strong bows with a band of bright blue half hidden in them. The old man's eyes slanted over, caught Henry's looking at the wings.

"Doesn't seem as if we'd had a duck feed since we left there," he said. His forehead wrinkled; he rubbed his neck, leaning forward over his plate, and his eyes met Henry's in the backbar mirror. He spoke to the mirror, ignoring the gobbling image of Schmeckebier between his own reflection and Henry's.

"You remember that set of china your mother used to have? The one she painted herself? Just the plain white china with the one design on each plate?"

Henry sat stiffly, angry that his mother's name should even be mentioned between them in this murky hole, and after what had passed. Gabble, gabble, gabble, he said to himself. If you can't think of anything else to gabble about, gabble about your dead wife. Drag her through the poolroom too. Aloud he said, "No, I guess I don't."

"Blue-wing teal," his father said, and nodded at the wings tacked to the mirror frame. "Just the wings, like that. Awful pretty. She thought a teal was about the prettiest little duck there was."

His vaguely rubbing hand came around from the back of his neck and rubbed along the cheek, pulling the slack flesh and distorting the mouth. Henry said nothing, watching the pouched hound eyes in the mirror.

It was a cold, skin-tightening shock to realize that the hound eyes were cloudy with tears. The rubbing hand went over them, shaded them like a hatbrim, but the mouth below remained distorted. With a plunging movement his father was off the stool.

"Oh, God damn!" he said in a strangling voice, and went past Henry on hard, heavy feet, down the steps and past Billy Hammond, who neither looked up nor broke the sad thin whistling.

Schmeckebier had swung around. "Vot's duh matter? Now vot's duh matter?"

With a short shake of the head, Henry turned away from him, staring after his father down the dark poolhall. He felt as if orderly things were breaking and flying apart in his mind; he had a moment of white blind terror that this whole scene upon whose reality he counted was really only a dream, something conjured up out of the bottom of his consciousness where he was accustomed to comfort himself into total sleep. His mind was still full of the anguished look his father had hurled at the mirror before he ran.

The hell with you, the look had said. The hell with you, Schmeckebier, and you, my son Henry. The hell with your ignorance, whether you're stupid or whether you just don't know all you think you know. You don't know enough to kick dirt down a hole. You know nothing at all, you know less than nothing because you know things wrong.

He heard Billy's soft whistling, saw him move around his one lighted table—a well-brought-up boy from some suburban town, a polite soft gentle boy lost and wandering among pimps and prostitutes, burying himself for some reason among people who never even touched his surface. Did he shoot pool in his bed at night, tempting sleep, as Henry did? Did his mind run carefully to angles and banks and englishes, making a reflecting mirror of them to keep from looking through them at other things?

Almost in terror he looked out across the sullen cave, past where the light came down in an intense isolated cone above Billy's table, and heard the lugubrious whistling that went on without intention of audience, a recurrent and deadening and only half-conscious sound. He looked toward the back, where his father had disappeared in the gloom, and wondered if in his bed before sleeping the old man worked through a routine of little jobs: cleaning the steam table, ordering a hundred pounds of coffee, jacking up the janitor about the mess in the hall. He wondered if it was possible to wash yourself to sleep with restaurant crockery, work yourself to sleep with chores, add yourself to sleep with columns of figures, as you could play yourself to sleep with a pool cue and a green table and fifteen colored balls. For a moment, in the sad old light with the wreckage of the duck feast at his elbow, he wondered if there was anything more to his life, or his father's life, or Billy Hammond's life, or anyone's life, than playing the careful games that deadened you into sleep.

Schmeckebier, beside him, was still groping in the fog of his mind for an explanation of what had happened. "Vere'd he go?" he said, and nudged Henry fiercely. "Vot's duh matter?"

Henry shook him off irritably, watching Billy Hammond's oblivious bent head under the light. He heard Schmeckebier's big lip flop and heard him sucking his teeth.

"I tell you," the guttural voice said. "I got somet'ing dot fixes him if he feels bum."

He too went down the stairs past the lighted table and into the gloom at the back. The light went on in his room, and after a minute or two his voice was shouting, "John! Say, come here, uh? Say, John!"

Eventually John Lederer came out of the toilet and they walked together between the tables. In his fist Schmeckebier was clutching a square bottle. He waved it in front of Henry's face as they passed, but Henry was watching his father. He saw the crumpled face, oddly rigid, like the face of a man in the grip of a barely controlled rage, but his father avoided his eyes.

"Kümmel," Schmeckebier said. He set four ice cream dishes on the counter and poured three about a third full of clear liquor. His squinted eyes lifted and peered toward Billy Hammond, but Henry said, on an impulse, "Let him alone. He's walking in his sleep."

So there were only the three. They stood together a moment and raised their glasses. "Happy days," John Lederer said automatically. They drank.

Schmeckebier smacked his lips, looked at them one after another, shook his head in admiration of the quality of his kümmel, and waddled back toward his room with the bottle. John Lederer was already drawing hot water to wash the dishes.

In the core of quiet which even the clatter of crockery and the whistling of Billy Hammond did not break into, Henry said what he had to say. "I'll be leaving," he said. "Probably tonight."

But he did not say it in anger, or with the cold command of himself that he had imagined in advance. He said it like a cry, and with the feeling he might have had on letting go the hand of a friend too weak and too exhausted to cling any longer to their inadequate shared driftwood in a wide cold sea.

With its hulking size, oddly shaped antlers, and enormous nose, the moose lends itself to caricature, as stuffed toys and cartoon characters come to mind. Like deer or elk, however, moose are game animals and are hunted in some places. This story is a satire on a moose hunt in New Brunswick. Its witty style creates a memorable adventure and is typical of the work of Irvin S. Cobb (1876–1944). Born in Paducah, Kentucky, Cobb was a well-known writer of humorous fiction, authoring numerous stories and books. He also acted in movies and wrote several screenplays, and he was a highly skilled hunter and fisherman. One reviewer said about Cobb: "He has inherited to some degree and worn modestly the mantle of Mark Twain."

Irvin S. Cobb

THE PLURAL OF MOOSE IS MISE (1921)

AT THE OUTSET, WHEN OUR expedition was still in the preparatory stages, we collectively knew a few sketchy details regarding the general architectural plan and outward aspect of the moose. One of us had once upon a time, years and years before, shot at or into—this point being debatable—a moose up in Maine. Another professed that in his youth he had seriously annoyed a moose with buckshot somewhere in Quebec. The rest of us had met the moose only in zoos with iron bars between us and him or in dining halls, where his head, projecting in a stuffed and mounted condition from the wall, gave one the feeling of dining with somebody out of the Old Testament. Speaking with regard to his family history, we understood he was closely allied to the European elk—the Unabridged told us that—and we gathered that, viewed at a distance, he rather suggested a large black mule with a pronounced Roman nose and a rustic hatrack sprouted out between his ears. Also, through our reading upon the subject, we knew that next to the buffalo he was the largest vegetarian in North America, and, next to a man who believes in the forecast of a campaign manager on the eve of an election, the stupidest native mammal that we have. By hearsay we had been made aware that he possessed a magnificent sense of smell and a perfectly wonderful sense of hearing, but was woefully shy on the faculty of thought, the result being that while by the aid of his nose and his ear he might all day elude you, if then perchance you did succeed in getting within gunning range of him he was prone to remain right where he was, peering blandly at you and accommodatingly shifting his position so as to bring his shape broadside on, thereby offering a better target until you, mastering the tremors of eagerness, succeeded in implanting a leaden slug in one of his vital areas.

But, offhand, we couldn't decide what the plural of him was. Still if the plural of goose were geese and the plural of mouse were mice it seemed reasonable to assume that the plural of moose should be mise. Besides, we figured that when we had returned and met friends and told them about our trip it would sound more impressive, in fact more plural, to say that we had slain mise rather than that we had slaughtered moose. In the common acceptance of the term as now used, moose might mean one moose or a herd of them, but mise would mean at least a bag of two of these mighty creatures and from two on up to any imaginable number.

One mentally framed the conversation:

"Well, I hear you've been up in Canada moose hunting." This is the other fellow speaking. "Kill any moose?"

"Kill any moose? Huh, we did better than that—we killed mise."

So by agreement we arranged that mise it should be. This being settled we went ahead with plans for outfitting ourselves against our foray into the game country. We equipped ourselves with high-powered rifles, with patent bedding rolls, with fanciful conceits in high boots and blanket overcoats. We bought everything that the clerk in the shop, who probably had never ventured north of the Bronx in all the days of his sheltered life, thought we should buy, including wicked-looking sheath knives and hand axes to be carried in the belt, tomahawk fashion, and pocket compasses. Personally, I have never been able to figure out the exact value of a compass to a man adrift in a strange country. What is the use of knowing where north is if you don't know where *you* are? Nevertheless, I was prevailed upon to purchase a compass, along with upward of a great gross of other articles large and small which the clerk believed would be needful to one starting upon such an expedition as we contemplated.

On my account he did a deal of thinking. Not since the fall of 1917, when we were making the world safe for the sporting-goods dealers of America, could he have spent so busy and so happy an afternoon as the afternoon when I dropped in on him.

By past experience I should have known better than to permit myself to be swept off my feet by this trademan's flood of suggestions and recommendations. Already I had an ample supply of khaki shirts that were endeared to me by associations of duck-hunting forays in North Carolina and chill evenings in an Adirondack camp and a memorable journey to Wyoming, where the sage hen abides. I treasured a pair of comfortable hunting boots that had gone twice to European battlefields and down into the Grand Canyon and up again and across the California desert, without ever breeding a blister or chafing a shin. Among my most valued possessions I counted an ancient shooting coat, wearing which I had missed quail in Kentucky, snipe on Long Island, grouse in Connecticut, doves in Georgia, and woodcock in New York State. Finally, had I but taken time for sober second consideration, I should have recalled that the guides I have from time to time known considered themselves properly accoutred for the chase when they put on the oldest suit of store clothes they owned and stuck an extra pair of wool socks in their pockets. But to the city-bred sportsman half the joy of going on a camping trip consists in getting ready for it. So eminent an authority as Emerson

Hough is much given to warning the amateur sportsman against burdening himself with vain adornments, and yet I am reliably informed that the said Hough has a larger individual collection of pretty devices in canvas and leather than any person in this republic.

That clerk had a seductive way about him; he had a positive gift. Otherwise I suppose he would have been handling some line which practically sells itself, such as oil stocks or mining shares. Under the influence of his blandishments I invested in a sweater of a pattern which he assured me was being favored by the really prominent moose hunters in the current season, and a pair of corduroy hunting pants which, when walked in, gave off a pleasant swishing sound like a softshoe dancer starting to do a sand jig. I was particularly drawn to these latter garments as being the most vocal pants I had ever seen. As I said before, I bought ever and ever so many other things; I am merely mentioning some of the main items.

We assembled the most impassive group of guides in the whole Dominion—men who, filled with the spirit of the majestic wilds, had never been known publicly to laugh at the expense of a tender-footed stranger. They did not laugh at Harry Leon Wilson's conception of the proper equipment for a man starting upon such an excursion as this one. Wilson on being wired an invitation to go on a hunt for moose promptly telegraphed back that to the best of his recollection he had not lost any moose, but that if any of his friends had been so unfortunate or so careless as to mislay one he gladly would join in the quest for the missing. He brought along an electric flashlight, in case the search should be prolonged after nightfall, a trout rod and a camera. The guides did not laugh at Colonel Tillinghast Houston's unique notion of buying an expensive rifle and a hundred rounds of ammunition and then spending his days in camp sitting in his tent reading a history of the Maritime Provinces in two large volumes. They did not laugh at Colonel Bozeman Bulger's overseas puttees or at Damon Runyon's bowie knife, or at Major McGeehan's eight-pound cartridge belt—it weighed more than that when loaded; I am speaking of it, *net*—or at Frank Stevens' sleeping-cap or at Bill MacBeth's going-away haircut—the handiwork of a barber who plainly was a person looking with abhorrence upon the thought of leaving any hair upon the human neck when it is so easy to shave all exposed surfaces smooth and clean from a point drawn across the back of the head at the level of the tops of the ears on down as far as the rear collar button. He must have been a lover of the nude in necks, that barber.

The guides did not laugh even at my vociferous corduroys which, at every step I took, went *"Hist, hist,"* as though entreating their wearer to be more quiet so they might the better be heard.

By a series of relay journeys we moved up across the line into Quebec, thence back again below the boundary and across the State of Maine, thence out of Maine into New Brunswick and to the thriving city of St. John, with its justly celebrated reversible falls which, by reason of the eccentricities of the tide, tumble upstream part of the time and downstream part of the time, thence by steamer across that temperamental body of water known as the Bay of Fundy, and so on into the interior of Nova Scotia. If anywhere on this continent there is a lovelier spot than the southern part of Nova Scotia in mid-fall I earnestly desire that, come next October, someone shall take me by the hand and lead me to it and let me rave. It used to be the land of Evangeline and the Acadians; now it is the land of the apple. You ran out of the finnan haddie belt in and around Digby into the wonderful valley of the apples. On every hand are apples—on this side of the right-of-way, orchards stretching down to the blue waters of the most beautiful rivers in America; on that side, orchards climbing up the flanks of the rolling hills to where the combing of thick timber comes down and meets them; and everywhere, at roadside, on the verges of thickets, in pastures and old fields, are seedlings growing singly, in pairs and in clumps. They told us that the valley scenically considered is at its best in the spring after the bloom bursts out upon the trees and the whole countryside turns to one vast pink and white bridal bouquet, but hardly can one picture it revealing itself as a more delectable vision than when the first frosts have fallen and every bough of every tree is studded with red and green and yellow globes and the scent of the ripened fruit rises like an incense of spices and wine.

The transition from the pastoral to the wilderness is abrupt. You leave Annapolis Royal in a motor car—that is, you do if you follow in our footsteps—and almost immediately you strike into the big game country. Not that the big game does not lap over into the settlements and even into the larger towns on occasion, for it does. It is recorded that on a certain day a full-grown moose—and a full-grown moose is almost the largest full-grown thing you ever saw—strolled through one of the principal streets of St. John and sought to enter—this being in the old sinful times—a leading saloon. A prominent lawyer of the same city told me that some four weeks before our arrival a woman client of his, living some two miles from the corporate limits, called him on the telephone at his office to ask his professional advice as to how legally she might go about getting rid of a bull moose which insisted on frequenting her orchard and frightening her children when they went to gather pippins. She felt, she said, that a lawyer was the proper person to seek in the emergency that had arisen, seeing that the closed season for moose was still on and it would be unlawful to take a shot at the intruder, so what she particularly desired to know was whether she couldn't have him impounded for trespass or something of that nature.

But such things as these do not happen every day. Probably a man could spend months on end in St. John without seeing the first of the above-mentioned animals rambling down the sidewalk in the manner of a young moose-about-town and trying to drop into the place where the saloon used to be, only to back out again, with chagrin writ large upon his features, upon discovering that the establishment in question had been transformed into a hat store.

To meet the moose where frequently he is and not merely where occasionally he is, one must go beyond the outlying orchards and on into the vasty expanse of the real moose country—hundreds of hundreds of miles of virgin waste, trackless except for game trails and portages across the ridges between waterways. It is a country of tamaracks and hemlocks, of maples and beech and birch, of berries and flowering shrubs, of bogs and barrens and swampy swales, of great granite boulders left behind by the glaciers when the world was young and thawing, of countless lakes and brawling white rapids and deep blue pools where, in the spawning season, the speckled trout are so thick that the small trout have to travel on the backs of the larger ones to avoid being crushed in the jam. I did not see this last myself; my authority for the statement is my friend the veracious lawyer of St. John. But I saw all the rest of it—the woods wearing the flaunting warpaint colors of the wonderful Canadian Indian summer—crimson of huckleberry, tawny of tamarack, yellow of birch, scarlet of maple; the ruffed grouse strutting, unafraid as barnyard fowl and, thanks be to a three-year period of protection, almost as numerous as sparrows in a city street; the signs of hoofed and padded creatures crossing and crisscrossing wherever the earth was soft enough to register the foot tracks of wild things.

And if you want to know how interior New Brunswick looked after Nova Scotia, you are respectfully requested to reread the foregoing paragraph, merely leaving out some of the lakes and most of the boulders.

On a flawless morning, in a motorboat we crossed a certain lake, and I wish I knew the language that might serve to describe the glory of the colors that ringed that lake around and were reflected, to the last flame-tipped leaf and the last smooth white column of birchen trunk, in its still waters, but I don't. I'll go further and say I can't believe Noah Webster had the words to form the picture, and he had more words than anybody up until the time William J. Bryan went actively into politics. As for myself, I can only say that these colors fairly crackled. There were hues and combinations of hues, shadings and contrasts such as no artist ever has painted and no artist will care to paint, either, for fear of being called a nature faker.

The scene shifts to our main camp. We have met our guides and have marveled at their ability to trot over steep up-and-down-hill portages carrying, each one of them, upon his back a load which no humane man would load on a mule, and have marveled still more when these men, having deposited their mountainous burdens at the farther end of the carry, go hurrying back across the ridge presently to reappear bearing upon their shoulders upturned canoes, their heads hidden inside the inverted interiors and yet by some magic gift peculiar to their craft, managing somehow to dodge the overhanging boughs of trees and without losing speed or changing gait to skip along from one slick round-topped boulder top to another.

Now we are in the deep woods, fifty miles from a railroad and thirty miles from a farmhouse. We sleep at night in canvas lean-tos, with log fires at our feet; we wash our faces and hands in the lake and make high resolves—which we never carry out—to take dips in that same frosty water; we breakfast at sun-up and sup at dusk in a log shanty set behind the cluster of tents, and between breakfast and supper we seek, under guidance, for fresh meat and dining-room trophies.

We have come too late for the calling season, it seems. In the calling season Mr. Moose desires female society, and by all accounts desires it mightily. So the guide takes a mean advantage of his social cravings. Generally afoot, but sometimes in a canoe, he escorts the gunner to a likely feeding ground or a drinking place, and through a scroll of birch bark rolled up in a megaphone shape, he delivers a creditable imitation of the call of the flirtatious cow moose. There are guides who can sound the love note through their cupped hands, but most of the fraternity favor the birchen cornucopia. The sound—part lonely bleat, part plaintive bellow—travels across the silent reaches for an incredible distance. Once when the wind was right there is a record of a moose call having been heard six miles away from where it was uttered, but in this case the instrumentalist was Louis Harlowe, a half-breed Micmac Indian, the champion moose caller of Nova Scotia and perhaps of the world.

In the bog where he is lying, or on the edge of the barren where he is feeding, the bull hears the pleading entreaty and thereby is most grossly deceived. Forgetting the caution which guides his course at other times, he hurries to where the deceiver awaits him, in his haste smashing down saplings, clattering his great horns against the tree boles, splashing through the brooks. And then when he bursts forth into the open, snorting and puffing and grunting, the hunter beholds before him a target which in that setting and with that background must loom up like a grain elevator. Yet at a distance of twenty yards or thirty, he has been known to miss the mark clean and to keep on missing it, the while the vast creature stands there, its dull brain filled with wonder that the expected cow should not be where he had had every vocal assurance that she would be, and seemingly only mildly disturbed by the crashing voice of the repeater and by the unseen, mysterious things which pass whistling over his back or under his belly as the gun quivers in the uncertain grasp of the overanxious or mayhap the buckague-stricken sportsman.

Once though he has made up his sluggish mind that all is not well for him in that immediate vicinity, he vanishes into deep cover as silently as smoke and as suddenly as a wink.

The mating time comes in mid-September and lasts about a month, more or less; and since the open season does not begin until October the first, it behooves the hunter who wishes to bag his moose with the least amount of physical exertion to be in camp during the first two weeks of October, for after that the bull moose is reverting to bachelorhood again. He may answer the call, but the chances are that he will not.

A little later on, after the snows have come, one may trail him with comparative ease. Besides, he is browsing more liberally then and consequently is moving pretty constantly. But between the time when the leaves begin to fall and the time when the snow begins to fly he is much given to staying in the densest coverts he can find and doing the bulk of his grazing by night.

So he must be still-hunted, as the saying goes, and it was still-hunting that we are called upon to do. The guide takes his birch-bark horn along each morning when he starts out, carrying it under one arm and an axe under the other, and upon his back a pouch containing the ingredients for the midday lunch and the inevitable fire-blackened teapot which he calls always by the affectionate name of "kittle." He never speaks of stopping for lunch. When the sun stands overhead and your foreshortened shadow has snuggled up close beneath your feet like a friendly black puppy, he suggests the advisability of "biling a kittle," by which he means building a fire and making tea. So the pack between his shoulders is necessary but the moose call is largely ornamental; it is habit for him to tote it and tote it he does; but mainly he depends upon his eyes and his ears and his uncanny knowledge of the ways of the thing we aim to destroy.

Yes, they call it still-hunting and still-hunting it truly is so far as Louis Harlowe, the half-breed, or Sam Glode, the full-blood Micmac, or Charley Charlton, the head guide, is concerned, as he goes worming his way through the undergrowth in his soft-soled moccasins, instinctively avoiding the rotted twig, the loose bit of stone and the swishy bough. But the pair of us, following in his footsteps, in our hard-bottomed, hob-nailed boots, our creaky leather gear and our noisy waterproofed nether garments, cannot, by the widest latitude in descriptive terminology, be called still-hunters. Carrying small avalanches with us, we slide down rocky slopes which the guide on ahead of us negotiated in pussy-footed style; and we blunder into undergrowth; and we trip over logs and we flounder into bogs and out of them again with loud, churning sounds. Going into second on a hillside we pant like switch engines. I was two weeks behind with my panting when I came out of Canada and in odd times now I still pant briskly, trying to catch up.

Reaching level ground we reverse gears and halt to blow. Toward mid-afternoon, on the homebound hike, our weary legs creak audibly at the joints and our tired feet blunder and fumble among the dried leaves. We create all the racket which, without recourse to bass drums or slide trom-bones, it is humanly possible for a brace of overdressed, city-softened so-journers to create in deep woods. And still our guide—that person so utterly lacking in a sense of humor—speaks of our endeavor as still-hunting. If an ethical Nova Scotian guide—and all professional guides everywhere, so far as I have observed, are most ethical—were hired to chaperon Sousa's band on a still-hunt through the wilderness and on the way Mr. Sousa should think up a new march full of oom-pahs and every-thing, and the band should practice it while cruising from bog to barren, the guide, returning to the settlements after the outing, would undoubt-edly refer to it as a still-hunt.

In our own case, I trust that our eagerness in some measure compen-sated for our awkwardness. At least, we worked hard—worked until mus-cles that we never before knew we had achingly forced themselves upon out attention. Yes, if for the first day or two our exertion brought us no reward in the shape of antlered frontlets or great black pelts drying on the rocks at the canoe landing or savory moose steaks in the frying pan;

if it seemed that after all we would have to content ourselves with taking home a stuffed guide's head or so; if twilight found us reuniting at the supper table each with tales of endless miles of tramping to our credit but no game, nevertheless and notwithstanding, the labor we spent was not without its plenteous compensations.

To begin with, there was ever the hope that beyond the next thicket or across the next swale old Mr. Sixty-Inch Spread would be browsing about waiting for us to come stealing upon him with all the stealthy approach of a runaway moving van and blow him over. There was the joy of watching our guide trailing, he reading the woods as a scholar reads a book and seeing there plain as print what we never would have seen—the impress of a great splayed hoof in the yellowed moss, the freshly gnawed twigs of the moose wood, the scarred bark high up on a maple to show that here a bull had whetted his horns, the scuffed earth where a bear had been digging for grubs, the wallow a buck deer had made at a crossing. And when he told us that the moose had passed this way, trotting, less than an hour before, but that the deer's bed was at least two nights old, while the bear's scratching dated back for days, we knew that he knew. Real efficiency in any line carries its own credentials and needs no bolstering affidavits. There may be better eyes in some human head than the pair Louis Harlowe owns or than that equally keen pair belonging to Harry Allen, the dean of New Brunswick guides, but I have yet to see their owner, and I am quite sure that for woodcraft there are no better equipped men anywhere than the two I have named.

We couldn't decide which was the finer—the supper at night with a great log fire chasing back the dense shadows, and the baked beans and the talk and the crisp bacon and the innocent lies passing back and forth, or the midday lunch out in the tangy, painted forest, miles and miles away from anywhere at all, with the chickadees and the snowbirds and the robins flittering about, waiting their chance to gather the crumbs they knew we would leave behind for them and with the moose birds informally dropping in on us before ever the kettle had begun to sing.

Naturalists know the moose bird, I believe, as the Canada jay and over the line in the States they call him the venison hawk, but by any name he is a handsome, saucy chap, as smart as Satan and as impudent as they make 'em. The first thin wisp of your fire, rising above the undergrowth, is his signal. For some of the denizens of the wilderness it may be just twelve o'clock, but to him it's feeding time. Here he comes in his swooping flight, a graceful, slate-blue figure with his snowy bib and tucker like a trencherman prepared. And there, following close behind him, are other members of his tribe. There always is one in the flock more daring than the rest. If you sit quietly, this fellow will flit closer and closer, his head cocked on one side, uttering half-doubtful, half-confident cheeps until he is snatching up provender right under your feet or even out of your hand. His preference is for meat—raw meat for choice, but his taste is catholic; he'll eat anything. Small morsels he swallows on the spot; larger tidbits he takes in his bill and flies away with to hide in a nearby tree crotch. His friends watch him, and by the time he has returned for another helping they have stolen his cache, so that chiefly what he gets out of the burden of his thriftful industry is the exercise. I do not know whether this should teach us that it is better to strive to lay something against a rainy day and take a chance on the honesty of the neighbors or to seize our pleasure when and where we find it and forget the morrow. Aesop might be able to figure it out, but, being no Aesop, I must continue to register uncertainty.

Campfire suppers and high noon barbecues and glorious sunrises and shooting the rapids in the rivers and paddling across the blue lakes, scaring up the black duck and the loons from before us, and all the rest of it, was fine enough in its way, but it was not killing the bull moose. So we hunted and we hunted. We dragged our reluctant feet through moose bogs—beaver meadows these are in the Adirondacks—and we ranged the high ground and the low. Cow moose we encountered frequently and calves aplenty. But the adult male was what we sought.

We had several close calls, or perhaps I should say he did. One of our outfit—nameless here because I have no desire to heap shame upon an otherwise well-meaning and always dependable companion—had been cruising through thick timber all day without seeing anything to fire at. Emerging into an open glade over a ridge above Little Red Lake, he was moved to try his new and virgin automatic at a target. So he loosed off at one of the big black crows of the North that was perched, like a disconsolate undertaker, with bunched shoulders and drooping head, on a dead tamarack fifty yards away. He did not hit Brother Corbie but he tore the top out of the tamarack snag. And then when he and the guide had rounded the shoulder of the little hill and descended to a swamp below they read in certain telltale signs a story which came near to moving the marksman to tears.

Moving up the slope from the other side the guide had been calling, a bull moose—and a whaling big one, to judge by his hoof marks—had been stirred to inquire into the circumstances. He had quitted the swamp and had ambled up the hill to within a hundred yards of the crest when—as the guide deduced it—the sound of the shot just above caused him to halt and swing about and depart from that neighborhood at his very best gait. But for that unlucky rifle report he probably would have walked right into the enemy. My friend does not now feel toward crows as he formerly felt. He thinks they should be abolished.

An experience of mine was likewise fraught with the germs of a tragic disappointment. In a densely thicketed district, my guide, with a view to getting a view of the surrounding terrain above the tops of the saplings, scaled the steep side of a boulder that was as big as an icehouse and then beckoned to me to follow.

But as a scaler I am not a conspicuous success. By main strength and awkwardness I managed to clamber up. Just as I reached the top and put my rifle down so that I might fan breath into myself with both hands, my boot soles slipped off the uncertain surface and I slid off my perch into space. Wildly I threw out both arms in a general direction. My clutching fingers closed on a limb of a maple which overshadowed the rock and I swung out into the air twelve feet or so above the inhospitable earth, utterly unable to reach with my convulsively groping feet the nearermost juts of granite. For an agonized moment it seemed probable that the only thing that might break my fall would be myself. But I kept my presence of mind. I flatter myself that in emergencies I am a quick thinker. As I dangled there an expedient came to me. I let go gradually.

And then as I plumped with a dull sickening thud into the herbage below and lay there weaponless, windless and jarred I saw, vanishing into the scrub not a hundred feet away, the black shape of a big and startled moose. I caught one fleeting glimpse of an enormous head, of a profile which might have belonged to one of the major prophets, of a set of horns outspreading even as the fronded palm outspreads itself, of a switching tail and a slab-sided rump, and then the shielding bushes closed and the apparition was gone, and gone for keeps. For my part there was nothing to do but to sit there for a spell and cherish regrets. Under the circumstances, trailing a frightened bull moose would have been about as satisfactory as trailing a comet, and probably not a bit more successful as to results.

For the majority of the members of our troupe the duration of the hunt had a time limit. On the afternoon of the last day in camp two of the party strolled into the immediate presence of a fair-sized bull and, firing together, one of them put a slug of lead in a twitching ear which he turned toward them. It must have been his deaf ear, else he would have been aware of their approach long before. But one moose was singular and the achievement of the plural number was our ambition. So four of us crossed back into New Brunswick, where, according to all native New Brunswickers, the moose grow larger than they do in the sister province; Nova Scotians taking the opposing side and being willing to argue it at all times.

With unabated determination the gallant quarter of us hunted and hunted. Three big deer died to make holiday for us but the moose displayed a coyness and diffidence which might be accounted for only on the ground that they heard we were coming. Indeed they could not very well help hearing it.

Each morning under the influences of the frost the flaming frost colors showed a dimming hue. Day before yesterday they had been like burning brands, yesterday there were dulled embers, today smoldering coals; and tomorrow they would be as dead ashes. Each night the sun went down in a nimbus of cold gray clouds. There was a taste and a smell as of snow in the air. The last tardy robin packed up and went south; the swarms of juncos grew thicker; wedge-shaped flights of coot and black duck passed overhead, their bills all pointing toward the Gulf of Mexico. Then on the last day there fell a rain which turned to sleet and the sleet to snow—four inches of it—and in the snow on that last day the reward which comes—sometimes—to the persevering was ours.

To know the climactic sensation which filled the triumphant amateur you must first of all care for the outdoors and for big-game shooting, and in the second place you must have known the feeling of hope deferred, and in the third place you must have reached the eleventh hour, so to speak, of your stay in these parts with the anticipation you had been nurturing for all these weeks since the trip was first proposed still unrealized in your soul.

You and your camp mate and your guide were on the last lap of the journey back to camp; the sun was slipping down the western wall of the horizon; the shadows were deepening under the spruces; you rounded the shoulder of a ridge and stood for a moment at your guide's back looking out across a fire-burned barren. He stiffened like a pointer on a warm scent and pointed straight ahead. Your eye followed where his finger aimed, and two hundred yards away you saw a dark blot against a background of faded tamarack—a bull standing head-on. You shot together, you and your companion. Apparently, the animal swung himself about and started moving at the seemingly languid lope of the moose, which really is a faster gait than you would suppose until you measure the length of his stride. You kept on firing, both of you, as rapidly almost as you could pull the triggers of your automatics. Twice he shook himself and humped his hindquarters as though stung, but he did not check his speed. You emptied your magazine—five shots. Your mate's fifth shell jammed in the chamber, putting him out of the running for the moment. In desperate haste you fumbled one more shell into your rifle, and just as the fugitive topped a little rise before disappearing for good into the shrouding second growth you got your sight full on the mark and sent a farewell bullet whistling on its way. The black hulk vanished magically.

"That'll do," said your guide, grinning broadly. "You got 'im. But load up again before we go down there. He's down and down for keeps, I think, judgin' by the way he flopped, but he might get up again."

But he didn't get up again. You came on him where he lay, still feebly twitching, with two flesh wounds in his flanks and a third hole right through him behind the shoulders—a thousand pounds of meat, a head worth saving and mounting and bragging about in the years to come, a pelt as a big as a double blanket and at last the accomplished plural of moose was mise.

So then you did what man generally does when language fails to express what he feels. You harked back sundry thousands of years and you did as your remote ancestor, the cave dweller, did when he slew the sabre-toothed whatyoumaycallhim. About the carcass of your kill you executed a war dance; at least you did if you chambered the emotions which filled the present writer to the choking point.

And then the next day, back in the settlements, when you reunited with two remaining members of the outfit who had been in camp eight miles away from the camp where you stayed, and when you learned that now there was a total tally of three deceased beasties, the war dance was repeated, only this time it was a four-handed movement instead of a solo number.

*One of the greatest French authors, Guy de Maupassant (1850–1893) is un-
surpassed as a master of the short story. What follows is one of his highly
polished gems. The duck hunting trip has a perfectly crafted ending that will
tug at your heartstrings. It reveals a tender side to this usually tough-minded
writer.*

Guy de Maupassant

LOVE (1885)

I HAVE JUST READ AMONG the general news in one of the papers a
drama of passion. He killed her and then he killed himself, so he must
have loved her. What matters He or She? Their love alone matters to me;
and it does not interest me because it moves me or astonishes me, or because it softens me or makes me think, but because it recalls to my mind
a remembrance of my youth, a strange recollection of a hunting adventure where Love appeared to me, as the Cross appeared to the early Chris-
tians, in the midst of the heavens.

I was born with all the instincts and the senses of primitive man, tempered by the arguments and the restraints of a civilized being. I am passionately fond of shooting, yet the sight of the wounded animal, of the blood on its feathers and on my hands, affects my heart so as almost to make it stop.

That year the cold weather set in suddenly toward the end of autumn, and I was invited by one of my cousins, Karl de Rauville, to go with him and shoot ducks on the marshes, at daybreak.

My cousin was a jolly fellow of forty, with red hair, very stout and bearded, a country gentlemen, an amiable semi-brute, of a happy disposition and endowed with that Gallic wit which makes even mediocrity agreeable. He lived in a house, half farmhouse, half château, situated in a broad valley through which a river ran. The hills right and left were covered with woods, old manorial woods where magnificent trees still remained, and where the rarest feathered game in that part of France was to be found. Eagles were shot there occasionally, and birds of passage, such as rarely venture into our overpopulated part of the country, invariably lighted amid these giant oaks, as if they knew or recognized some little corner of a primeval forest which had remained there to serve them as a shelter during their short nocturnal halt.

In the valley there were large meadows watered by trenches and separated by hedges; then, farther on, the river, which up to that point had been kept between banks, expanded into a vast marsh. That marsh was the best shooting ground I ever saw. It was my cousin's chief care, and he kept it as a preserve. Through the rushes that covered it, and made it rustling and rough, narrow passages had been cut, through which the flat-bottomed boats, impelled and steered by poles, passed along silently over dead water, brushing up against the reeds and making the swift fish take refuge in the weeds, and the wild fowl, with their pointed, black heads, dive suddenly.

I am passionately fond of the water: of the sea, though it is too vast, too full of movement, impossible to hold; of the rivers which are so beautiful, but which pass on, and flee away; and above all of the marshes, where the whole unknown existence of aquatic animals palpitates. The marsh is an entire world in itself on the world of earth—a different world, which has its own life, its settled inhabitants and its passing travelers, its voices, its noises, and above all its mystery. Nothing is more impressive, nothing more disquieting, more terrifying occasionally, than a fen. Why should a vague terror hang over these low plains covered with water? Is it the low rustling of the rushes, the strange will-o'-the-wisp lights, the silence which prevails on calm nights, the still mists which hang over the surface like a shroud; or is it the almost inaudible splashing, so slight and so gentle, yet sometimes more terrifying than the cannons of men or the thunders of the skies, which makes these marshes resemble countries one has dreamed of, terrible countries holding an unknown and dangerous secret?

No, something else belongs to it—another mystery, perhaps the mystery of the creation itself! For was it not in stagnant and muddy water, amid the heavy humidity of moist land under the heat of the sun, that the first germ of life pulsated and expanded to the day?

I arrived at my cousin's in the evening. It was freezing hard enough to split the stones.

During dinner, in the large room whose sideboards, walls, and ceiling were covered with stuffed birds, with wings extended or perched on branches to which they were nailed—hawks, herons, owls, nightjars, buzzards, tiercels, vultures, falcons—my cousin, who, dressed in a sealskin jacket, himself resembled some strange animal from a cold country, told me what preparations he had made for that same night.

We were to start at half past three in the morning, so as to arrive at the place which he had chosen for our watching place at about half past four. On that spot a hut had been built of lumps of ice, so as to shelter us somewhat from the trying wind which precedes daybreak, a wind so cold as to tear the flesh like a saw, cut it like the blade of a knife, prick it like a poisoned sting, twist it like a pair of pincers, and burn it like fire.

My cousin rubbed his hands: "I have never known such a frost," he said; "it is already twelve degrees below zero at six o'clock in the evening."

I threw myself onto my bed immediately after we had finished our meal, and went to sleep by the light of a bright fire burning in the grate.

At three o'clock he woke me. In my turn, I put on a sheepskin, and found my cousin Karl covered with a bearskin. After having each swallowed two cups of scalding coffee, followed by glasses of liqueur brandy, we started, accompanied by a gamekeeper and our dogs, Plongeon and Pierrot.

From the first moment that I got outside, I felt chilled to the very marrow. It was one of those nights on which the earth seems dead with cold. The frozen air becomes resisting and palpable, such pain does it cause; no breath of wind moves it, it is fixed and motionless; it bites you, pierces through you, dries you, kills the trees, the plants, the insects, the small birds themselves, who fall from the branches onto the hard ground, and become stiff themselves under the grip of the cold.

The moon, which was in her last quarter and was inclining all to one side, seemed fainting in the midst of space, so weak that she was unable to wane, forced to stay up yonder, seized and paralyzed by the severity of the weather. She shed a cold, mournful light over the world, that dying and wan light which she gives us every month, at the end of her period.

Karl and I walked side by side, our backs bent, our hands in our pockets and our guns under our arms. Our boots, which were wrapped in wool so that we might be able to walk without slipping on the frozen river, made no sound, and I looked at the white vapor which our dogs' breath made.

We were soon on the edge of the marsh, and entered one of the lanes of dry rushes which ran though the low forest.

Our elbows, which touched the long, ribbonlike leaves, left a slight noise behind us, and I was seized, as I had never been before, by the powerful and singular emotion which marshes cause in me. This one was dead, dead from cold, since we were walking on it, in the middle of its population of dried rushes.

Suddenly, at the turn of one of the lanes, I perceived the ice hut which had been constructed to shelter us. I went in, and as we had nearly an hour to wait before the wandering birds would awake, I rolled myself up in my rug in order to try and get warm. Then, lying on my back, I began to look at the misshapen moon, which had four horns, through the vaguely transparent walls of this polar house. But the frost of the frozen marshes, the cold of these walls, the cold from the firmament penetrated me so terribly that I began to cough. My cousin Karl became uneasy.

"No matter if we do not kill much today," he said: "I do not want you to catch cold; we will light a fire." And he told the gamekeeper to cut some rushes.

We made a pile in the middle of our hut, which had a hole in the middle of the roof to let out the smoke, and when the red flames rose up to the clear, crystal blocks they began to melt, gently, imperceptibly, as if they were sweating. Karl, who had remained outside, called out to me: "Come and look here!" I went out of the hut and remained struck with astonishment. Our hut, in the shape of a cone, looked like an enormous diamond with a heart of fire, which had been suddenly planted there in the midst of the frozen water of the marsh. And inside, we saw two fantastic forms, those of our dogs, who were warming themselves at the fire.

But a peculiar cry, a lost, a wandering cry, passed over our heads, and the light from our hearth showed us the wild birds. Nothing moves one so much as the first clamor of a life which one does not see, which passes through the somber air so quickly and so far off, just before the first streak of a winter's day appears on the horizon. It seems to me, at this glacial hour of dawn, as if that passing cry which is carried away by the wings of a bird is the sigh of a soul from the world!

"Put out the fire," said Karl, "it is getting daylight."

The sky was, in fact, beginning to grow pale, and the flights of ducks made long, rapid streaks which were soon obliterated on the sky.

A stream of light burst out into the night; Karl had fired, and the two dogs ran forward.

And then, nearly every minute, now he, now I, aimed rapidly as soon as the shadow of a flying flock appeared above the rushes. And Pierrot and Plongeon, out of breath but happy, retrieved the bleeding birds, whose eyes still, occasionally, looked at us.

The sun had risen, and it was a bright day with a blue sky, and we were thinking of taking our departure, when two birds with extended necks and outstretched wings glided rapidly over our heads. I fired, and one of them fell almost at my feet. It was a teal, with a silver breast, and then, in the blue space above me, I heard a voice, the voice of a bird. It was a short, repeated, heart-rending lament; and the bird, the little animal that had been spared, began to turn round in the blue sky, over our heads, looking at its dead companion which I was holding in my hand.

Karl was on his knees, his gun to his shoulder watching it eagerly, until it should be within shot. "You have killed the duck," he said, "and the drake will not fly away."

He certainly did not fly away; he circled over our heads continually, and continued his cries. Never have any groans of suffering pained me so much as that desolate appeal, as that lamentable reproach of this poor bird which was lost in space.

Occasionally he took flight under the menace of the gun which followed his movements, and seemed ready to continue his flight alone, but as he could not make up his mind to this, he returned to find his mate.

"Leave her on the ground," Karl said to me, "he will come within shot by and by." And he did indeed come near us, careless of danger, infatuated by his animal love, by his affection for his mate, which I had just killed.

Karl fired, and it was as if somebody had cut the string which held the bird suspended. I saw something black descend, and I heard the noise of a fall among the rushes. And Pierrot brought it to me.

I put them—they were already cold—into the same gamebag, and I returned to Paris the same evening.

A boy and his father, hunting moose in Montana, come across a dangerous bear. Their misfortune generates a steely display of courage. This is one of the truly great hunting stories and an astonishing piece of literature. David Quammen, another of the talented Montana writers represented in this book, has worked as a science writer and fishing guide. Among his books are To Walk the Line *(1970),* The Zolta Configuration *(1983), and* Wild Thoughts from Wild Places *(1998). This story first appeared in* TriQuarterly.

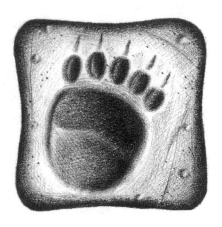

David Quammen

WALKING OUT (1980)

AS THE TRAIN ROCKED DEAD at Livingston he saw the man, in a worn khaki shirt with button flaps buttoned, arms crossed. The boy's hand sprang up by reflex, and his face broke into a smile. The man smiled back gravely, and nodded. He did not otherwise move. The boy turned from the window and, with the awesome deliberateness of a fat child harboring reluctance, began struggling to pull down his bag. His father would wait on the platform. First sight of him had reminded the boy that nothing was simple enough now for hurrying.

They drove in the old open Willys toward the cabin beyond town. The windshield of the Willys was up, but the fine cold sharp rain came into their faces, and the boy could not raise his eyes to look at the road. He wore a rain parka his father had handed him at the station. The man, protected by only the khaki, held his lips strung in a firm silent line that seemed more grin than wince. Riding through town in the cold rain, open topped and jaunty, getting drenched as though by necessity, was—the boy understood vaguely—somehow in the spirit of this season.

"We have a moose tag," his father shouted.

The boy said nothing. He refused to care what it meant, that they had a moose tag.

"I've got one picked out. A bull. I've stalked him for two weeks. Up in the Crazies. When we get to the cabin, we'll build a good roaring fire." With only the charade of a pause, he added, "Your mother." It was said like a question. The boy waited. "How is she?"

"All right, I guess." Over the jeep's howl, with the wind stealing his voice, the boy too had to shout.

"Are you friends with her?"

"I guess so."

"Is she still a beautiful lady?"

"I don't know. I guess so. I don't know that."

"You must know that. Is she starting to get wrinkled like me? Does she seem worried and sad? Or is she just still a fine beautiful lady? You must know that."

"She's still a beautiful lady, I guess."

"Did she tell you any messages for me?"

"She said . . . she said I should give you her love," the boy lied, impulsively and clumsily. He was at once embarrassed that he had done it.

"Oh," his father said. "Thank you, David."

They reached the cabin on a mile of dirt road winding through meadow to a spruce grove. Inside, the boy was enwrapped in the strong syncretic smell of all seasonal mountain cabins: pine resin and insect repellent and a mustiness suggesting damp bathing trunks stored in a drawer. There were yellow pine floors and rope-work throw rugs and a bead curtain to the bedroom and a cast-iron cook stove with none of the lids or handles missing and a pump in the kitchen sink and old issues of *Field and Stream,* and on the mantel above where a fire now finally burned was a picture of the boy's grandfather, the railroad telegrapher, who had once owned the cabin. The boy's father cooked a dinner of fried ham, and though the boy did not like ham he had expected his father to cook canned stew or Spam, so he said nothing. His father asked him about school and the boy talked and his father seemed to be interested. Warm and dry, the boy began to feel safe from his own anguish. Then his father said:

"We'll leave tomorrow around ten."

Last year on the boy's visit they had hunted birds. They had lived in the cabin for six nights, and each day they had hunted pheasant in the wheat stubble, or blue grouse in the woods, or ducks along the irrigation slews. The boy had been wet and cold and miserable at times, but each evening they returned to the cabin and to the boy's suitcase of dry clothes. They had eaten hot food cooked on a stove, and had smelled the cabin smell, and had slept together in a bed. In six days of hunting, the boy had not managed to kill a single bird. Yet last year he had known that, at least once a day, he would be comfortable, if not happy. This year his father planned that he should not even be comfortable. He had said in his letter to Evergreen Park, before the boy left Chicago but when it was too late for him not to leave, that he would take the boy camping in the mountains, after big game. He had pretended to believe that the boy would be glad.

The Willys was loaded and moving by ten minutes to ten. For three hours they drove, through Big Timber, and then north on the highway, and then back west again on a logging road that took them winding and bouncing higher into the mountains. Thick cottony streaks of white cloud hung in among the mountaintop trees, light and dense dollops against the bulking sharp dark olive, as though in a black-and-white photograph. They followed the gravel road for an hour, and the boy thought they would soon have a flat tire or break an axle. If they had a flat, the boy knew, his father would only change it and drive on until they had the second, farther from the highway. Finally they crossed a creek and his father plunged the Willys off into a bed of weeds.

His father said, "Here."

The boy said, "Where?"

"Up that little drainage. At the head of the creek."

"How far is it?"

"Two or three miles."

"Is that where you saw the moose?"

"No. That's where I saw the sheepman's hut. The moose is farther. On top."

"Are we going to sleep in a hut? I thought we were going to sleep in a tent."

"No. Why should we carry a tent up there when we have a perfectly good hut?"

The boy couldn't answer that question. He thought now that this might be the time when he would cry. He had known it was coming.

"I don't much want to sleep in a hut," he said, and his voice broke with the simple honesty of it, and his eyes glazed. He held his mouth tight against the trembling.

As though something had broken in him too, the boy's father laid his forehead down on the steering wheel, against his knuckles. For a moment he remained bowed, breathing exhaustedly. But he looked up again before speaking.

"Well, we don't have to, David."

The boy said nothing.

"It's an old sheepman's hut made of logs, and it's near where we're going to hunt, and we can fix it dry and good. I thought you might like that. I thought it might be more fun than a tent. But we don't have to do it. We can drive back to Big Timber and buy a tent, or we can drive back to the cabin and hunt birds, like last year. Whatever you want to do. You have to forgive me the kind of ideas I get. I hope you will. We don't have to do anything that you don't want to do."

"No," the boy said. "I want to."

"Are you sure?"

"No," the boy said. "But I just want to."

They bushwhacked along the creek, treading a thick soft mixture of moss and humus and needles, climbing upward through brush. Then the brush thinned and they were ascending an open creek bottom, thirty yards wide, darkened by fir and cedar. Farther, and they struck a trail, which led them upward along the creek. Farther still, and the trail received a branch, then another, then forked.

"Who made this trail? Did the sheepman?"

"No," his father said. "Deer and elk."

Gradually the creek's little canyon narrowed, steep wooded shoulders funneling closer on each side. For a while the game trails forked and converged like a maze, but soon again there were only two branches, and finally one, heavily worn. It dodged through alder and willow, skirting tangles of browned raspberry, so that the boy and his father could never see more than twenty feet ahead. When they stopped to rest, the boy's father unstrapped the .270 from his pack and loaded it.

"We have to be careful now," he explained. "We may surprise a bear."

Under the cedars, the creek bottom held a cool dampness that seemed to be stored from one winter to the next. The boy began at once to feel chilled. He put on his jacket, and they continued climbing. Soon he was sweating again in the cold.

On a small flat where the alder drew back from the creek, the hut was built into one bank of the canyon, with the sod of the hillside lapping out over its roof. The door was a low dark opening. Forty or fifty years ago, the boy's father explained, this hut had been built and used by a Basque shepherd. At that time there had been many Basques in Montana, and they had run sheep all across this ridge of the Crazies. His father forgot to explain what a Basque was, and the boy didn't remind him.

They built a fire. His father had brought sirloin steaks and an onion for dinner, and the boy was happy with him about that. As they ate, it grew dark, but the boy and his father had stocked a large comforting pile of naked deadfall. In the darkness, by firelight, his father made chocolate pudding. The pudding had been his father's surprise. The boy sat on a piece of canvas and added logs to the fire while his father drank coffee. Sparks rose on the heat and the boy watched them climb toward the cedar limbs and the black pools of sky. The pudding did not set.

"Do you remember your grandfather, David?"

"Yes," the boy said, and wished it were true. He remembered a funeral when he was three.

"Your grandfather brought me up on this mountain when I was seventeen. That was the last year he hunted." The boy knew what sort of thoughts his father was having. But he knew also that his own home was in Evergreen Park, and that he was another man's boy now, with another man's name, though this indeed was his father. "Your grandfather was fifty years older than me."

The boy said nothing.

"And I'm thirty-four years older than you."

"And I'm only eleven," the boy cautioned him.

"Yes," said his father. "And someday you'll have a son and you'll be forty years older than him, and you'll want so badly for him to know who you are that you could cry."

The boy was embarrassed.

"And that's called the cycle of life's infinite wisdom," his father said, and laughed at himself unpleasantly.

"What did he die of?" the boy asked, desperate to escape the focus of his father's rumination.

"He was eighty-seven then. Christ. He was tired." The boy's father went silent. Then he shook his head, and poured himself the remaining coffee.

Through that night the boy was never quite warm. He slept on his side with his knees drawn up, and this was uncomfortable but his body seemed to demand it for warmth. The hard cold mountain earth pressed upward through the mat of fir boughs his father had laid, and drew heat from the boy's body like a pallet of leeches. He clutched the bedroll around his neck and folded the empty part at the bottom back under his legs. Once he woke to a noise. Though his father was sleeping between him and the door of the hut, for a while the boy lay awake, listening worriedly, and then woke again on his back to realize time had passed. He heard droplets begin to hit the canvas his father had spread over the sod roof of the hut. But he remained dry.

He rose to the smell of a fire. The tarp was rigid with sleet and frost. The firewood and the knapsacks were frosted. It was that gray time of dawn before any blue and, through the branches above, the boy was unable to tell whether the sky was murky or clear. Delicate sheet ice hung on everything, but there was no wetness. The rain seemed to have been hushed by the cold.

"What time is it?"

"Early yet."

"How early?" The boy was thinking about the cold at home as he waited outside on 96th Street for his school bus. That was the cruelest moment of his day, but it seemed a benign and familiar part of him compared to this.

"Early. I don't have a watch. What difference does it make, David?"

"Not any."

After breakfast they began walking up the valley. His father had the .270, and the boy carried an old Winchester .30–30, with open sights. The walking was not hard, and with this gentle exercise in the cold morning the boy soon felt fresh and fine. Now I'm hunting for moose with my father, he told himself. That's just what I'm doing. Few boys in Evergreen Park had ever been moose hunting with their fathers in Montana, he knew. I'm doing it now, the boy told himself.

Reaching the lip of a high meadow, a mile above the shepherd's hut, they had not seen so much as a magpie.

Before them, across hundreds of yards, opened a smooth lake of tall lifeless grass, browned by September drought and killed by the frosts and beginning to rot with November's rain. The creek was here a deep quiet channel of smooth curves overhung by the grass, with a dark surface like heavy oil. When they had come fifty yards into the meadow, his father turned and pointed out to the boy a large ponderosa pine with a forked crown that marked the head of their creek valley. He showed the boy a small aspen grove midway across the meadow, toward which they were aligning themselves.

"Near the far woods is a beaver pond. The moose waters there. We can wait in the aspens and watch the whole meadow without being seen. If

205

he doesn't come, we'll go up another canyon, and check again on the way back."

For an hour, and another, they waited. The boy sat with his hands in his jacket pockets, bunching the jacket tighter around him, and his buttocks drew cold moisture from the ground. His father squatted on his heels like a country man, rising periodically to inspect the meadow in all directions. Finally he stood up; he fixed his stare on the distant fringe of woods and, like a retriever, did not move. He said, "David."

The boy stood beside him. His father placed a hand on the boy's shoulder. The boy saw a large dark form rolling toward them like a great slug in the grass.

"Is it the moose?"

"No," said his father. "That is a grizzly bear, David. An old male grizzly."

The boy was impressed. He sensed an aura of power and terror and authority about the husky shape, even at two hundred yards.

"Are we going to shoot him?"

"No."

"Why not?"

"We don't have a permit," his father whispered. "And because we don't want to."

The bear plowed on toward the beaver pond for a while, then stopped. It froze in the grass and seemed to be listening. The boy's father added: "That's not hunting for the meat. That's hunting for the fear. I don't need the fear. I've got enough in my life already."

The bear turned and moiled off quickly through the grass. It disappeared back into the far woods.

"He heard us."

"Maybe," the boy's father said. "Let's go have a look at that beaver pond."

A sleek furred carcass lay low in the water, swollen grotesquely with putrescence and coated with glistening blowflies. Four days, the boy's father guessed. The moose had been shot at least eighteen times with a .22 pistol. One of its eyes had been shot out; it had been shot twice in the jaw; and both quarters on the side that lay upward were ruined with shots. Standing up to his knees in the sump, the boy's father took the trouble of counting the holes, and probing one of the slugs out with his knife. That only made him angrier. He flung the lead away.

For the next three hours, with his father withdrawn into a solitary and characteristic bitterness, the boy felt abandoned. He did not understand why a moose would be slaughtered with a light pistol and left to rot. His father did not bother to explain; like the bear, he seemed to understand it as well as he needed to. They walked on, but they did not really hunt.

They left the meadow for more pine, and now tamarack, naked tamarack, the yellow needles nearly all down and going ginger where they coated the trail. The boy and his father hiked along a level path into another canyon, this one vast at the mouth and narrowing between high ridges of bare rock. They crossed and recrossed the shepherd's creek, which in this canyon was a tumbling free-stone brook. Following five yards behind his father, watching the cold, unapproachable rage that shaped the line of the man's shoulders, the boy was miserably uneasy because his father had grown so distant and quiet. They climbed over deadfalls blocking the trail, skirted one boulder large as a cabin, and blundered into a garden of nettles that stung them fiercely through their trousers. They saw fresh elk scat, and they saw bear, diarrhetic with late berries. The boy's father eventually grew bored with brooding, and showed the boy how to stalk. Before dusk that day they had shot an elk.

An open and gently sloped hillside, almost a meadow, ran for a quarter mile in quaking aspen, none over fifteen feet tall. The elk was above. The boy's father had the boy brace his gun in the notch of an aspen and take the first shot. The boy missed. The elk reeled and bolted down and his father killed it before it made cover. It was a five-point bull. They dressed the elk out and dragged it down to the cover of large pines, near the stream, where they would quarter it tomorrow, and then they returned under twilight to the hut.

That night even the fetal position could not keep the boy warm. He shivered wakefully for hours. He was glad that the following day, though full of walking and butchery and oppressive burdens, would be their last in the woods. He heard nothing. When he woke, through the door of the hut he saw whiteness like bone.

Six inches had fallen, and it was still snowing. The boy stood about in the campsite, amazed. When it snowed three inches in Evergreen Park, the boy would wake before dawn to the hiss of sand trucks and the ratchet of chains. Here there had been no warning. The boy was not much colder than he had been yesterday, and the transformation of the woods seemed mysterious and benign and somehow comic. He thought of Christmas. Then his father barked at him.

His father's mood had also changed, but in a different way; he seemed serious and hurried. As he wiped the breakfast pots clean with snow, he gave the boy orders for other chores. They left camp with two empty pack frames, both rifles, and a handsaw and rope. The boy soon understood why his father felt pressure of time: it took them an hour to climb the mile to the meadow. The snow continued. They did not rest until they reached the aspens.

"I had half a mind at breakfast to let the bull lie and pack us straight down out of here," his father admitted. "Probably smarter and less trouble in the long run. I could have come back on snowshoes next week. But by then it might be three feet deep and starting to drift. We can get two quarters out today. That will make it easier for me later." The boy was surprised by two things: that his father would be so wary in the face of a gentle snowfall and that he himself would have felt disappointed to be taken out of the woods that morning. The air of the meadow teemed with white.

"If it stops soon, we're fine," said his father.

It continued.

The path up the far canyon was hard climbing in eight inches of snow. The boy fell once, filling his collar and sleeves, and the gun-sight put a small gouge in his chin. But he was not discouraged. That night they would be warm and dry at the cabin. A half mile on and he came up beside his father, who had stopped to stare down at dark splashes of blood.

Heavy tracks and a dragging belly mark led up to the scramble of deepening red, and away. The tracks were nine inches long and showed claws.

The boy's father knelt. As the boy watched, one shining maroon splotch the size of a saucer sank slowly beyond sight into the snow. The blood was warm.

Inspecting the tracks carefully, his father said, "She's got a cub with her."

"What happened?"

"Just a kill. Seems to have been a bird. That's too much blood for a grouse, but I don't see signs of any four-footed creature. Maybe a turkey." He frowned thoughtfully. "A turkey without feathers. I don't know. What I dislike is coming up on her with a cub." He drove a round into the chamber of the .270.

Trailing red smears, the tracks preceded them. Within fifty feet they found the body. It was half-buried. The top of its head had been shorn away, and the cub's brains had been licked out.

His father said "Christ," and plunged off the trail. He snapped at the boy to follow closely.

They made a wide crescent through brush and struck back after a quarter mile. His father slogged ahead in the snow, stopping often to stand holding his gun ready and glancing around while the boy caught up and passed him. The boy was confused. He knew his father was worried, but he did not feel any danger himself. They met the trail again, and went on to the aspen hillside before his father allowed them to rest. The boy spat on the snow. His lungs ached badly.

"Why did she do that?"

"She didn't. Another bear got her cub. A male. Maybe the one we saw yesterday. Then she fought him for the body, and she won. We didn't miss them by much. She may even have been watching. Nothing could put her in a worse frame of mind."

He added: "If we so much as see her, I want you to pick the nearest big tree and start climbing. Don't stop till you're twenty feet off the ground. I'll stay down and decide whether we have to shoot her. Is your rifle cocked?"

"No."

"Cock it, and put on the safety. She may be a black bear and black bears can climb. If she comes up after you, lean down, and stick your gun in her mouth and fire. You can't miss."

He cocked the Winchester, as his father had said.

They angled downhill to the stream, and on to the mound of their dead elk. Snow filtered down steadily in purposeful silence. The boy was thirsty. It could not be much below freezing, he was aware, because with the exercise his bare hands were comfortable, even sweating between the fingers.

"Can I get a drink?"

"Yes. Be careful you don't wet your feet. And don't wander anywhere. We're going to get this done quickly."

He walked the few yards, ducked through the brush at streamside, and knelt in the snow to drink. The water was painful to his sinuses and bitterly cold on his hands. Standing again, he noticed an animal body ahead near the stream bank. For a moment he felt sure it was another dead cub. During that moment his father called:

"David! Get up here right now!"

The boy meant to call back. First he stepped closer to turn the cub with his foot. The touch brought it alive. It rose suddenly with a high squealing growl and whirled its head like a snake and snapped. The boy shrieked. The cub had his right hand in its jaws. It would not release.

It thrashed senselessly, working its teeth deeper and tearing flesh with each movement. The boy felt no pain. He knew his hand was being damaged and that realization terrified him and he was desperate to get the hand back before it was ruined. But he was helpless. He sensed the same furious terror racking the cub that he felt in himself, and he screamed at the cub almost reasoningly to let him go. His screams scared the cub more. Its head snatched back and forth. The boy did not think to shout for his father. He did not see him or hear him coming.

His father moved at full stride in a slowed laboring run through the snow, saying nothing and holding the rifle he did not use, crossed the last six feet still gathering speed, and brought his right boot up into the cub's belly. That kick seemed to lift the cub clear of the snow. It opened its jaws to another shrill piggish squeal, and the boy felt dull relief on his hand, as though his father had pressed open the blades of a spring trap with his foot. The cub tumbled once and disappeared over the stream bank, then surfaced downstream, squalling and paddling. The boy looked at his hand and was horrified. He still had no pain, but the hand was unrecognizable. His fingers had been peeled down through the palm like flaps on a banana. Glands at the sides of his jaw threatened that he would vomit, and he might have stood stupidly watching the hand bleed if his father had not grabbed him.

He snatched the boy by the arm and dragged him toward a tree without even looking at the boy's hand. The boy jerked back in angry resistance as though he had been struck. He screamed at his father. He screamed that his hand was cut, believing his father did not know, and as he screamed he began to cry. He began to feel hot throbbing pain. He began to worry about the blood he was losing. He could imagine his blood melting red holes in the snow behind him and he did not want to look. He did not want to do anything until he had taken care of his hand. At that instant he hated his father. But his father was stronger. He all but carried the boy to a tree.

He lifted the boy. In a voice that was quiet and hurried and very unlike the harsh grip with which he had taken the boy's arm, he said:

"Grab hold and climb up a few branches as best you can. Sit on a limb and hold tight and clamp the hand under your other armpit, if you can do that. I'll be right back to you. Hold tight because you're going to get dizzy." The boy groped desperately for a branch. His father supported him from beneath, and waited. The boy clambered. His feet scraped at the trunk. Then he was in the tree. Bark flakes and resin were stuck to the raw naked meat of his right hand. His father said:

"Now here, take this. Hurry."

The boy never knew whether his father himself had been frightened enough to forget for the moment about the boy's hand, or whether his father was still thinking quite clearly. His father may have expected that much. By the merciless clarity of his own standards, he may have expected that the boy should be able to hold onto a tree, and a wound, and a rifle, all with one hand. He extended the stock of the Winchester toward the boy.

The boy wanted to say something, but his tears and his fright would not let him gather a breath. He shuddered, and could not speak. "David," his father urged. The boy reached for the stock and faltered and clutched at the trunk with his good arm. He was crying and gasping, and he wanted to speak. He was afraid he would fall out of the tree. He released his grip once again, and felt himself tip. His father extended the gun higher, holding the barrel. The boy swung out his injured hand, spraying his father's face with blood. He reached and he tried to close torn dangling fingers around the stock and he pulled the trigger.

The bullet entered low on his father's thigh and shattered the knee and traveled down the shin bone and into the ground through his father's heel.

His father fell, and the rifle fell with him. He lay in the snow without moving. The boy thought he was dead. Then the boy saw him grope for the rifle. He found it and rolled onto his stomach, taking aim at the sow grizzly. Forty feet up the hill, towering on hind legs, she canted her head to one side, indecisive. When the cub pulled itself up a snowbank from the stream, she coughed at it sternly. The cub trotted straight to her with its head low. She knocked it off its feet with a huge paw, and it yelped. Then she turned quickly. The cub followed.

The woods were silent. The gunshot still echoed awesomely back to the boy but it was an echo of memory, not sound. He felt nothing. He saw his father's body stretched on the snow and he did not really believe he was where he was. He did not want to move: he wanted to wake. He sat in the tree and waited. The snow fell as gracefully as before.

His father rolled onto his back. The boy saw him raise himself to a sitting position and look down at the leg and betray no expression, and then slump back. He blinked slowly and lifted his eyes to meet the boy's eyes. The boy waited. He expected his father to speak. He expected his father to say *Shinny down using your elbows and knees and get the first-aid kit and boil water and phone the doctor. The number is taped to the dial.* His father stared. The boy could see the flicker of thoughts behind his father's eyes.

His father said nothing. He raised his arms slowly and crossed them over his face, as though to nap in the sun.

The boy jumped. He landed hard on his feet and fell onto his back. He stood over his father. His hand dripped quietly onto the snow. He was afraid that his father was deciding to die. He wanted to beg him to reconsider. The boy had never before seen his father hopeless. He was afraid.

But he was no longer afraid of his father.

Then his father uncovered his face and said, "Let me see it."

They bandaged the boy's hand with a sleeve cut from the other arm of his shirt. His father wrapped the hand firmly and split the sleeve end with his deer knife and tied it neatly in two places. The boy now felt searing pain in his torn palm, and his stomach lifted when he thought of the damage, but at least he did not have to look at it. Quickly the plaid flannel bandage began to soak through maroon. They cut a sleeve from his father's shirt to tie over the wound in his thigh. They raised the trouser leg to see the long swelling bruise down the calf where he was hemorrhaging into the bullet's tunnel. Only then did his father realize that he was bleeding also from the heel. The boy took off his father's boot and placed a half-clean handkerchief on the insole where the bullet had exited, as his father instructed him. Then his father laced the boot on again tightly. The boy helped his father to stand. His father tried to step, then collapsed in the snow with a blasphemous howl of pain. They had not known that the knee was shattered.

The boy watched his father's chest heave with the forced sighs of suffocating frustration, and heard the air wheeze through his nostrils. His father relaxed himself with the breathing, and seemed to be thinking. He said,

"You can find your way back to the hut."

The boy held his own breath and did not move.

"You can, can't you?"

"But I'm not. I'm not going alone. I'm only going with you."

"All right, David, listen carefully," his father said. "We don't have to worry about freezing. I'm not worried about either of us freezing to death. No one is going to freeze in the woods in November, if he looks after himself. Not even in Montana. It just isn't that cold. I have matches and I have a fresh elk. And I don't think this weather is going to get any worse. It may be raining again by morning. What I'm concerned about is the bleeding. If I spend too much time and effort trying to walk out of here, I could bleed to death.

"I think your hand is going to be all right. It's a bad wound, but the doctors will be able to fix it as good as new. I can see that. I promise you that. You'll be bleeding some too, but if you take care of that hand it won't bleed any more walking than if you were standing still. Then you'll be at the doctor's tonight. But if I try to walk out on this leg it's going to bleed and keep bleeding and I'll lose too much blood. So I'm staying here and bundling up warm and you're walking out to get help. I'm sorry about this. It's what we have to do.

"You can't possibly get lost. You'll just follow this trail straight down the canyon the way we came up, and then you'll come to the meadow. Point yourself toward the big pine tree with the forked crown. When you get to that tree you'll find the creek again. You may not be able to see it, but make yourself quiet and listen for it. You'll hear it. Follow that down off the mountain and past the hut till you get to the jeep."

He struggled a hand into his pocket. "You've never driven a car, have you?"

The boy's lips were pinched. Muscles in his cheeks ached from clenching his jaws. He shook his head.

"You can do it. It isn't difficult." His father held up a single key and began telling the boy how to start the jeep, how to work the clutch, how to find reverse and then first and then second. As his father described the positions on the floor shift the boy raised his swaddled right hand. His father stopped. He rubbed at his eye sockets, like a man waking.

"Of course," he said. "All right. You'll have to help me."

Using the saw with his left hand, the boy cut a small forked aspen. His father showed the boy where to trim it so that the fork would reach just to his armpit. Then they lifted him to his feet. But the crutch was useless on a steep hillside of deep grass and snow. His father leaned over the boy's shoulders and they fought the slope for an hour.

When the boy stepped in a hole and they fell, his father made no exclamation of pain. The boy wondered whether his father's knee hurt as badly as his own hand. He suspected it hurt worse. He said nothing about his hand, though several times in their climb it was twisted or crushed. They reached the trail. The snow had not stopped, and their tracks were veiled. His father said:

"We need one of the guns. I forgot. It's my fault. But you'll have to go back down and get it."

The boy could not find the tree against which his father said he had leaned the .270, so he went toward the stream and looked for blood. He saw none. The imprint of his father's body was already softened beneath an inch of fresh silence. He scooped his good hand through the snowy depression and was startled by cool slimy blood, smearing his fingers like phlegm. Nearby he found the Winchester.

"The lucky one," his father said. "That's all right. Here." He snapped open the breach and a shell flew and he caught it in the air. He glanced dourly at the casing, then cast it aside in the snow. He held the gun out for the boy to see, and with his thumb let the hammer down one notch.

"Remember?" he said. "The safety."

The boy knew he was supposed to feel great shame, but he felt little. His father could no longer hurt him as he once could, because the boy was coming to understand him. His father could not help himself. He did not want the boy to feel contemptible, but he needed him to, because of the loneliness and the bitterness and the boy's mother; and he could not help himself.

After another hour they had barely traversed the aspen hillside. Pushing the crutch away in angry frustration, his father sat in the snow. The boy did not know whether he was thinking carefully of how they might get him out, or still laboring with the choice against despair. The light had wilted to something more like moonlight than afternoon. The sweep of snow had gone gray, depthless, flat, and the sky warned sullenly of night. The boy grew restless. Then it was decided. His father hung himself piggyback over the boy's shoulders, holding the rifle. The boy supported him with elbows crooked under his father's knees. The boy was tall for eleven years old, and heavy. The boy's father weighed 164 pounds.

The boy walked.

He moved as slowly as drifting snow: a step, then time, then another step. The burden at first seemed to him overwhelming. He did not think he would be able to carry his father far.

He took the first few paces expecting to fall. He did not fall, so he kept walking. His arms and shoulders were not exhausted as quickly as he had thought they would be, so he kept walking. Shuffling ahead in the deep powder was like carrying one end of an oak bureau up stairs. But for a surprisingly long time the burden did not grow any worse. He found balance. He found rhythm. He was moving.

Dark blurred the woods, but the snow was luminous. He could see the trail well. He walked.

"How are you, David? How are you holding up?"

"All right."

"We'll stop for a while and let you rest. You can set me down here." The boy kept walking. He moved so ponderously, it seemed after each step that he had stopped. But he kept walking.

"You can set me down. Don't you want to rest?"

The boy did not answer. He wished that his father would not make him talk. At the start he had gulped air. Now he was breathing low and regularly. He was watching his thighs slice through the snow. He did not want to be disturbed. After a moment he said, "No."

He walked. He came to the cub, shrouded beneath new snow, and did not see it, and fell over it. His face was smashed deep into the snow by his father's weight. He could not move. But he could breathe. He rested. When he felt his father's thigh roll across his right hand, he remembered the wound. He was lucky his arms had been pinned to his sides, or the hand might have taken the force of their fall. As he waited for his father to roll himself clear, the boy noticed the change in temperature. His sweat chilled him quickly. He began shivering.

His father had again fallen in silence. The boy knew that he would not call out or even mention the pain in his leg. The boy realized that he did not want to mention his hand. The blood soaking the outside of his flannel bandage had grown sticky. He did not want to think of the alien tangle of flesh and tendons and bones wrapped inside. There was pain, but he kept the pain at a distance. It was not *his* hand any more. He was not counting on ever having it back. If he was resolved about that, then the pain was not his either. It was merely pain of which he was aware. His good hand was numb.

"We'll rest now."

"I'm not tired," the boy said. "I'm just getting cold."

"We'll rest," said his father. "I'm tired."

Under his father's knee, the boy noticed, was a cavity in the snow, already melted away by fresh blood. The dark flannel around his father's thigh did not appear sticky. It gleamed.

His father instructed the boy how to open the cub with the deer knife. His father stood on one leg against a deadfall, holding the Winchester ready, and glanced around on all sides as he spoke. The boy used his left hand and both his knees. He punctured the cub low in the belly, to a soft squirting sound, and sliced upward easily. He did not gut the cub. He merely cut out a large square of belly meat. He handed it to his father, in exchange for the rifle.

His father peeled off the hide and left the fat. He sawed the meat in half. One piece he rolled up and put in his jacket pocket. The other he divided again. He gave the boy a square thick with glistening raw fat.

"Eat it. The fat too. Especially the fat. We'll cook the rest farther on. I don't want to build a fire here and taunt Momma."

The meat was chewy. The boy did not find it disgusting. He was hungry.

His father sat back on the ground and unlaced the boot from his good foot. Before the boy understood what he was doing, he had relaced the boot. He was holding a damp wool sock.

"Give me your left hand." The boy held out his good hand, and his father pulled the sock down over it. "It's getting a lot colder. And we need that hand."

"What about yours? We need your hands too. I'll give you my—"

"No, you won't. We need your feet more than anything. It's all right. I'll put mine inside your shirt."

He lifted his father, and they went on. The boy walked.

He moved steadily through cold darkness. Soon he was sweating again, down his ribs and inside his boots. Only his hands and ears felt as though crushed in a cold metal vise. But his father was shuddering. The boy stopped.

His father did not put down his legs. The boy stood on the trail and waited. Slowly he released his wrist holds. His father's thighs slumped. The boy was careful about the wounded leg. His father's grip over the boy's neck did not loosen. His fingers were cold against the boy's bare skin.

"Are we at the hut?"

"No. We're not even to the meadow."

"Why did you stop?" his father asked.

"It's so cold. You're shivering. Can we build a fire?"

"Yes," his father said hazily. "We'll rest. What time is it?"

"We don't know," the boy said. "We don't have a watch."

The boy gathered small deadwood. His father used the Winchester stock to scoop snow away from a boulder, and they placed the fire at the boulder's base. His father broke up pine twigs and fumbled dry toilet paper from his breast pocket and arranged the wood, but by then his fingers were shaking too badly to strike a match. The boy lit the fire. The boy stamped down the snow, as his father instructed, to make a small ovenlike recess before the fire boulder. He cut fir boughs to floor the recess. He added more deadwood. Beyond the invisible clouds there seemed to be part of a moon.

"It stopped snowing," the boy said.

"Why?"

The boy did not speak. His father's voice had sounded unnatural. After a moment his father said:

"Yes, indeed. It stopped."

They roasted pieces of cub meat skewered on a green stick. Dripping fat made the fire spatter and flare. The meat was scorched on the outside and raw within. It tasted as good as any meat the boy had ever eaten. They burned their palates on hot fat. The second stick smoldered through before they had noticed, and that batch of meat fell in the fire. The boy's father cursed once and reached into the flame for it and dropped it and clawed it out, and then put his hand in the snow. He did not look at the blistered fingers. They ate. The boy saw that both his father's hands had gone clumsy and almost useless.

The boy went for more wood. He found a bleached deadfall not far off the trail, but with one arm he could only break up and carry small loads. They lay down in the recess together like spoons, the boy nearer the fire. They pulled fir boughs into place above them, resting across the snow. They pressed close together. The boy's father was shivering spastically now, and he clenched the boy in a fierce hug. The boy put his father's hands back inside his own shirt. The boy slept. He woke when the fire faded and added more wood and slept. He woke again and tended the fire and changed places with his father and slept. He slept less soundly with his father between him and the fire. He woke again when his father began to vomit.

The boy was terrified. His father wrenched with sudden vomiting that brought up cub meat and yellow liquid and blood and sprayed them across the snow by the grayish-red glow of the fire and emptied his stomach dry and then would not release him. He heaved on pathetically. The boy pleaded to be told what was wrong. His father could not or would not answer. The spasms seized him at the stomach and twisted the rest of his body taut in ugly jerks. Between the attacks he breathed with a wet rumbling sound deep in his chest, and did not speak. When the vomiting subsided, his breathing stretched itself out into long bubbling sighs, then shallow gasps, then more liquidy sighs. His breath caught and froth rose in his throat and into his mouth and he gagged on it and began vomiting again. The boy thought his father would choke. He knelt beside him and held him and cried. He could not see his father's face well and he did not want to look closely while the sounds that were coming from inside his father's body seemed so unhuman. The boy had never been more frightened. He wept for himself, and for his father. He knew from the noises and movements that his father must die. He did not think his father could ever be human again.

When his father was quiet, he went for more wood. He broke limbs from the deadfall with fanatic persistence and brought them back in bundles and built the fire up bigger. He nestled his father close to it and held him from behind. He did not sleep, though he was not awake. He waited. Finally he opened his eyes on the beginnings of dawn. His father sat up and began to spit.

"One more load of wood and you keep me warm from behind and then we'll go."

The boy obeyed. He was surprised that his father could speak. He thought it strange now that his father was so concerned for himself and so little concerned for the boy. His father had not even asked how he was.

The boy lifted his father, and walked.

Sometime while dawn was completing itself, the snow had resumed. It did not filter down soundlessly. It came on a slight wind at the boy's back, blowing down the canyon. He felt as though he were tumbling forward with the snow into a long vertical shaft. He tumbled slowly. His father's body protected the boy's back from being chilled by the wind. They were both soaked through their clothes. His father was soon shuddering again.

The boy walked. Muscles down the back of his neck were sore from yesterday. His arms ached, and his shoulders and thighs, but his neck hurt him most. He bent his head forward against the weight and the pain, and he watched his legs surge through the snow. At his stomach he felt the dull ache of hunger, not as an appetite but as an affliction. He thought of the jeep. He walked.

He recognized the edge of the meadow but through the snow-laden wind he could not see the cluster of aspens. The snow became deeper where he left the wooded trail. The direction of the wind was now variable, sometimes driving snow into his face, sometimes whipping across him from the right. The grass and snow dragged at his thighs, and he moved by stumbling forward and then catching himself back. Twice he stepped into small overhung fingerlets of the stream, and fell violently, shocking the air from his lungs and once nearly spraining an ankle. Farther out into the meadow, he saw the aspens. They were a hundred yards off to his right. He did not turn directly toward them. He was afraid of crossing more hidden creeks on the intervening ground. He was not certain now whether the main channel was between him and the aspen grove or behind him to the left. He tried to project from the canyon trail to the aspens and on to the forked pine on the far side of the meadow, along what he remembered as almost a straight line. He pointed himself toward the far edge, where the pine should have been. He could not see a forked crown. He could not even see trees. He could see only a vague darker corona above the curve of white. He walked.

He passed the aspens and left them behind. He stopped several times with the wind rasping against him in the open meadow, and rested. He did not set his father down. His father was trembling uncontrollably. He had not spoken for a long time. The boy wanted badly to reach the far side of the meadow. His socks were soaked and his boots and cuffs were glazed with ice. The wind was chafing his face and making him dizzy. His thighs felt as if they had been bruised with a club. The boy wanted to give up and set his father down and whimper that this had gotten to be very unfair; and he wanted to reach the far trees. He did not doubt which he would do. He walked.

He saw trees. Raising his head painfully, he squinted against the rushing flakes. He did not see the forked crown. He went on, and stopped again, and craned his neck, and squinted. He scanned a wide angle of pines, back and forth. He did not see it. He turned his body and his burden to look back. The snow blew across the meadow and seemed, whichever way he turned, to be streaking into his face. He pinched his eyes tighter. He could still see the aspens. But he could not judge where the canyon trail met the meadow. He did not know from just where he had come. He looked again at the aspens, and then ahead to the pines. He considered the problem carefully. He was irritated that the forked ponderosa did not show itself yet, but not worried. He was forced to estimate. He estimated, and went on in that direction.

When he saw a forked pine it was far off to the left of his course. He turned and marched toward it gratefully. As he came nearer, he bent his head up to look. He stopped. The boy was not sure that this was the right tree. Nothing about it looked different, except the thick cakes of snow weighting its limbs, and nothing about it looked especially familiar. He had seen thousands of pine trees in the last few days. This was one like the others. It definitely had a forked crown. He entered the woods at its base.

He had vaguely expected to join a trail. There was no trail. After two hundred yards he was still picking his way among trees and deadfalls and brush. He remembered the shepherd's creek that fell off the lip of the meadow and led down the first canyon. He turned and retraced his tracks to the forked pine.

He looked for the creek. He did not see it anywhere near the tree. He made himself quiet, and listened. He heard nothing but the wind, and his father's tremulous breathing.

"Where is the creek?"

His father did not respond. The boy bounced gently up and down, hoping to jar him alert.

"Where is the creek? I can't find it."

"What?"

"We crossed the meadow and I found the tree but I can't find the creek. I need you to help."

"The compass is in my pocket," his father said.

He lowered his father into the snow. He found the compass in his father's breast pocket, and opened the flap, and held it level. The boy noticed with a flinch that his right thigh was smeared with fresh blood. For an instant he thought he had a new wound. Then he realized that the blood was his father's. The compass needle quieted.

"What do I do?"

His father did not respond. The boy asked again. His father said nothing. He sat in the snow and shivered.

The boy left his father and made random arcs within sight of the forked tree until he found a creek. They followed it onward along the flat and then where it gradually began sloping away. The boy did not see what else he could do. He knew that this was the wrong creek. He hoped that it would flow into the shepherd's creek, or at least bring them out on the same road where they had left the jeep. He was very tired. He did not want to stop. He did not care any more about being warm. He wanted only to reach the jeep, and to save his father's life.

He wondered whether his father would love him more generously for having done it. He wondered whether his father would ever forgive him for having done it.

If he failed, his father could never again make him feel shame, the boy thought naively. So he did not worry about failing. He did not worry about dying. His hand was not bleeding, and he felt strong. The creek swung off and down to the left. He followed it, knowing that he was lost. He did not want to reverse himself. He knew that turning back would make him feel confused and desperate and frightened. As long as he was following some pathway, walking, going down, he felt strong.

That afternoon he killed a grouse. He knocked it off a low branch with a heavy short stick that he threw like a boomerang. The grouse fell in the snow and floundered and the boy ran up and plunged on it. He felt it thrashing against his chest. He reached in and it nipped him and he caught it by the neck and squeezed and wrenched mercilessly until long after it stopped writhing. He cleaned it as he had seen his father clean grouse and built a small fire with matches from his father's breast pocket and seared the grouse on a stick. He fed his father. His father could not chew. The boy chewed mouthfuls of grouse, and took the chewed gobbets in his hand, and put them into his father's mouth. His father could swallow. His father could no longer speak.

The boy walked. He thought of his mother in Evergreen Park, and at once he felt queasy and weak. He thought of his mother's face and her voice as she was told that her son was lost in the woods in Montana with a damaged hand that would never be right, and with his father, who had been shot and was unconscious and dying. He pictured his mother receiving the news that her son might die himself, unless he could carry his father out of the woods and find his way to the jeep. He saw her face change. He heard her voice. The boy had to stop. He was crying. He could not control the shape of his mouth. He was not crying with true sorrow, as he had in the night when he held his father and thought his father would die; he was crying in sentimental self-pity. He sensed the difference. Still he cried.

He must not think of his mother, the boy realized. Thinking of her could only weaken him. If she knew where he was, what he had to do, she could only make it impossible for him to do it. He was lucky that she knew nothing, the boy thought.

No one knew what the boy was doing, or what he had yet to do. Even the boy's father no longer knew. The boy was lucky. No one was watching, no one knew, and he was free to be capable.

The boy imagined himself alone at his father's grave. The grave was open. His father's casket had already been lowered. The boy stood at the foot in his black Christmas suit, and his hands were crossed at his groin, and he was not crying. Men with shovels stood back from the grave, waiting for the boy's order for them to begin filling it. The boy felt a horrible swelling sense of joy. The men watched him, and he stared down into the hole. He knew it was a lie. If his father died, the boy's mother would rush out to Livingston and have him buried and stand at the grave in a black dress and veil squeezing the boy to her side like he was a child. There was nothing the boy could do about that. All the more reason he must keep walking.

Then she would tow the boy back with her to Evergreen Park. And he would be standing on 96th Street in the morning dark before his father's cold body had even begun to grow alien and decayed in the buried box. She would drag him back, and there would be nothing the boy could do. And he realized that if he returned with his mother after the burial, he would never again see the cabin outside Livingston. He would have no more summers and no more Novembers anywhere but in Evergreen Park.

The cabin now seemed to be at the center of the boy's life. It seemed to stand halfway between this snowbound creek valley and the train station in Chicago. It would be his cabin soon.

The boy knew nothing about his father's will, and he had never been told that legal ownership of the cabin was destined for him. Legal ownership did not matter. The cabin might be owned by his mother, or sold to pay his father's debts, or taken away by the state, but it would still be the boy's cabin. It could only forever belong to him. His father had been telling him *Here, this is yours. Prepare to receive it.* The boy had sensed that much. But he had been threatened, and unwilling. The boy realized now that he might be resting warm in the cabin in a matter of hours, or he might never see it again. He could appreciate the justice of that. He walked.

He thought of his father as though his father was far away from him. He saw himself in the black suit at the grave, and he heard his father speak to him from aside: *That's good. Now raise your eyes and tell them in a man's voice to begin shoveling. Then turn away and walk slowly back down the hill. Be sure you don't cry. That's good.* The boy stopped. He felt his glands quiver, full of new tears. He knew that it was a lie. His father would never be there to congratulate him. His father would never know how well the boy had done.

He took deep breaths. He settled himself. Yes, his father would know somehow, the boy believed. His father had known all along. His father knew.

He built the recess just as they had the night before, except this time he found flat space between a stone bank and a large fallen cottonwood trunk. He scooped out the snow, he laid boughs, and he made a fire against each reflector. At first the bed was quite warm. Then the melt from the fire began to run down and collect in the middle, forming a puddle of wet boughs under them. The boy got up and carved runnels across the packed snow to drain the fires. He went back to sleep and slept warm, holding his father. He rose again each half hour to feed the fires.

The snow stopped in the night, and did not resume. The woods seemed to grow quieter, settling, sighing beneath the new weight. What was going to come had come.

The boy grew tired of breaking deadwood and began walking again before dawn and walked for five more hours. He did not try to kill the grouse that he saw because he did not want to spend time cleaning and cooking it. He was hurrying now. He drank from the creek. At one point he found small black insects like winged ants crawling in great numbers across the snow near the creek. He stopped to pinch up and eat thirty or forty of them. They were tasteless. He did not bother to feed any to his father. He felt he had come a long way down the mountain. He thought he was reaching the level now where there might be roads. He followed the creek, which had received other branches and grown into a stream. The ground was flattening again and the drainage was widening, opening to daylight. As he carried his father, his head ached. He had stopped noticing most of his other pains. About noon of that day he came to the fence.

It startled him. He glanced around, his pulse drumming suddenly, preparing himself at once to see the long empty sweep of snow and broken fence posts and thinking of Basque shepherds fifty years gone. He saw the cabin and the smoke. He relaxed, trembling helplessly into laughter. He relaxed, and was unable to move. Then he cried, still laughing. He cried shamelessly with relief and dull joy and wonder, for as long as he wanted. He held his father, and cried. But he set his father down and washed his own face with snow before he went to the door.

He crossed the lot walking slowly, carrying his father. He did not now feel tired.

The young woman's face was drawn down in shock and revealed at first nothing of friendliness.

"We had a jeep parked somewhere, but I can't find it," the boy said. "This is my father."

They would not talk to him. They stripped him and put him before the fire wrapped in blankets and started tea and made him wait. He wanted to talk. He wished they would ask him a lot of questions. But they went about quickly and quietly, making things warm. His father was in the bedroom.

The man with the face full of dark beard had telephoned for a doctor. He went back into the bedroom with more blankets, and stayed. His wife went from room to room with hot tea. She rubbed the boy's naked shoulders through the blanket, and held a cup to his mouth, but she would not talk to him. He did not know what to say to her, and he could not move his lips very well. But he wished she would ask him some questions. He was restless, thawing in silence before the hearth.

He thought about going back to their own cabin soon. In his mind he gave the bearded man directions to take him and his father home. It wasn't far. It would not require much of the man's time. They would thank him, and give him an elk steak. Later he and his father would come back for the jeep. He could keep his father warm at the cabin as well as they were doing here, the boy knew.

While the woman was in the bedroom, the boy overheard the bearded man raise his voice:

"He what?"

"He carried him out," the woman whispered.

"What do you mean, carried him?"

"Carried him. On his back. I saw."

"Carried him from where?"

"Where it happened. Somewhere on Sheep Creek, maybe."

"Eight miles?"

"I know."

"*Eight miles?* How could he do that?"

"I don't know. I suppose he couldn't. But he did."

The doctor arrived in half an hour, as the boy was just starting to shiver. The doctor went into the bedroom and stayed for five minutes. The woman poured the boy more tea and knelt beside him and hugged him around the shoulders.

When the doctor came out, he examined the boy without speaking. The boy wished the doctor would ask him some questions, but he was afraid he might be shivering too hard to answer in a man's voice. While the doctor touched him and probed him and took his temperature, the boy looked the doctor directly in the eye, as though to show him he was really all right.

The doctor said:

"David, your father is dead. He has been dead for a long time. Probably since yesterday."

"I know that," the boy said.

E. Annie Proulx's distinction as a writer has been widely acknowledged. She won the 1994 Pulitzer Prize, the 1993 National Book Award, and the Irish Times *International Fiction Prize for her novel* The Shipping News. *Her first novel,* Postcards, *won the 1993 PEN/Faulkner Award. Proulx's articles and stories have appeared in many periodicals, especially the* New Yorker. *The story below was originally published in* Gray's Sporting Journal. *A wealthy young man hires a grizzled guide to teach him how to hunt grouse. Proulx's strong, supple prose and often lyrical images are nicely displayed.*

E. Annie Proulx

THE UNCLOUDED DAY (1985)

IT WAS A RARE THING, A DRY, warm spring that swelled into summer so ripe and full that gleaming seed bent the grass low a month before its time; a good year for grouse. When the season opened halfway through September, the heat of summer still held, dust lay like yellow flour on the roads, and a perfume of decay came from the thorned mazes where blackberries fell and rotted on the ground. Grouse were in the briars, along the water-courses, and, drunk on fermenting autumn juices, they flew recklessly, their wings cleaving the shimmering heat of the day.

Santee did not care to hunt birds in such high-colored weather. Salty sweat stung the whipped-branch welts on his neck and arms, the dog worked badly and the birds spoiled in an hour. In their sour, hot intestines he smelled imminent putrefaction. The feathers stuck to his hands, for Earl never helped gut them. Noah, the dog, lay panting in the shade.

The heat wave wouldn't break. Santee longed for the cold weather and unclouded days that lay somewhere ahead, for the sharp chill of spruce shadow, icy rime thickening over osier twigs and a hard autumnal sky cut by the parabolic flights of birds in the same way pond ice was cut by skaters. Ah goddamn, thought Santee, there were better things to do than hunt partridge with a fool in these burning days.

Earl had come to Santee the year before and begged him to teach him how to hunt birds. He had a good gun, he said, a Tobias Hume. Santee thought it overrated and overpriced, but it was a finer instrument than his own field-grade Jorken with the cracked stock he'd meant to replace for years. (The rough walnut blank lay on the workbench out in the barn, cans of motor oil and paint standing on it; the kids had ruined the checkering files by picking out butternut meats with them.) Santee's gun, like its owner, was inelegant and long in the tooth, but it worked well.

Earl had come driving up through the woods to Santee's place, overlooking the mess in the yard, nodding to Verna, and he had flattered Santee right out of his mind.

"Santee," he said, measuring him, seeing how he was inclined, "I've talked to people around and they say you're a pretty good hunter. I want to learn how to hunt birds. I want you to teach me. I'll pay you to teach me everything about them."

Santee could see that Earl had money. He wore nice boots, rich corduroy trousers in a golden syrup color, his hands were shaped like doves and his voice rolled out of this throat like sweet batter. He was not more than thirty, Santee thought, looking at the firm cheek slabs and thick yellow hair.

"I usually hunt birds by myself. Or with my boys." Santee gave each word its fair measure of weight. "Me'n the dog." Noah, lying on the porch under the rusty glider, raised his head at the sound of "birds" and watched them.

"Nice dog," said Earl in his confectionary voice. Santee folded his arms across his chest rather than let them hang by his sides. Hands in the pockets was even worse, he thought, looking at Earl, a wastrel's posture.

Earl oiled Santee with his voice. "All I ask, Santee, is that you try it two or three times, and if you don't want to continue, why then, I'll pay you for your time." He gave Santee a smile, the leaf-colored eyes under the gleaming lids shifting from Santee to the warped screen door, to the scabby paint on the clapboards, to the run-down yard. Santee looked off to the side as though the muscles in his own eyes were weak.

"Maybe give it a try. Rather go on a weekday than a weekend. You get away on Monday?"

Earl could get away any day Santee wanted. He worked at home.

"What doin'?" asked Santee, letting his arms hang down.

"Consulting. I analyze stocks and economic trends." Santee saw that Earl was younger than his own oldest son, Derwin, whose teeth were entirely gone and who worked up at the veneer mill at Potumsic Falls breathing fumes and tending a machine with whirling, curved blades. Santee said he would go out with Earl on Monday. He didn't know how to say no.

The first morning was a good one, a solid bright day with a spicy taste to the air. Noah was on his mettle, eager to find birds and showing off a little for the stranger. Santee set Earl some distance away on his right until he could see how he shot.

Noah worked close. He stiffened two yards away from birds in front, he pointed birds to the left, the right. A single step from Santee or Earl sent partridge bursting out of the cover and into straightaway flight. He pinned them in trees and bushes, scented them feeding on fallen fruit or dusting on powdery bowls of fine earth, marked them as they pattered through wood sorrel. He worked like two dogs, his white sides gliding through the grass, his points so rigid he might have been a glass animal.

The grouse tore up the air and the shotguns bellowed. Earl, Santee saw, didn't know enough to say "Nice dog" when it counted.

Santee held himself back in order to let his pupil learn, but Earl was a slow, poor shot. The bird would be fifty yards out and darting through safe holes in the air when he finally got the gun around and pulled the trigger. Sometimes a nervous second bird would go up before Earl fired at the first one. He couldn't seem to catch the rhythm, and had excuses for each miss.

"Caught the butt end in my shirt pocket flap," he'd say, laughing a little, and, "My fingers are stiff from carrying the gun," and "Oh, that one was gone before I could get the bead on him."

Santee tried over and over again to show him that you didn't aim at the bird, that you just threw up the gun and fired in the right place.

"You have to shoot where they're goin', not where they are." He made Earl watch him on the next one, how the gun notched into place on his shoulder, how his right elbow lifted smoothly as his eyes bent toward the empty air the bird was about to enter. *Done!* went the shotgun, and the bird fell like a nut.

"Now you do it," said Santee.

But when a grouse blustered out of the wild rose haws, Earl only got the gun to his hip, then twisted his body in an odd backward contortion as he fired. The train of shot cut a hole in the side of a tamarack and the bird melted away through the trees.

"I'n see you need a lot of practice," said Santee.

"What I need *is* practice," agreed Earl, "and that is what I am paying for."

"Try movin' the stock up to your shoulder," said Santee, thinking that his kids had shot better when they were eight years old.

They worked through the morning, Santee illustrating swift reaction and tidy speed, and Earl sweating and jerking like an old Vitagraph film, trying to line up the shotgun with the bird. Santee shot seven grouse and gave four to Earl who had missed every one. Earl gave Santee a hundred dollars and said he wanted to do it again.

"I can practice all the rest of this week," he said, making it sound like a piano lesson.

The next three Mondays were the same. They went out and worked birds. Earl kept shooting from the hip. With his legs spraddled out he looked like an old-time gangster spraying the rival mob with lead.

"Listen here," said Santee, "there are six more weeks left in the season, which means we go out six more times. No, I am not after more money, but you might want to think about goin' out a little more often." Earl was eager and said he'd pay.

"Three times a week. I can go Monday, Wednesday and Friday." They tried it that way. Then they tried Monday, Tuesday and Wednesday for continuity. Earl was paying Santee three hundred dollars a week and he hadn't shot a single bird.

"How's about this?" said Santee, feeling more and more like a cheating old whore every time they went out. "How's about I come over to your place on the weekend with a box of clay pigeons and you practice shootin' them up? No charge! Just to sort of get your eye in, and the gun up to your shoulder."

"Yes, but I'm not upset about missing the birds, you know," said Earl, looking in the trees. "I've read the books and I know it takes years before you develop that fluid, almost instinctive response to the grouse's rising thunder. I know, believe me, how difficult a target these speedy fliers really are, and I'm willing to work on it, even if it takes years."

Santee had not heard shooting birds was that hard, but he knew Earl was no good; he had the reflexes of a snowman. He said to Verna, "That Earl has got to get it together or I can't keep takin' his money. I feel like I'm goin' to the salt mines every time we go out. I don't have the heart to hunt any more on my own, out of fear I'll bust up a bunch of birds he needs for practice. Dammit, all the fun is goin' out of it."

"The money is good," said Verna, giving the porch floor a shove that set the glider squeaking. Her apron was folded across her lap, her arms folded elbow over elbow with her hands on her shoulders, her ankles crossed against the coolness of the night. She wore the blue acrylic slippers Santee had given her for Mother's Day.

"I just wonder how I got into it," he said, closing his eyes and gliding.

Santee bought a box of a hundred clay pigeons and drove up to Earl's house on a Sunday afternoon. It was the kind of day people decided to go for a ride.

"I wish I hadn't come," said Verna, looking through the cloudy windshield at Earl's home, an enormous Swiss chalet with windows like tan bubbles in the roof and molded polystyrene pillars holding up a portico roof. She wouldn't get out of the truck, but sat for two hours with the window ground up. Santee knew how she felt, but he had to go. He was hired to teach Earl how to shoot birds.

There was a big porch and on it was Earl's wife, as thin as a folded dollar bill, her hand as narrow and cold as a trout. A baby crawled around inside a green plastic-mesh pen playing with a tomato. Earl told them to watch.

"Watch Daddy shoot the birdy!" he said.

"Beady!" said the baby.

"Knock those beadies dead, Earl," said the wife, drawing her fingernail through a drop of moisture that had fallen from her drink onto the chair arm.

Santee cocked his arm back again and again and sent the clay discs flying out over a garden of dark shrubs. His ears rang. The baby screamed every time the gun went off, but Earl wouldn't let the woman take him inside.

"Watch!" he cried. "Dammit, watch Daddy shoot the beady!" He would get the gun to his hip and bend his back into the strange posture he had made his trademark. Him and Al Capone, thought Santee, saying, "Put it to your shoulder," like a broken record. "It won't backfire."

He looked to see if Earl shut his eyes behind the yellow spectacles when he pulled the trigger, but couldn't tell. After a long time a clay round flew into three black pieces and Earl shrieked, "I got it!" as if it were a wooly mammoth. It was the first object he had hit since Santee had met him.

"Pretty good," he lied. "*Now* you're doin' it."

Verna called all the kids home for dinner a week later. There was home-cured ham basted with Santee's hard cider, baked Hubbard squash, mashed potato with Jersey cream spattered over each mound and a platter of roast partridge glazed with chokecherry jelly.

Before they sat down at the table Verna got everybody out in the yard to clean it up. They all counted one-two-three and heaved the carcass of Santee's 1952 Chevrolet in with the torn chicken wire, rotted fence posts and dimpled oil cans. Derwin drove the load to the dump after dinner and brought back a new lawn mower Verna had told him to get.

The next day she waded the brook, feeling for spherical stones of a certain size with her feet. Santee carried them up to the house in a grain bag. When they had dried on the porch she painted them snow white and set them in a line along the driveway. Santee saw the beauty of it—the green shorn grass, the gleaming white stones. It all had something to do with teaching Earl how to hunt, but aside from the money he didn't know what.

After a while he did. It was that she wouldn't let him quit. She would go out into the yard at the earliest light of hunting days—Santee had come to think of them as work days—walking in the wet grass and squinting at the sky to interpret the character of the new day. She got back into bed and put her cold feet on Santee's calves.

"It's cloudy," she would say. "Rain by noon." Santee would groan, because Earl did not like to get his gun wet.

"Won't it hurt it?" Earl always asked, as though he knew it would.

"Don't be no summer soldier," said Santee. "Wipe it down when you get back home and put some WD-40 to it, all good as new." It took him a while to understand that it wasn't the gun. Earl didn't like to get rain down his neck or onto his shooting glasses with the yellow lenses, didn't care to feel the cold drops trace narrow trails down his back and forearms, nor to taste the salty stuff that trickled from his hatband to the corners of his mouth.

They were walking through the deep wet grass, the rain drumming hard enough to make the curved blades bounce up and down. Earl's wet twill pants were plastered to him like blistered skin. Something in the way he pulled at the sodden cloth with an arched finger and thumb told Santee he was angry at the rain, at Santee, maybe mad enough to quit shelling out three hundred dollars a week for no birds and a wet nature walk. Good, thought Santee.

But the rain stopped and a watery sun warmed their backs. Noah found tendrils of rich hot grouse scent lying on the moist air as solidly as cucumber vines on the garden earth. He locked into his catatonic point again and again, and they sent the birds flying in arcs of shaken raindrops. Earl didn't connect, but he said he knew it took years before shooters got the hang of it.

The only thing he shot that season was the clay pigeon, and the year ended with no birds for Earl, money in Santee's bank account and a row of white stones under the drifting snow. Santee thought it was all over, a bad year to be buried with the memory of other bad years.

Through the next spring and summer he never thought of Earl without a shudder. The droughty grouse summer held into September. Santee bored the replacement stock for the Jorken. He bought a new checkering file and sat on the porch after dinner making a good job of it and waiting for the heat to break, thinking about going out by himself in the chill October days as the woods and fields faded and clods of earth froze hard. He hunched toward the west on the steps, catching the last of the good light; the days were getting shorter in spite of the lingering heat from the baked earth. Verna fanned her damp neck with a sale flier that had come in the mail.

"Car's comin'," she said. Santee stopped rasping and listened.

"It's that Earl again," said Verna, recognizing the Saab before it was in sight.

He was a little slicker in his talk, and wore an expensive game vest with a rubber pocket in the back where the birds would lie, their dark blood seeping into the seams.

"My wife gave me this," he said, and showed them the new leather case for his shotgun, stamped with his initials and a design of three flying grouse.

"No," Santee tried to say, "I've taught you all I can. I don't want to take your money no more." But Earl wasn't going to let him go. Now he wanted a companion with a dog and Santee was it, with no pay.

"After all, we got to know each other very well last year. We're a good team—friends," Earl said, looking at the fresh paint on the clapboards. "Nice job," he said.

Santee went because he had taken Earl's money. Until the fool shot a bird on his own or gave up, Santee was obliged to keep going out with him. The idea that Earl might ruin every fall for the rest of his life made Santee sick.

"I've come to hate partridge huntin'," he told Verna in the sultry night. "I hate those white stones, too." She knew what he was talking about.

Derwin heard Earl bragging down at the store, some clam dip and a box of Triscuits in front of him on the counter. Earl's new game vest hung open casually, his yellow shooting glasses dangled outside the breast pocket, one earpiece tucked in through the buttonhole.

"Yes," he said, "we did quite well today. Limited out. I hunt with Santee, you know—grand old fellow."

"He didn't know who I was," raged Derwin, who had wanted to say something deadly but hadn't found any words until he drove up home and sat on the edge of the porch. "Whyn't you tell him where to head in, Pa? At least quit givin' him birds he makes like he shot hisself."

"I wish I could," groaned Santee. "If he would just get one bird I could cut loose, or if he decided to go in for somethin' else and quit comin' around. But I feel like I owe him part of a bargain. I took a lot of his money and all he got out of it was a clay pigeon."

"You don't owe him nothin'," said Derwin.

Earl came up again the next morning. He parked his Saab in the shade and beeped the horn in Santee's truck until he came out on the porch.

"Where you want to hit today?" called Earl. It wasn't a question. In some way he'd gotten ahead of Santee. "Might as well take your truck, it's already scratched up. Maybe go to the Africa covert and then hit White Birch Heaven."

Earl had given fanciful names to the different places they hunted. "Africa" because there was long yellow grass on the edge of a field Earl said looked like the veldt. "White Birch Heaven" because Noah had pointed six birds in twenty minutes. Santee had taken two, leaving the rest for seed after Earl shot the tops out of the birches. They were grey birches, but Santee had not cared enough to say so, any more than he pointed out that the place had been called "Ayer's high pasture" for generations.

It was breathlessly close as they climbed toward the upper fields of the old farm. The sky was a slick white color. Noah lagged, the dust filling his nose. Santee's shirt was wet and he could hear thunder in the ground, the storm that had been building for weeks of drumming heat. Deerflies and gnats bit furiously at their ears and necks.

"Gonna be a hell of a storm," said Santee.

Nothing moved. They might have been in a painted field, walking slowly across the fixed landscape where no bird could ever fly, nor tree fall. The leaves hung limp, soil crumbled under their feet.

"You won't put no birds up in this weather," said Santee.

"What?" asked Earl, the yellow glasses shining like insect eyes.

"I said, it's gonna be a corker of a storm. See there?" Santee dropped his arm toward the west where a dark humped line illuminated by veins of lightning lay across the horizon. "Comin' right for us like a house on fire. Time to go home and try again another day."

He started back down, paying no attention to Earl's remarks that the storm was a long way off and there were birds up there. He was dogged enough, thought Santee sourly.

As they went down the hill, slipping on the drought-polished grass, the light thickened to a dirty ocher. Little puffs of wind raised dust and started the poplars vibrating.

"You might be right," said Earl, passing Santee. "It's coming along pretty fast. I just felt a drop."

Santee looked back over his shoulder and saw the black wall of cloud swelling into the sky. Bursts of wind ripped across the slope and the rolling grind of thunder shook the earth. Noah scampered fearfully, his tail clamped between his legs, his eyes seeking Santee's again and again.

"We're goin', boy," said Santee encouragingly.

The first raindrops hit like bird shot, rattling down on them and striking the trees with flat smacks. White hail pellets bounced and stung where they hit flesh. They ran into a belt of spruce where there was a narrow opening in the trees like a bowling alley. Halfway down its length a panicky grouse flew straight away from them. It was at least eighty yards out, an impossible distance, when Earl heaved his shotgun onto his hip and fired. As he pulled the trigger, lightning struck behind them. The grouse dropped low and skimmed away, but Earl believed he had hit it. Buried in the sound of his crashing gun he had not even heard the lightning strike.

"Get it!" he shouted at Noah, who had pasted himself to Santee's legs when the lightning cracked the spruce. "Make your dog get it!" yelled Earl, pointing in the direction the grouse had flown. The rain roared down on them. Earl ran for evergreen shelter in the direction his bird had vanished, still pointing through the bursting rain. "Fetch! Fetch! Oh, you damn thing, fetch my bird!"

Santee, trusting the principle that lightning never strikes twice in the same place, went under the smoking spruce. The bolt had entered the pith and exploded the heartwood in a column of live steam. White wood welled out of the riven bark. Almost at his feet, lying where they had fallen from the needled canopy of the top branches, were three dead grouse. They steamed gently in the cold rain. The hard drops struck the breast feathers like irregular heartbeats. Santee picked them up and looked at them. He turned them around and upside down. As soon as the rain slackened he pulled his shirt up over his head and made a run for Earl's tree.

"You don't need to yell at my dog. Here's your birds. Three in one shot, mister man, is somethin' I never seen before. You sure have learned how to shoot." He shook his head.

Earl's eyes were hidden behind the rain-streaked yellow shooting glasses. His thick cheeks were wet and his lips flapped silently. "Something felt right," he gabbled, seizing the birds. "I knew something was going to happen today. I guess I was ready for the big breakthrough."

He talked all the way back to Santee's truck, and as they drove through the woods, the windshield wipers beating, the damp air in the cab redolent of wet dog, explained how he'd felt the birds were there, how he'd felt the gun fall into line on them, how he saw the feathers fountain up.

"I saw right where they went down," he said. Santee thought he probably believed he had. "But that dog of yours . . ."

Santee pulled up his yard beside Earl's Saab and set the hand brake. The rain flowed over the windshield in sheets. Santee cleared his throat.

"This is the parting of our ways," he said. "I can take a good deal, but I won't have my dog called down."

Earl smirked; he knew Santee was jealous. "That's okay with me," he said, and ran through the hammering rain to his car, squeezing the grouse in his arms.

Santee woke before dawn, jammed up against Verna. He could see the pale mist of breath floating from her nostrils. Icy air flowed through an inch of open window. He slipped out of bed to close it, saw the storm had cleared the weather. Stars glinted like chips of mica in the paling sky, hoarfrost coated the fields and the row of stones along the drive. The puddles in the road were frozen solid. It was going to be a cold, un-clouded day. He laughed to himself as he got back into the warm bed, wondering what Earl had said when he plucked three partridges that were already cooked.

This story is "told" by a big whitetail buck who is trying to get through another hunting season. It reverberates with the wonders of nature and the rituals of survival in the wilderness. Originally published in Sports Afield, it was later included in The Best of Sports Afield (1996). Author Sigurd Olson (1899–1982) hailed from the boundary waters area of Ely, Minnesota. A noted naturalist and environmentalist, he was dean of the junior college in Ely and wrote many stories and popular books, such as The Singing Wilderness (1956), The Hidden Forest (1969), and Reflections From the North Country (1976). Olson was an active hunter well into his seventies.

Sig Olson

TRAIL'S END
(1933)

IT WAS EARLY MORNING IN the northern wilderness, one of those rare breathless mornings, that come only in November, and though it was not yet light enough to see, the birds were stirring. A covey of partridge whirred up from their cozy burrows in the snow and lit in the top of a white birch, where they feasted noisily upon the frozen brown buds. The rolling tattoo of a downy woodpecker, also looking for his breakfast, reverberated again and again through the timber.

They were not the only ones astir however, for far down the trail leading from the Tamarack Swamp to Kennedy Lake browsed a big buck. He worked his way leisurely along, stopping now and then to scratch away the fresh snow and nibble daintily the still tender green things underneath. A large buck he was, even as deer run, and as smooth and sleek as good feeding could make him. His horns, almost too large, were queerly shaped, for instead of being rounded as in other deer, they were broad and palmate, the horns of a true swamp buck.

The eastern skyline was just beginning to tint with lavender as he reached the summit of the ridge overlooking the lake. He stopped for his usual morning survey of the landscape below him. For some reason, ever since his spike-buck days, he had always stopped there to look the country over before working down to water. He did not know that for countless generations before him, in the days when the pine timber stood tall and gloomy round the shores of the lake, other swamp bucks had also stopped, to scent the wind and listen, before going down to drink.

As he stood on the crest of the ridge, his gaze took in the long reaches of dark blue water far below him; the ice rimmed shores with long white windfalls reaching like frozen fingers out into the shallows, and the mottled green and gray of the brush covered slopes. His attention was finally centered on a little log cabin tucked away on the opposite shore in a clump of second growth spruce and balsam. Straight above it rose a thin wreath of pale blue smoke, almost as blue as the clear morning air. The metallic chuck, chuck of an axe ringing on a dry log came clearly across the water, and a breath of air brought to him strange odors that somehow filled him with a vague misgiving.

He was fascinated by the cabin and could not take his gaze from it. On other mornings, it had seemed as much a part of the shoreline as the trees themselves, but now it was different. A flood of almost forgotten memories surged back to him, of days long ago, when similar odors and sounds had brought with them a danger far greater than that of any natural enemy. He rubbed the top of a low hazel bush and stamped his forefeet nervously, undecided what to do. Then, in a flash, the full realization came to him. He understood the meaning of it all. This was the season of the year when man was no longer his friend, and it was not safe to be seen in the logging roads or in the open clearings near the log houses. He sniffed the air keenly a moment longer, to be sure, then snorted loudly as if to warn all the wilderness folk of their danger, and bounded back up the trail the way he had come.

Not until he had regained the heavy protecting timber of the Tamarack Swamp, north of Kennedy Lake, did he feel safe. What he had seen, made him once again the wary old buck who had lived by his cunning and strength through many a hunting season. Although he was safe for the time being, he was too experienced not to know, that before many days had passed, the Tamarack Swamp would no longer be a haven of refuge.

As he worked deeper into the heavy moss hung timber, he stopped frequently to look into the shadows. The trail here was knee-deep in moss and criss-crossed by a labyrinth of narrow rabbit runways. Soon his search was rewarded, for a sleek yearling doe met him at a place where two trails crossed. After nosing each other tenderly, by way of recognition, they began feeding together on the tender shoots of blueberries and still green tufts of swamp grass underneath the protecting blanket of snow.

All that morning they fed leisurely and when the sun was high in the heavens, they worked cautiously over to the edge of the swamp. Here was a warm sunny opening hedged in by huge windfalls grown over with a dense tangle of blackberry vines. They often came here for their afternoon sunning, as the ice-encrusted ovals in the snow attested. Leaping a big windfall that guarded the entrance to the opening, they carefully examined the ground, then picked their beds close together. There they rested contentedly with the warm sun shining upon them, little thinking that soon their peace would be broken.

The snow had fallen early that autumn and good feed had been scarce everywhere, except in the depths of the Tamarack Swamp, where the protecting timber had sheltered the grass and small green things. The plague had killed off most of the rabbits, and the few which survived were already forced to feed upon the bark of the poplar. The heavy crust, forming suddenly the night after the first heavy snow, had imprisoned countless partridge and grouse in their tunnels. As a result, small game was scarce and the wolves were lean and gaunt, although it was yet hardly winter. The stark famine months ahead gave promise of nothing but star-vation and death, and the weird discordant music of the wolf pack had sounded almost every night since the last full moon.

The swamp buck and his doe had not as yet felt the pinch of hunger, but instinct told them to keep close to the shelter of the Tamarack Swamp, so except for the morning strolls of the buck to the shore of Kennedy Lake, they had seldom ventured far from the timber. They had often heard the wolf pack, but always so far away that there was little dan-ger as long as they stayed under cover.

Several days had passed since the buck had been to the shore of Kennedy Lake. As yet the silence of the swamp had been unbroken ex-cept for the crunching of their own hoofs through the icy crust on the trails, and the buck was beginning to wonder if there was really anything to fear. Then one day, as they were again leisurely working their way over to the sunning place in the clearing, they were startled by the strange noises far toward the east end of the swamp. They stopped, every nerve on edge. At times they could hear them quiet plainly, then again they would be so faint as to be almost indistinguishable from the other sounds of the forest.

The two deer were not much concerned at first. After satisfying them-selves that there was no real danger, they started again down the trail to-ward the clearing. They could still hear the noises occasionally, but could not tell whether they were coming closer or going further away.

Then just as they neared the edge of the swamp, the sound of heavy footsteps seemed suddenly to grow louder and more distinct. Once more they stopped and stood with heads high, ears pricked up, listening in-tently. This time they were thoroughly alarmed. Closer and closer came the racket. Now they could hear distinctly the crunching of snow and the crackling of twigs, and then the whole east end of the timber seemed to be fairly alive with tumult, and the air reeked with danger.

The buck ran in a circle, sniffing keenly. The same scent that had come to him from the cabin, now rankled heavily in the air, and he knew the time had come to leave the shelter of the Tamarack Swamp. He hesitated, however, not knowing which way to turn. Back and forth he ran, stopping now and then to paw the ground, or to blow the air through his nostrils with the sharp whistling noise that all deer use when in danger.

A branch cracked sharply close at hand, and the scent came doubly strong from the east. With a wild snort the buck wheeled and led the way toward the western end of the swamp followed closely by the doe. Their only hope lay in reaching a heavy belt of green hemlock timber which they knew was separated from the western end of the Tamarack Swamp by a broad stretch of barren, burned-over slashing. As they neared the edge of the swamp they stopped, dreading to leave its protection. From where they stood they could see the dark wall of timber half a mile away. A brushy gully ran diagonally toward it across the open slashing, offering some protection, but the hills on either side were as stark and bare as an open field.

Again came the crack and crunch, now so close that the very air burned with danger. It was time to go. They bounded out of the timber, their white flags waving defiance, and were soon in the brush gully, going like the wind. Just as they sailed over a windfall, the buck caught a glimpse of something moving on a big black pine stump on top of the ridge to their right. Then the quiet was shattered by a succession of rending crashes and strange singing and whining sounds filled the air above them.

Again and again came the crashes. Suddenly the little doe stopped dead in her tracks. She gave a frightened baa-aa-a of pain and terror as the blood burst in a stream from a jagged wound in her throat. The buck stopped and ran back to where she stood, head down and swaying unsteadily. He watched her a moment, then, growing nervous, started down the trail again. The doe tried bravely to follow, but fell half way across a windfall too high for her to clear. Again the buck stopped and watched her anxiously. The snow by the windfall was soon stained bright red with blood, and the head of the little doe sank lower and lower in spite of her brave efforts to hold it up.

Hurriedly the buck looked about him. Several black figures were coming rapidly down the ridge. He nosed his doe gently, but this time she did not move. Raising his head he looked toward the approaching figures. Danger was close, but he could not leave his mate.

A spurt of smoke came from one of the figures, followed by another crash. This time the buck felt a blow so sharp that it made him stumble. Staggering to his feet, he plunged blindly down the gully. His flag was down, the sure sign of a wounded deer. Again and again came the crashes and the air above him whined and sang as the leaden pellets searched for their mark. The bark flew from a birch tree close by, spattering him with fragments. In spite of his wound, he ran swiftly and was soon out of range in the protecting green timber. He knew that he would not be tracked for at least an hour, as his pursuers would wait for him to lie down and stiffen.

He was bleeding badly from a long red scar cutting across his flank, and his back trail was sprinkled with tiny red dots. Where he stopped to rest and listen, little puddles of blood would form that quickly turned bluish black in the snow. For two hours he ran steadily, and then was so weakened by loss of blood that at last he was forced to lie down.

After a short rest, he staggered to his feet, stiffened badly. The bed he had melted in the snow was stained dark red from his bleeding flank. The cold, however, had contracted the wound and had stopped the bleeding a little. He limped painfully down the trail, not caring much which direction it led. Every step was torture. Once when crossing a small gully, he stumbled and fell on his wounded leg. It rested him to lie there, and it was all he could do to force himself on.

While crossing a ridge, the wind bore the man scent strongly to him, and he knew that now he was being trailed. Once, he heard the brush crack behind him, and was so startled that the wound was jerked open and the bleeding started afresh. He watched his back trail nervously, expecting to see his pursuer at any moment and hear again the rending crash that would mean death.

He grew steadily weaker and knew that unless night came soon, he would be overtaken. He had to rest more often now, and when he did move it was to stagger aimlessly down the trail, stumbling on roots and stubs. It was much easier now to walk around the windfalls, than to try to jump over as he had always done before.

The shadows were growing longer and longer, and in the hollows it was already getting dusk. If he could last until nightfall he would be safe. But the man scent was getting still stronger, and he realized at last that speed alone could not save him. Strategy was the only course. If this pursuer could be thrown off the trail, only long enough to delay him half an hour, darkness would be upon the wilderness and he could rest.

So waiting until the trail ran down onto a steep ravine filled with brush and windfalls, the buck suddenly turned and walked back on his own trail as far as he dared. It was the old trick of back tracking that deer have used for ages to elude their pursuers. Then stopping suddenly, he jumped as far to the side as his strength would permit, landing with all four feet tightly bunched together in the very center of a scrubby hazel bush. From there, he worked his way slowly into a patch of scrub spruce and lay down exhausted under an old windfall. Weakened as he was from loss of blood and from the throbbing pain in his flank, it was all he could do to keep his eyes riveted on his back trail, and his ears strained for the rustling and crunching that he feared would come, unless darkness came first.

It seemed that he had barely lain down, when without warning, the brush cracked sharply, and not 100 yards away appeared a black figure. The buck was petrified with terror. His ruse had failed. He shrank as far down as he could in the grass under the windfall and his eyes almost burst from their sockets. Frantically he thought of leaving his hiding place, but knew that would only invite death. The figure came closer and closer, bending low over the trail and peering keenly into the spruce thicket ahead. In the fading light the buck was well hidden by the windfall, but the blood spattered trail led straight to his hiding place. Discovery seemed certain.

The figure picked its way still nearer. It was now within 30 feet of the windfall. The buck watched, hardly daring to breathe. Then, in order to get a better view into the thicket, the hunter started to climb a snow covered stump close by. Suddenly, losing his balance, he slipped and plunged backwards into the snow. The buck saw his chance. Gathering all his remaining strength, he dashed out of his cover and was soon hidden in the thick growth of spruce.

It was almost dark now and he knew that as far as the hunter was concerned, he was safe. Circling slowly around, he soon found a sheltered hiding place in a dense clump of spruce where he could rest and allow his wound to heal.

Night came swiftly, bringing with it protection and peace. The stars came out one by one, and a full November moon climbed into the sky, flooding the snowy wilderness with its radiance.

Several hours had passed since the buck had lain down to rest in the spruce thicket. The moon was now riding high in the heavens and in the open places it was almost as light as day. Although well hidden, he dozed fitfully, waking at times with a start, thinking that again he was being trailed. He would then lie and listen, with nerves strained to the breaking point, for any sounds of the wild that might mean danger. An owl hooted over in a clump of timber, and the new forming ice on the shores of Kennedy Lake, half a mile away, rumbled ominously. Then he heard a long quavering call, so faint and far away that it almost blended with the whispering of the wind. The coarse hair on his shoulders bristled as he recognized the hunting call of the age-old enemy of his kind. It was answered again and again. The wolf pack was gathering, and for the first time in his life, the buck knew fear. In the shelter of the Tamarack Swamp there had been little danger, and even if he had been driven to the open, his strength and speed would have carried him far from harm. Now, sorely wounded and far from shelter, he would have hardly a fighting chance should the pack pick up his trail.

They were now running in full cry, having struck a trail in the direction of the big swamp far to the west. To the buck, the weird music was as a song of death. Circling and circling, for a time they seemed to draw no nearer. As yet he was not sure whether it was his own blood bespattered trail that they were unraveling, or that of some other one of his kind. Then, suddenly, the cries grew in fierceness and volume and sounded much closer than before. He listened spellbound as he finally realized the truth it was his own trail they were following. The fiendish chorus grew steadily louder and more venomous, and now had a new note of triumph in it that boded ill for whatever came in its way.

He could wait no longer and sprang to his feet. To his dismay, he was so stiffened and sore, that he could hardly take a step. Forcing himself on, he hobbled painfully through the poplar brush and clumps of timber in the direction of the lake. Small windfalls made him stumble, and having to walk around hummocks and hollows made progress slow and difficult. How he longed for his old strength and endurance. About two-thirds of the distance to the lake had been covered and already occasional glimpses of water appeared between the openings.

Suddenly the cries of the pack burst out in redoubled fury behind him, and the buck knew they had found his warm blood-stained bed. Plunging blindly on, he used every ounce of strength and energy that he had left, for now the end was only a matter of minutes. The water was his only hope, for by reaching that he would at least escape being torn to shreds by the teeth of the pack. He could hear them coming swiftly down the ridge behind him and every strange shadow he mistook for one of the gliding forms of his pursuers. They were now so close that he could hear their snarls and yapping. Then a movement caught his eye in the checkered moonlight. A long gray shape had slipped out of the darkness and was easily keeping pace with him. Another form crept in silently on the other side and both ran like phantoms with no apparent effort. He was terror stricken, but kept on desperately. Other ghost-like shapes filtered in from the timber, but still they did not close. The water was just ahead. They would wait till he broke from the brush that lined the shore. With a crash, he burst through the last fringe of alders and charged forward. As he did so, a huge gray form shot out of the shadows and launched itself at his throat. He saw the movement in time and caught the full force of the blow on his horns. A wild toss and the snarling shape splashed into the ice rimmed shallows. At the same instant the two that had been running along side closed, one for his throat and the other for his hamstrings. The first he hit a stunning blow with his sharp front hoof, but as he did so the teeth of the other fastened on the tendon of his hind leg. A frantic leap loosened his hold and the buck half plunged and half slid over the ice into the waters of Kennedy

Lake. Then the rest of the pack tore down to the beach with a deafening babble of snarls and howls, expecting to find their quarry down or at bay. When they realized that they had been outwitted, their anger was hideous and the air was rent with howls and yaps.

The cold water seemed to put new life into the buck and each stroke was stronger than the one before. Nevertheless, it was a long hard swim, and before he was half way across the benumbing cold had begun to tell. He fought on stubbornly, his breath coming in short, choking sobs and finally, after what seemed ages, touched the hard sandy bottom of the other shore. Dragging himself painfully out, he lay down exhausted in the snow. All sense of feeling had left his tortured body, but the steady lap, lap of the waves against the tinkling shore ice soothed him into sleep.

When he awoke, the sun was high in the heavens. For a long time he lay as in a stupor, too weak and sorely stiffened to move. Then with a mighty effort he struggled to his feet, and stood motionless, bracing himself unsteadily. Slowly his strength returned and leaving his bed, he picked his way carefully along the beach, until he struck the trail, down which he had so often come to drink. He followed it to the summit of the ridge overlooking the lake.

The dark blue waters sparkled in the sun, and the rolling spruce covered ridges were green as they had always been. Nothing had really changed, yet never again would it be the same. He was a stranger in the land of his birth, a lonely fugitive where once he had roamed at will, his only choice to leave forever the ancient range of his breed. For a time he wavered torn between his emotions, then finally turned to go. Suddenly an overwhelming desire possessed him, to visit again the place where last he had seen his mate. He worked slowly down the trail to the old Tamarack Swamp and did not stop until he came to the old meeting place deep in the shadows where the two trails crossed. For a long time he did not move, then turned and headed into the north to a new wilderness far from the old, a land as yet untouched, the range of the Moose and Caribou.

A fine piece of literary artistry, this story may remind readers of James Dickey's Deliverance. *A commercial fisherman and two boys go duck hunting on Christmas morning. They manage to find ducks but experience horrific twists of fate. The story came out in the* Hudson Review, *was honored by first prize in the O. Henry Awards and inclusion in* The Best American Short Stories, 1960, *and appears in* The Best American Short Stories of the Century (*1999*). *Lawrence Sargent Hall received his Ph.D. in English from Yale University in 1941. He enjoyed a long career as a professor of English at Bowdoin College in Maine. Hall's first novel was* Stowaway (*1961*).

Lawrence Sargent Hall

THE LEDGE (1959)

ON CHRISTMAS MORNING BEFORE SUNUP the fisherman embraced his warm wife and left his close bed. She did not want him to go. It was Christmas morning. He was a big, raw man, with too much strength, whose delight in winter was to hunt the sea ducks that flew in to feed by the outer ledges, bare at low tide.

As his bare feet touched the cold floor and the frosty air struck his nude flesh, he might have changed his mind in the dark of this special day. It was a home day, which made it seem natural to think of the outer ledges merely as some place he had shot ducks in the past. But he had promised his son, thirteen, and his nephew, fifteen, who came from in-land. That was why he had given them his present of an automatic shot-gun each the night before, on Christmas Eve. Rough man though he was known to be, and no spoiler of boys, he kept his promises when he understood what they meant. And to the boys, as to him, home meant where you came for rest after you had had your Christmas fill of action and excitement.

His legs astride, his arms raised, the fisherman stretched as high as he could in the dim privacy of his bedroom. Above the snug murmur of his wife's protest he heard the wind in the pines and knew it was easterly as the boys had hoped and he had surmised the night before. Conditions would be ideal, and when they were, anybody ought to take advantage of them. The birds would be flying. The boys would get a man's sport their first time outside on the ledges.

His son at thirteen, small but steady and experienced, was fierce to grow up in hunting, to graduate from sheltered waters and the blinds along the shores of the inner bay. His nephew at fifteen, an overgrown farm boy, had a farm boy's love of the sea, though he could not swim a stroke and was often sick in choppy weather. That was the reason his father, the fisherman's brother, was a farmer and chose to sleep in on the holiday morning at his brother's house. Many of the ones the farmer had grown up with were regularly seasick and could not swim, but they were unafraid of the water. They could not have dreamed of being anything but fishermen. The fisherman himself could swim like a seal and was never sick, and he would sooner die than be anything else.

He dressed in the cold and dark, and woke the boys gruffly. They tumbled out of bed, their instincts instantly awake while their thoughts still fumbled slumbrously. The fisherman's wife in the adjacent bedroom heard them apparently trying to find their clothes, mumbling sleepily and happily to each other, while her husband went down to the hot kitchen to fry eggs—sunny-side up, she knew, because that was how they all liked them.

Always in winter she hated to have them go outside, the weather was so treacherous and there were so few others out in case of trouble. To the fisherman these were no more than woman's fears, to be taken for granted and laughed off. When they were first married they fought miserably every fall because she was after him constantly to put his boat up until spring. The fishing was all outside in winter, and though prices were high the storms made the rate of attrition high on gear. Nevertheless he did well. So she could do nothing with him.

People thought him a hard man, and gave him the reputation of being all out for himself because he was inclined to brag and be disdainful. If it was true, and his own brother was one of those who strongly felt it was, they lived better than others, and his brother had small right to criticize. There had been times when in her loneliness she had yearned to leave him for another man. But it would have been dangerous. So over the years she had learned to shut her mind to his hard-driving, and take what comfort she might from his unsympathetic competence. Only once or twice, perhaps, had she gone so far as to dwell guiltily on what it would be like to be a widow.

The thought that her boy, possibly because he was small, would not be insensitive like his father, and the rattle of dishes and smell of frying bacon downstairs in the kitchen shut off from the rest of the chilly house, restored the cozy feeling she had had before she was alone in bed. She heard them after a while go out and shut the back door.

Under her window she heard the snow grind dryly beneath their boots, and her husband's sharp, exasperated commands to the boys. She shivered slightly in the envelope of her own warmth. She listened to the noise of her son and nephew talking elatedly. Twice she caught the glimmer of their lights on the white ceiling above the window as they went down the path to the shore. There would be frost on the skiff and freezing suds at the water's edge. She herself used to go gunning when she was younger; now, it seemed to her, anyone going out like that on Christmas morning had to be incurably male. They would none of them think about her until they returned and piled the birds they had shot on top of the sink for her to dress.

Ripping into the quiet predawn cold she heard the hot snarl of the outboard taking them out to the boat. It died as abruptly as it had burst into life. Two or three or four or five minutes later the big engine broke into a warm reassuring roar. He had the best of equipment, and he kept it in the best of condition. She closed her eyes. It would not be too long before the others would be up for Christmas. The summer drone of the exhaust deepened. Then gradually it faded in the wind until it was lost at sea, or she slept.

The engine had started immediately in spite of the temperature. This put the fisherman in a good mood. He was proud of his boat. Together he and the two boys heaved the skiff and outboard onto the stern and secured it athwartships. His son went forward along the deck, iridescent in the ray of the light the nephew shone through the windshield, and cast the mooring pennant loose into darkness. The fisherman swung to starboard, glanced at his compass, and headed seaward down the obscure bay.

There would be just enough visibility by the time they reached the headland to navigate the crooked channel between the islands. It was the only nasty stretch of water. The fisherman had done it often in fog or at night—he always swore he could go anywhere in the bay blindfolded—but there was no sense in taking chances if you didn't have to. From the mouth of the channel he could lay a straight course for Brown Cow Island, anchor the boat out of sight behind it, and from the skiff set their tollers off Devil's Hump three hundred yards to seaward. By then the tide would be clearing the ledge and they could land and be ready to shoot around half-tide.

It was early, it was Christmas, and it was farther out than most hunters cared to go in this season of the closing year, so that he felt sure no one would be taking possession ahead of them. He had shot thousands of ducks there in his day. The Hump was by far the best hunting. Only thing was you had to plan for the right conditions because you didn't have too much time. About four hours was all, and you had to get it before three in the afternoon when the birds left and went out to sea ahead of nightfall.

They had it figured exactly right for today. The ledge would not be going under until after the gunning was over, and they would be home for supper in good season. With a little luck the boys would have a skiff-load of birds to show for their first time outside. Well beyond the legal limit, which was no matter. You took what you could get in this life, or the next man made out and you didn't.

The fisherman had never failed to make out gunning from Devil's Hump. And this trip, he had a hunch, would be above ordinary. The easterly wind would come up just stiff enough, the tide was right, and it was going to storm by tomorrow morning so the birds would be moving. Things were perfect.

The old fierceness was in his bones. Keeping a weather eye to the murk out front and a hand on the wheel, he reached over and cuffed both boys playfully as they stood together close to the heat of the exhaust pipe running up through the center of the house. They poked back at him and shouted above the drumming engine, making bets as they always did on who would shoot the most birds. This trip they had the thrill of new guns, the best money could buy, and a man's hunting ground. The black retriever wagged at them and barked. He was too old and arthritic to be allowed in December water, but he was jaunty anyway at being brought along.

Groping in his pocket for his pipe the fisherman suddenly had his high spirits rocked by the discovery that he had left his tobacco at home. He swore. Anticipation of a day out with nothing to smoke made him incredulous. He searched his clothes, and then he searched them again, unable to believe the tobacco was not somewhere. When the boys inquired what was wrong he spoke angrily to them, blaming them for being in some devious way at fault. They were instantly crestfallen and willing to put back after the tobacco, though they could appreciate what it meant only through his irritation. But he bitterly refused. That would throw everything out of phase. He was a man who did things the way he set out to do.

He clamped his pipe between his teeth, and twice more during the next few minutes he ransacked his clothes in disbelief. He was no stoic. For one relaxed moment he considered putting about and gunning somewhere nearer home. Instead he held his course and sucked the empty pipe, consoling himself with the reflection that at least he had whiskey enough if it got too uncomfortable on the ledge. Peremptorily he made the boys check to make certain the bottle was really in the knapsack with the lunches where he thought he had taken care to put it. When they reassured him he despised his fate a little less.

The fisherman's judgment was as usual accurate. By the time they were abreast of the headland there was sufficient light so that he could wind his way among the reefs without slackening speed. At last he turned his bows toward open ocean, and as the winter dawn filtered upward through long layers of smoky cloud on the eastern rim his spirits rose again with it.

He opened the throttle, steadied on his course, and settled down to the two-hour run. The wind was stronger but seemed less cold coming from the sea. The boys had withdrawn from the fisherman and were talking together while they watched the sky through the windows. The boat churned solidly through a light chop, flinging spray off her flaring bows. Astern the headland thinned rapidly till it lay like a blackened sill on the gray water. No other boats were abroad.

The boys fondled their new guns, sighted along the barrels, worked the mechanisms, compared notes, boasted, and gave each other contradictory advice. The fisherman got their attention once and pointed at the horizon. They peered through the windows and saw what looked like a black scum floating on top of gently agitated water. It wheeled and tilted, rippled, curled, then rose, strung itself out and became a huge raft of ducks escaping over the sea. A good sign.

The boys rushed out and leaned over the washboards in the wind and spray to see the flock curl below the horizon. Then they went and hovered around the hot engine, bewailing their lot. If only they had been already set out and waiting. Maybe these ducks would be crazy enough to return later and be slaughtered. Ducks were known to be foolish.

In due course and right on schedule they anchored at midmorning in the lee of Brown Cow Island. They put the skiff overboard and loaded it with guns, knapsacks, and tollers. The boys showed their eagerness by being clumsy. The fisherman showed his in bad temper and abuse which they silently accepted in the absorbed tolerance of being boys. No doubt they laid it to lack of tobacco.

By outboard they rounded the island and pointed due east in the direction of a ridge of foam which could be seen whitening the surface three hundred yards away. They set the decoys in a broad, straddling vee opening wide into the ocean. The fisherman warned them not to get their hands wet, and when they did he made them carry on with red and painful fingers, in order to teach them. Once the last toller was bobbing among his fellows, brisk and alluring, they got their numbed fingers inside their oilskins and hugged their warm crotches. In the meantime the fisherman had turned the skiff toward the patch of foam where as if by magic, like a black glossy rib of earth, the ledge had broken through the belly of the sea.

Carefully they inhabited their slippery nub of the North American continent, while the unresting Atlantic swelled and swirled as it had for eons round the indomitable edges. They hauled the skiff after them, established themselves as comfortably as they could in a shallow sump on top, lay on their sides a foot or so above the water, and waited, guns in hand.

In time the fisherman took a thermos bottle from the knapsack and they drank steaming coffee, and waited for the nodding decoys to lure in the first flight to the rock. Eventually the boys got hungry and restless. The fisherman let them open the picnic lunch and eat one sandwich apiece, which they both shared with the dog. Having no tobacco the fisherman himself would not eat.

Actually the day was relatively mild, and they were warm enough at present in their woolen clothes and socks underneath oilskins and hip boots. After a while, however, the boys began to feel cramped. Their nerves were agonized by inactivity. The nephew complained and was severely told by the fisherman—who pointed to the dog, crouched unmoving except for his white-rimmed eyes—that part of doing a man's hunting was learning how to wait. But he was beginning to have misgivings of his own. This could be one of those days where all the right conditions masked an incalculable flaw.

If the fisherman had been alone, as he often was, stopping off when the necessary coincidence of tide and time occurred on his way home from hauling trawls, and had plenty of tobacco, he would not have fidgeted. The boys' being nervous made him nervous. He growled at them again. When it came it was likely to come all at once, and then in a few moments be over. He warned them not to slack off, never to slack off, to be always ready. Under his rebuke they kept their tortured peace, though they could not help shifting and twisting until he lost what patience he had left and bullied them into lying still. A duck could see an eyelid twitch. If the dog could go without moving so could they.

"Here it comes!" the fisherman said tersely at last.

The boys quivered with quick relief. The flock came in downwind, quartering slightly, myriad, black, and swift.

"Beautiful—" breathed the fisherman's son.

"All right," said the fisherman, intense and precise. "Aim at singles in the thickest part of the flock. Wait for me to fire and then don't stop shooting till your gun's empty." He rolled up onto his left elbow and spread his legs to brace himself. The flock bore down, arrowy and vibrant, then a hundred yards beyond the decoys it veered off.

"They're going away!" the boys cried, sighting in.

"Not yet!" snapped the fisherman. "They're coming round."

The flock changed shape, folded over itself, and drove into the wind in a tight arc. "Thousands—" the boys hissed through their teeth. All at once a whistling storm of black and white broke over the decoys.

"Now!" the fisherman shouted. "Perfect!" And he opened fire at the flock just as it hung suspended in momentary chaos above the tollers. The three pulled at their triggers and the birds splashed into the water, until the last report went off unheard, the last smoking shell flew unheeded over their shoulders, and the last of the routed flock scattered diminishing, diminishing, diminishing in every direction.

Exultantly the boys dropped their guns, jumped up and scrambled for the skiff.

"I'll handle that skiff!" the fisherman shouted at them. They stopped. Gripping the painter and balancing himself he eased the skiff into the water stern first and held the bow hard against the side of the rock shelf the skiff had rested on. "You stay here," he said to his nephew. "No sense in all three of us going in the boat."

The boy on the reef gazed at the gray water rising and falling hypnotically along the glistening edge. It had dropped about a foot since their arrival. "I want to go with you," he said in a sullen tone, his eyes on the streaming eddies.

"You want to do what I tell you if you want to gun with me," answered the fisherman harshly. The boy couldn't swim, and he wasn't going to have him climbing in and out of the skiff any more than necessary. Besides he was too big.

The fisherman took his son in the skiff and cruised round and round among the decoys picking up dead birds. Meanwhile the other boy stared unmoving after them from the highest part of the ledge. Before they had quite finished gathering the dead birds, the fisherman cut the outboard and dropped to his knees in the skiff. "Down!" he yelled. "Get down!" About a dozen birds came tolling in. "Shoot—shoot!" his son hollered from the bottom of the boat to the boy on the ledge.

The dog, who had been running back and forth whining, sank to his belly, his muzzle on his forepaws. But the boy on the ledge never stirred. The ducks took late alarm at the skiff, swerved aside and into the air, passing with a whirr no more than fifty feet over the head of the boy, who remained on the ledge like a statue, without his gun, watching the two crouching in the boat.

The fisherman's son climbed onto the ledge and held the painter. The bottom of the skiff was covered with feathery black and white bodies with feet upturned and necks lolling. He was jubilant. "We got twenty-seven!" he told his cousin. "How's that? Nine apiece. Boy—" he added, "what a cool Christmas!"

The fisherman pulled the skiff onto its shelf and all three went and lay down again in anticipation of the next flight. The son, reloading, patted his shotgun affectionately. "I'm going to get me ten next time," he said. Then he asked his cousin, "Whatsamatter—didn't you see the strays?"

"Yeah," the boy said.

"How come you didn't shoot at 'em?"

"Didn't feel like it," replied the boy, still with a trace of sullenness.

"You stupid or something?" The fisherman's son was astounded. "What a highlander!" But the fisherman, though he said nothing, knew that the older boy had had an attack of ledge fever.

"Cripes!" his son kept at it. "I'd at least of tried."

"Shut up," the fisherman finally told him, "and leave him be."

At slack water three more flocks came in, one right after the other, and when it was over, the skiff was half full of clean, dead birds. During the subsequent lull they broke out the lunch and ate it all and finished the hot coffee. For a while the fisherman sucked away on his cold pipe. Then he had himself a swig of whiskey.

The boys passed the time contentedly jabbering about who shot the most—there were ninety-two all told—which of their friends they would show the biggest ones to, how many each could eat at a meal provided they didn't have to eat any vegetables. Now and then they heard sporadic distant gunfire on the mainland, at its nearest point about two miles to the north. Once far off they saw a fishing boat making the direction of home.

At length the fisherman got a hand inside his oilskins and produced his watch.

"Do we have to go now?" asked his son.

"Not just yet," he replied. "Pretty soon." Everything had been perfect. As good as he had ever had it. Because he was getting tired of the boys' chatter he got up, heavily in his hip boots, and stretched. The tide had turned and was coming in, the sky was more ashen, and the wind had freshened enough so that whitecaps were beginning to blossom. It would be a good hour before they had to leave the ledge and pick up the tollers. However, he guessed they would leave a little early. On account of the rising wind he doubted there would be much more shooting. He stepped carefully along the back of the ledge, to work his kinks out. It was also getting a little colder.

The whiskey had begun to warm him, but he was unprepared for the sudden blaze that flashed upward inside him from belly to head. He was standing looking at the shelf where the skiff was. Only the foolish skiff was not there!

For the second time that day the fisherman felt the deep vacuity of disbelief. He gaped, seeing nothing but the flat shelf of rock. He whirled, started toward the boys, slipped, recovered himself, fetched a complete circle, and stared at the unimaginably empty shelf. Its emptiness made him feel as if everything he had done that day so far, his life so far, he had dreamed. What could have happened? The tide was still nearly a foot below. There had been no sea to speak of. The skiff could hardly have slid off by itself. For the life of him, consciously careful as he inveterately was, he could not now remember hauling it up the last time. Perhaps in the heat of hunting he had left it to the boy. Perhaps he could not remember which was the last time.

"Christ—" he exclaimed loudly, without realizing it because he was so entranced by the invisible event.

"What's wrong, Dad?" asked his son, getting to his feet.

The fisherman went blind with uncontainable rage. "Get back down there where you belong!" he screamed. He scarcely noticed the boy sink back in amazement. In a frenzy he ran along the ledge thinking the skiff might have been drawn up at another place, though he knew better. There was no other place.

He stumbled, half falling, back to the boys who were gawking at him in consternation, as though he had gone insane. "God damn it!" he yelled savagely, grabbing both of them and yanking them to their knees. "Get on your feet!"

"What's wrong?" his son repeated in a stifled voice.

"Never mind what's wrong," he snarled. "Look for the skiff—it's adrift!" When they peered around he gripped their shoulders, brutally facing them about. "Down-wind—" He slammed his fist against his thigh. "Jesus!" he cried, struck to madness at their stupidity.

At last he sighted the skiff himself, magically bobbing along the grim sea like a toller, a quarter of a mile to leeward on a direct course for home. The impulse to strip himself naked was succeeded instantly by a queer calm. He simply sat down on the ledge and forgot everything except the marvelous mystery.

As his awareness partially returned he glanced toward the boys. They were still observing the skiff speechlessly. Then he was gazing into the clear young eyes of his son.

"Dad," asked the boy steadily, "what do we do now?"

That brought the fisherman upright. "The first thing we have to do," he heard himself saying with infinite tenderness as if he were making love, "is think."

"Could you swim it?" asked his son.

He shook his head and smiled at them. They smiled quickly back, too quickly. "A hundred yards, maybe, in this water. I wish I could," he added. It was the most intimate and pitiful thing he had ever said. He walked in circles round them, trying to break the stall his mind was left in.

He gauged the level of the water. To the eye it was quite stationary, six inches from the shelf at this second. The fisherman did not have to mark it on the side of the rock against the passing of time to prove to his reason that it was rising, always rising. Already it was over the brink of reason, beyond the margins of thought—a senseless measurement. No sense to it.

All his life the fisherman had tried to lick the element of time, by getting up earlier and going to bed later, owning a faster boat, planning more than the day would hold, and tackling just one other job before the deadline fell. If, as on rare occasions he had the grand illusion, he ever really had beaten the game, he would need to call on all his reserves of practice and cunning now.

He sized up the scant but unforgivable three hundred yards to Brown Cow Island. Another hundred yards behind it his boat rode at anchor, where, had he been aboard, he could have cut in a fathometer to plumb the profound and occult seas, or a ship-to-shore radio on which in an interminably short time he would have heard his wife's voice talking to him over the air about homecoming.

"Couldn't we wave something so somebody would see us?" his nephew suggested.

The fisherman spun round. "Load your guns!" he ordered. They loaded as if the air had suddenly gone frantic with birds. "I'll fire once and count to five. Then you fire. Count to five. That way they won't just think it's only somebody gunning ducks. We'll keep doing that."

"We've only got just two and a half boxes left," said his son.

The fisherman nodded, understanding that from beginning to end their situation was purely mathematical, like the ticking of the alarm clock in his silent bedroom. Then he fired. The dog, who had been keeping watch over the decoys, leaped forward and yelped in confusion. They all counted off, fired the first five rounds by threes, and reloaded. The fisherman scanned first the horizon, then the contracting borders of the ledge, which was the sole place the water appeared to be climbing. Soon it would be over the shelf.

They counted off and fired the second five rounds. "We'll hold off a while on the last one," the fisherman told the boys. He sat down and pondered what a trivial thing was a skiff. This one he and the boy had knocked together in a day. Was a gun, manufactured for killing.

His son tallied up the remaining shells, grouping them symmetrically in threes on the rock when the wet box fell apart. "Two short," he announced. They reloaded and laid the guns on their knees.

Behind thickening clouds they could not see the sun going down. The water, coming up, was growing blacker. The fisherman thought he might have told his wife they would be home before dark since it was Christmas day. He realized he had forgotten about its being any particular day. The tide would not be high until two hours after sunset. When they did not get in by nightfall, and could not be raised by radio, she might send somebody to hunt for them right away. He rejected this arithmetic immediately, with a sickening shock, recollecting it was a two-and-a-half-hour run at best. Then it occurred to him that she might send somebody on the mainland who was nearer. She would think he had engine trouble.

He rose and searched the shoreline, barely visible. Then his glance dropped to the toy shoreline at the edges of the reef. The shrinking ledge, so sinister from a boat, grew dearer minute by minute as though the whole wide world he gazed on from horizon to horizon balanced on its contracting rim. He checked the water level and found the shelf awash.

Some of what went through his mind the fisherman told to the boys. They accepted it without comment. If he caught their eyes they looked away to spare him or because they were not yet old enough to face what they saw. Mostly they watched the rising water. The fisherman was unable to initiate a word of encouragement. He wanted one of them to ask him whether somebody would reach them ahead of the tide. He would have found it possible to say yes. But they did not inquire.

The fisherman was not sure how much, at their age, they were able to imagine. Both of them had seen from the docks drowned bodies put ashore out of boats. Sometimes they grasped things, and sometimes not.

He supposed they might be longing for the comfort of their mothers, and was astonished, as much as he was capable of any astonishment except the supreme one, to discover himself wishing he had not left his wife's dark, close, naked bed that morning.

"Is it time to shoot now?" asked his nephew.

"Pretty soon," he said, as if he were putting off making good on a promise. "Not yet."

His own boy cried softly for a brief moment, like a man, his face averted in an effort neither to give or show pain.

"Before school starts," the fisherman said, wonderfully detached, "we'll go to town and I'll buy you boys anything you want."

With great difficulty, in a dull tone as though he did not in the least desire it, his son said after a pause, "I'd like one of those new thirty-horse outboards."

"All right," said the fisherman. And to his nephew, "How about you?"

The nephew shook his head desolately. "I don't want anything," he said.

After another pause the fisherman's son said, "Yes he does, Dad. He wants one too."

"All right—" the fisherman said again, and said no more.

The dog whined in uncertainty and licked the boys' faces where they sat together. Each threw an arm over his back and hugged him. Three strays flew in and sat companionably down among the stiff-necked decoys. The dog crouched, obedient to his training. The boys observed them listlessly. Presently, sensing something untoward, the ducks took off, splashing the wave tops with feet and wingtips, into the dusky waste.

The sea began to make up in the mounting wind, and the wind bore a new and deathly chill. The fisherman, scouring the somber, dwindling shadow of the mainland for a sign, hoped it would not snow. But it did. First a few flakes, then a flurry, then storming past horizontally. The fisherman took one long, bewildered look at Brown Cow Island three hundred yards dead to leeward, and got to his feet.

Then it shut in, as if what was happening on the ledge was too private even for the last wan light of the expiring day.

"Last round," the fisherman said austerely.

The boys rose and shouldered their tacit guns. The fisherman fired into the flying snow. He counted methodically to five. His son fired and counted. His nephew. All three fired and counted. Four rounds.

"You've got one left, Dad," his son said.

The fisherman hesitated another second, then he fired the final shell. Its pathetic report, like the spat of a popgun, whipped away on the wind and was instantly blanketed in falling snow.

Night fell all in a moment to meet the ascending sea. They were now barely able to make one another out through driving snowflakes, dim as ghosts in their yellow oilskins. The fisherman heard a sea break and glanced down where his feet were. They seemed to be wound in a snowy sheet. Gently he took the boys by the shoulders and pushed them in front of him, feeling with his feet along the shallow sump to the place where it triangulated into a sharp crevice at the highest point of the ledge. "Face ahead," he told them. "Put the guns down."

"I'd like to hold mine, Dad," begged his son.

"Put it down," said the fisherman. "The tide won't hurt it. Now brace your feet against both sides and stay there."

They felt the dog, who was pitch black, running up and down in perplexity between their straddled legs. "Dad," said his son, "what about the pooch?"

If he had called the dog by name it would have been too personal. The fisherman would have wept. As it was he had all he could do to keep from laughing. He bent his knees, and when he touched the dog hoisted him under one arm. The dog's belly was soaking wet.

So they waited, marooned in their consciousness, surrounded by a monstrous tidal space which was slowly, slowly closing them out. In this space the periwinkle beneath the fisherman's boots was king. While hovering airborne in his mind he had an inward glimpse of his house as curiously separate, like a June mirage.

Snow, rocks, seas, wind the fisherman had lived by all his life. Now he thought he had never comprehended what they were, and he hated them. Though they had not changed. He was deadly chilled. He set out to ask the boys if they were cold. There was no sense. He thought of the whiskey, and sidled backward, still holding the awkward dog, till he located the bottle under water with his toe. He picked it up squeamishly as though afraid of getting his sleeve wet, worked his way forward and bent over his son. "Drink it," he said, holding the bottle against the boy's ribs. The boy tipped his head back, drank, coughed hotly, then vomited.

"I can't," he told his father wretchedly.

"Try—try—" the fisherman pleaded, as if it meant the difference between life and death.

The boy obediently drank, and again he vomited hotly. He shook his head against his father's chest and passed the bottle forward to his cousin, who drank and vomited also. Passing the bottle back, the boys dropped it in the frigid water between them.

When the waves reached his knees the fisherman set the warm dog loose and said to his son, "Turn around and get up on my shoulders." The boy obeyed. The fisherman opened his oilskin jacket and twisted his hands behind him through his suspenders, clamping the boy's booted ankles with his elbows.

"What about the dog?" the boy asked.

"He'll make his own way all right," the fisherman said. "He can take the cold water." His knees were trembling. Every instinct shrieked for gymnastics. He ground his teeth and braced like a colossus against the sides of the submerged crevice.

The dog, having lived faithfully as though one of them for eleven years, swam a few minutes in and out around the fisherman's legs, not knowing what was happening, and left them without a whimper. He would swim and swim at random by himself, round and round in the blinding night, and when he had swum routinely through the paralyzing water all he could, he would simply, in one incomprehensible moment, drown. Almost the fisherman, waiting out infinity, envied him his pattern.

Freezing seas swept by, flooding inexorably up and up as the earth sank away imperceptibly beneath them. The boy called out once to his cousin. There was no answer. The fisherman, marveling on a terror without voice, was dumbly glad when the boy did not call again. His own boots were long full of water. With no sensation left in his straddling legs he dared not move them. So long as the seas came sidewise against his hips, and then sidewise against his shoulders, he might balance—no telling how long. The upper half of him was what felt frozen. His legs, disengaged from his nerves and his will, he came to regard quite scientifically. They were the absurd, precarious axis around which reeled and surged universal tumult. The waves would come on and on; he could not visualize how many tossing reinforcements lurked in the night beyond—inexhaustible numbers, and he wept in supernatural fury at each because it was higher, till he transcended hate and took them, swaying like a convert, one by one as they lunged against him and away aimlessly into their own undisputed, wild realm.

From his hips upward the fisherman stretched to his utmost as a man does whose spirit reaches out of dead sleep. The boy's head, none too high, must be at least seven feet above the ledge. Though growing larger every minute, it was a small light life. The fisherman meant to hold it there, if need be, through a thousand tides.

By and by the boy, slumped on the head of his father, asked, "Is it over your boots, Dad?"

"Not yet," the fisherman said. Then through his teeth he added, "If I fall—kick your boots off—swim for it—down-wind—to the island. . . ."

"You . . . ?" the boy finally asked.

The fisherman nodded against the boy's belly. "—Won't see each other," he said.

The boy did for the fisherman the greatest thing that can be done. He may have been too young for perfect terror, but he was old enough to know there were things beyond the power of any man. All he could do he did, by trusting his father to do all he could, and asking nothing more.

The fisherman, rocked to his soul by a sea, held his eyes shut upon the interminable night.

"Is it time now?" the boy said.

The fisherman could hardly speak. "Not yet," he said. "Not just yet. . . ."

As the land mass pivoted toward sunlight the day after Christmas, a tiny fleet of small craft converged off shore like iron filings to a magnet.

At daybreak they found the skiff floating unscathed off the headland, half full of ducks and snow. The shooting *had* been good, as someone hearing on the nearby mainland the previous afternoon had supposed. Two hours afterward they found the unharmed boat adrift five miles at sea. At high noon they found the fisherman at ebb tide, his right foot jammed cruelly into a glacial crevice of the ledge beside three shotguns, his hands tangled behind him in his suspenders, and under his right el-bow a rubber boot with a sock and a live starfish in it. After dragging un-lit depths all day for the boys, they towed the fisherman home in his own boat at sundown, and in the frost of evening, mute with discovering pur-gatory, laid him on his wharf for his wife to see.

She, somehow, standing on the dock as in her frequent dream, gazing at the fisherman pure as crystal on the icy boards, a small rubber boot still frozen under one clenched arm, saw him exaggerated beyond re-morse or grief, absolved of his mortality.

It's one thing to hunt and kill a large animal deep in the winter wilderness, and quite another to get the beast home. This story describes the dangerous and exhausting task of getting a butchered elk out of the wild. It is from the New Yorker. Author Rick Bass is another exceptionally fine writer from Montana. He is a contributing editor for Sports Afield *and has written for* Audubon, Esquire, Sierra, *and the* Paris Review. *His nonfiction work includes* Ninemile Wolves (*1992*) *and* The Lost Grizzlies (*1995*). *More recently, Bass's fiction has drawn considerable national attention:* In The Loyal Mountains (*1995*), The Sky, the Stars, the Wilderness (*1997*), *and* Where the Sea Used to Be (*1998*).

Rick Bass

ELK (1997)

IT WAS MATTHEW WHO KILLED the elk. I was only trying to learn how it was done.

My first year in the valley, I knew next to nothing, though when only a week of hunting season remained and still I had no meat, I knew enough to ask Matthew for help. People told me he didn't like new people coming into the valley and that he wouldn't help me, wouldn't help anyone—but when I went to his cabin and asked, he said he would, just this once, and that I would have to watch carefully, and learn: he would only hunt an elk for me once.

We canoed across the Yaak River and went into the wilderness. We found a bull's tracks, and followed the bull for three days, killing it on the fourth.

Afterward, Matthew built a fire in the woods next to the elk to warm us as we went to work. There was plenty of dry wood and it was easy to make a roaring fire: its flames grew almost as tall as we were, and they lit up the woods. The orange light danced against the elk's hide and against his antlers, making it seem as if he had come back to life. In his final death leap the elk had got tangled in the blowdown and now hung there, several feet off the ground. Matthew crawled underneath and began cutting. There was a rasping sound of his knife against the coarse hair and thick skin and cartilage, and from time to time he had to stop and sharpen his knife with a whetstone.

"Nothing in the world dulls a steel blade like elk hair," he said. He was doing a neat job. "I'd like a stone knife someday, black obsidian," he said. I added wood to the fire. I would not have believed that you could skin such an animal. It was surely enough meat for the coming year.

By morning we had the elk skinned and the immense antlers sawed off. Matthew had brought a small wood-handled folding saw—its blade was now ruined—and he tossed it into the fire. The bull's immense hindquarters—heavier than a man's body—were hanging from trees. So, too, were the shoulders.

We filled our packs with the loose meat—all the neck roasts, tenderloins, neck loins, and lengths of backstrap like deep-red anacondas. In lifting the hindquarters and shoulders, we became covered with blood. I was glad that the bears were already in hibernation.

The fire had sprawled and wandered through the night. Ashes and charred half-lengths of timber lay in a circle thirty feet across: a testament to what had happened here.

We roasted some of the ribs over the coals of the fire and chewed on them for a long time. We ate a whole side of the trimmings from the elk skeleton—the bones were stripped clean and gleaming when we were done—and then broke the other side in half with the hatchet. We tied the rib cages to our packs like a frame; they would help hold in place the shifting weight of the meat, which was still warm against our backs. I gathered a few stones as we were about to leave and, not knowing why, stacked them where the elk had fallen, now a pile of hooves, shins, and hair.

Matthew carried the antlers—settled them over his shoulders upside down—and with their long tips and tines furrowing the snow behind him he looked as if he were in a yoke and plowing the snow. I carried the wet hide atop my pack of meat, increasing the weight of my pack up to around a hundred and thirty pounds. Matthew said it was important to carry out the extraneous stuff first—the antlers, the hide—before our resolve weakened and we were tempted to leave them behind for the wolves.

It began to snow again. I wondered where the other elk were, if they knew that our hunt for them was over.

We stayed on the ridges. Under such a load, our steps were small and slow. We travelled a mile, dropped our weight, then went back to where we'd left all the other meat, and carried it to the point we'd got to before—each of us carrying a hindquarter on his back, or dragging it behind like a sled.

And so we moved across the valley, slowly, as if in some eternal meat relay—continuously undoing the progress we'd made, working hours to move the whole mass only one mile, at which point we then started all over again. The winter-short days passed quickly, and we slept soundly through the nights.

The snow kept coming. We dropped off one ridge down into a creek and ascended another, and Matthew said he knew where we were. After the second or third day, the ravens appeared. They landed in front of us and strutted with outstretched wings, drawing little tracings in the snow, barking and cawing in their voices that were alternately shrill and hoarse, as if they were hurling different languages at us. Sometimes they landed behind us, darted in and pecked at whatever section of the elk we were dragging, but usually they picked at the meat fragments in the snow.

On the third day there was a moment of startling beauty. We were walking in a fog so thick that we could barely see more than a few feet in front of us. We knew to stay on the ridge. Four ravens were following us, walking behind us in their penguin strut. And then to our left, to the west, a slot appeared in the fog, a slot of pale-blue sky, and through the slot there was a shaft of gold light illuminating the forest below us. The shaft was the only thing we could see in the storm. The wind was blowing north, the direction we were going, and for a while the shaft travelled with us. As it did, it kept revealing more of the same uncut, untouched forest. The impression it made was that the uncut forest would never end. In less than a minute, the shaft had moved on—the wind was about thirty miles an hour—but the sight has stayed with me, and neither Matthew nor I said anything about it to each other, though we did stop and watch it, as if unsure of what it was we were seeing.

We ate on the elk as we travelled, but after four days I wanted bread or potatoes. I was tired of all meat. I wanted an apple pie, dense with sugar, and a hot bath.

The massive antlers had sunk lower on Matthew's shoulders, and the plow they made cut deeper in the snow. Sometimes their heavy tips struck a rock beneath the snow and made a *clinking* sound. The weight of the antlers was starting to wear Matthew's skin raw, even though he had cut a small strip of hide to use as a cushion. A thin red "Y" now ran down his back, merging just below his shoulders. The furrows in the snow behind him, wide as the antlers, looked like the boundaries for a small road, a lane, and within them we sometimes spotted the tracks of the creatures that were following us: the ravens, coyotes, and wolves.

We were descending slowly, and were beginning to see the tracks of other animals again—deer, moose, and elk, though the elk tracks were those of cows and calves, not bulls.

We were down out of the high country and into the dense forest. It was growing warmer at the lower elevation, so that, rather than snow falling, there was a sleety drizzle, which was more chilling than any storm or blizzard. We came across a dropped moose antler, resting upright on the snow—

we could read his tracks leading to it, and leading away from it—and the antler, upturned, was full of water and slush from the sleet. We knelt and took turns drinking from it, without disturbing it. We were almost home. One more night, and the next day. A year's worth of meat, put away safely.

The "Y" on Matthew's back widened, but he was moving stronger again. I was shivering hard by now. I was drenched. For a long time the effort of hauling and skidding the meat had been enough to keep me warm, but now that effort wasn't enough. I was cold and I needed help from the outside. My body could no longer hold off the whole mass of winter. I was without reserves.

"Do you want to stop and light a fire?" Matthew asked, watching my slowing movements, my clumsiness, my giving-upness. I nodded, still lucid enough to know that hypothermia had arrived. Matthew seemed to be a great distance away, and I felt that he was studying me, evaluating me. We were no longer partners in the hunt, brothers in the hunt—brothers in anything—and as my mind began to close down, chamber by chamber, I had the feeling that Matthew was going to let me freeze: that he had run me into the ground, had let me haul out half the elk, and now, only a day's journey from town, he was going to let winter have me. He would carry the rest of the meat out himself, leaving me to disappear beneath the snow.

He stood there waiting. I knelt and slipped out of my pack. I then lost my balance and tipped over in the snow. Not thinking clearly—not thinking at all—I searched through my pack for matches, shivering. I found them, held the small box tightly in my gloved hands, then remembered that I needed wood.

Matthew continued watching me. He had not taken his pack off—as if he had no intention of stopping here anyway—and the antlers had been with him so long that they seemed to be growing out of him. I moved off into the trees and down a slope and began indiscriminately snapping twigs and gathering branches, dropping much of what I picked up. Matthew stayed up on the hill above, watching. The rain and sleet kept coming down. He was drenched, too—there was ice on his antlers—but he seemed to have a fire and a hardness in him that I knew I didn't have.

I heaped the branches, some green and some dry, into a small pile, and began striking matches; and the sodden pile of wood would not light. I tried until I was out of matches, then rose and went back up to my pack to look for more. I was moving slowly and wanted to lie down. I had to keep going, but I knew that I wasn't going to find any more matches.

"This way," Matthew said finally, taking a cigarette lighter of his pack. "Look at me," he said. "Watch." He walked down to the nearest dead tree, an old wind-blasted fir tree, shrouded dense with black hanging lichen. "This is what you do," he said. His words came in breaths of steam rising into the rain. He stood under the canopy of the tree's branches and moss cloak and snapped the lighter a couple of times, holding it right up against the lichen tendrils.

On the third snap the lichen caught, burned blue for a moment, then leapt into quick orange flame.

It was like something chemical—the whole tree, or the shell of lichen around it, metamorphosed into bright crackling fire: the lichen burning explosively and the sudden shock of heat, the updraft, in turn lighting the lichen above, accelerating the rush of flame as if climbing a ladder. It was a forty-foot-tall tree, and it was on fire from top to bottom in about five seconds.

"That's how you do it," Matthew said, stepping back. I had stopped shivering, my blood heated by one last squeeze of adrenaline at the sight; but now, even as I watched the flames, the chill, and then the shivering, returned.

"You'd better get on over there," he said. "They don't burn long."

I walked over to the burning tree. There was a lot of heat; the snow in all directions glistened—but I knew that the heat wasn't going to last. Flaming wisps of lichen separated from the tree and floated upward in curls before cooling and descending. By the time they landed on me, they were almost burnt out—charcoal skeletons of the lichen. A few of the tree's branches burned and crackled, but that was pretty much it; the fire was gone.

I wouldn't say I was warm, but I had stopped shivering.

"Come on," Matthew said. "Let's go find another one." He set off into the rain, the antlers behind him plowing a path.

And that was how we came out of the mountains, in that last night and the next day, moving from tree to tree—looking for the right one, properly dead—through the drizzle, from one tower of flame to the next, Matthew probing the right ones with his cigarette lighter, testing them, always choosing the right ones. That was how we walked through that night—the trees sizzling and steaming after we were done with them—and on into the gray rainy day. We were back into country that I knew well, even underneath all the snow. We were seeing the tracks of wolves, and finding some of their kills. I had stopped shivering, though we continued lighting tree torches—leaving a crooked, wandering path of them behind us.

I suspect that in twenty years I will still be able to trace our journey backward, back up the mountain from torched tree to torched tree. Some will be fallen and rotting black husks, others might still be standing. In twenty years, I'll be able to return to where it all started—that point where we first saw the elk, and then lost him, and then found him again, and killed him. From among the stones and ferns and forest, there will be a piece of charcoal, a fire-blackened rock, an antler in a tree, a rusting saw blade, even a scabbed-over set of initials, where Matthew marked his kill, although as the years go on, those initials will be harder to find, until finally you will have to know exactly where they are, and have some sort of guide, someone who has actually been there before, to show you.

The rut was on as we approached town the next day—the giant bucks chasing the does—and though we were exhausted, we could see that we had to shoot a deer.

As we drew nearer the village—the forest ripe with the scent of rut musk—we saw a swarm of antlers, dozens of bucks prowling the woods, mesmerized by sex, by creation, by the needs of the future, and we were almost home when we saw the buck we wanted.

We saw him because he had seen us, and was coming up the hill toward us—or, rather, toward Matthew. He was drawn by the sight of the giant antlers strapped to Matthew's back. We were moving through dense brush and it's possible that was all he could see, and he came forward with a strange aggression. He was wet from the rain. His antlers were black-brown, from his having lived in a dark forest, and rose three feet above his head and extended beyond the tips of his outstretched ears. It did not seem possible that he could carry such a weight on his head. Matthew dropped to his knees. The deer stopped, then came closer, still entranced by the antlers, and Matthew raised his rifle and shot the deer through the neck, now not twenty yards away.

The deer's head snapped back, and we saw a thin pattern of blood spray across the snow behind him, but the deer did not drop. Instead it whirled and ran down the hill, hard and strong.

I wondered if Matthew could ever finish anything gracefully.

We had to track it.

The snow was deep and slushy. There was little if any blood trail to follow, and the big buck's tracks merged with hundreds of others: the carnival of the rut. We stood there in the hissing, steady rain, breathing our own milky vapors.

"Fuck," Matthew said. He looked down toward the river in the direction the buck had run. He dropped his pack in the snow. The bloody "Y" on his chest was the same as the one on his back; the two together were like the delicate, perfect, world-shaped markings on the wings of some obscure tropical butterfly. I dropped my pack as well. A blood trail was beginning to form on my own back and chest.

Not to be wearing a pack after having carried one for so long gave us a feeling like flight; as if, suddenly, we could have gone for another seventy-five miles. We rested a moment, then donned our packs again. The rain and slush continued to beat down on us. We kept stopping to rest, ass-whipped. We began lighting trees again—tree after tree, following the wounded buck's tracks.

A drop of blood here; a loose hair there.

We found the buck down at the river, in a backwater slough, thrashing around in six feet of water, having broken through a skin of thawing ice as he tried to cross. We watched him for a moment as he swam in circles with only his head and the tower of antlers above the water. He was chok-ing on his blood, coughing sprays of it across the water with each exha-lation, and swallowing blood with each breath—the bullet had missed an artery, but severed a vessel—and his face was a red mask of blood.

He glared at us as he swam—a red king, defiant. It was a strange sight, those giant antlers going around and around in the small pond—like some new creature being born into the world. Matthew raised his rifle, waited for the deer to swim back around, closer to the edge of the shore.

The deer continued to watch us as it swam—head held high, drowning in blood. Matthew shot it in the neck again, breaking it this time, and the deer stopped swimming. The antlers sank.

We sat and stared at it for a long time—watching it motionless through the refraction of water—as if expecting it to come back to life.

Another buck, following the trail of the giant's hock musk, appeared on the other side of the pond, lowered its head, trying to decipher the cone of scent that had drifted its way.

We travelled upriver to where Matthew had left the canoe. It was un-der a shell of snow. We got it out and went and got the elk and loaded it, part by part, into the canoe, until the canoe was low in the water. Dusk was coming on again and we could see a few lights across the river, the lights of town. We had been gone only two weeks but it felt like a century.

I stayed behind while Matthew made two crossings with the meat; then he came back for me. The rain had stopped and the sky was clear-ing and Matthew said we had to get the deer out now as the pond would freeze thick if we waited until the next day.

We waded out into the pond together. The water was slightly warmer than the air. Under water the deer was light, and we were able to muscle him awkwardly up to the shore. Then we dragged him over to the canoe—gutted him quickly—loaded him, and set out across one more time, rid-ing lower than ever. Freezing seemed to be a more imminent danger than drowning, but we reached the other shore, sledded the canoe up onto the gravel, and finally we quit; abandoned the meat, hundreds of pounds of it, only a short distance from home, and ran stumbling and falling up the hill toward town.

Lights were on in the bar. We went straight in and lay down next to the big woodstove, shivering and in pain. The bartenders, Artie and Charlie, came over with blankets and hides and began helping us out of our wet clothes and wrapping the hides around us. They started heating water on the stove for baths and making hot tea for us to drink; it was the first fluid we'd had in days that was neither snow nor cold creek water, and the heat of it made us vomit the second the hot tea hit our stomachs. Artie looked at the meat we had spit up and said, "They got an elk."

*This story resembles Hemingway's "The Short Happy Life of Francis Ma-
comber" in that both feature African big game and are dangerous for the
hunters. But this is a spoof, set at a man-made hunting preserve outside
Bakersfield, California. Clearly inspired by Hemingway's classic, it is highly
original and splendidly carried off. T. Coraghessan Boyle is a frequent contributor to the* New Yorker, Playboy, Esquire, *and* Harper's. *He is the author of seven novels and, most recently,* T. C. Boyle Stories *(1999). Boyle is
the founder and director of the creative writing program at the University of
Southern California.*

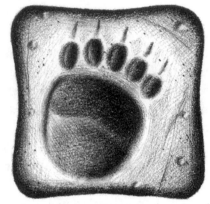

T. Coraghessan Boyle
BIG GAME (1994)

*The way to hunt is for as long as you live against as long as there is such and such
an animal.*

—Ernest Hemingway, *Green Hills of Africa*

YOU COULD SHOOT ANYTHING you wanted, for a price, even the
elephant, but Bernard tended to discourage the practice. It made an awful mess, for one thing, and when all was said and done it was the big animals—the elephant, the rhino, the water buff and giraffe—that gave the
place its credibility, not to mention ambiance. They weren't exactly easy
to come by, either. He still regretted the time he'd let the kid from the
heavy-metal band pot one of the giraffes—even though he'd taken a cool
twelve thousand dollars to the bank on that one. And then there was the
idiot from MGM who opened up on a herd of zebra and managed to

decapitate two ostriches and lame the Abyssinian ass in the process. Well, it came with the territory, he supposed, and it wasn't as if he didn't carry enough insurance on the big stuff to buy out half the L.A. Zoo if he had to. He was just lucky nobody had shot himself in the foot yet. Or the head. Of course, he was insured for that, too.

Bernard Puff pushed himself up from the big mahogany table and flung the dregs of his coffee down the drain. He wasn't exactly over-wrought, but he was edgy, his stomach sour and clenched round the im-permeable lump of his breakfast cruller, his hands afflicted with the little starts and tremors of the coffee shakes. He lit a cigarette to calm himself and gazed out the kitchen window on the dromedary pen, where one of the moth-eaten Arabians was methodically peeling the bark from an elm tree. He looked at the thing in amazement, as if he'd never seen it be-fore—the flexible lip and stupid eyes, the dully working jaw—and made a mental note to offer a special on camels. The cigarette tasted like tin, like death. Somewhere a catbird began to call out in its harsh mewling tones.

The new people were due any minute now, and the prospect of new people always set him off—there were just too many things that could go wrong. Half of them didn't know one end of a rifle from the other, they expected brunch at noon and a massage an hour later, and they bitched about everything, from the heat to the flies to the roaring of the lions at night. Worse: they didn't seem to know what to make of him, the men regarding him as a subspecies of the blue-collar buddy, regaling him with a nonstop barrage of lickerish grins, dirty jokes and fractured grammar, and the women treating him like a cross between a maître d' and a water carrier. Dudes and greenhorns, all of them. Parvenus. Moneygrubbers. The kind of people who wouldn't know class if it bit them.

Savagely snubbing out the cigarette in the depths of the coffee mug, Bernard wheeled round on the balls of his feet and plunged through the swinging doors and out into the high dark hallway that gave onto the foyer. It was stifling already, the overhead fans chopping uselessly at the dead air round his ears and the sweat prickling at his new-shaven jowls as he stomped down the hall, a big man in desert boots and khaki shorts, with too much belly and something overeager and graceless in his stride. There was no one in the foyer and no one at the registration desk. (Espinoza was out feeding the animals—Bernard could hear the hyenas whooping in the distance—and the new girl—what was her name?—hadn't made it to work on time yet. Not once.) The place seemed deserted, though he knew Orbalina would be making up the beds and Roland sneaking a drink somewhere—probably out behind the lion cages.

For a long moment Bernard stood there in the foyer, framed against a bristling backdrop of kudu and oryx heads, as he checked the reservation card for the tenth time that morning:

> Mike and Nicole Bender
> Bender Realty
> 15125 Ventura Blvd.
> Encino, California

Real estate people. Jesus. He'd always preferred the movie crowd—or even the rock-and-rollers, with their spiked wristbands and pouf hairdos. At least they were willing to buy into the illusion that Puff's African Game Ranch, situated on twenty-five hundred acres just outside Bakersfield, was the real thing—the Great Rift Valley, the Ngorongoro Crater, the Serengeti—but the real estate people saw every crack in the plaster. And all they wanted to know was how much he'd paid for the place and was the land subdividable.

He looked up into the yellow-toothed grin of the sable mounted on the wall behind him—the sable his father had taken in British East Africa back in the thirties—and let out a sigh. Business was business, and in the long run it didn't matter a whit who perforated his lions and gazelles— just as long as they paid. And they always paid, up front and in full. Bernard saw to that.

"What was it, Nik, six months ago when we went to Gino Parducci's for dinner? It was six months, wasn't it? And didn't I say we'd do the African thing in six months? Didn't I?"

Nicole Bender was curled up in the passenger seat of the white Jaguar XJS her husband had given her for Valentine's Day. A pile of knitting magazines lay scattered in her lap, atop a set of bamboo needles trailing an embryonic garment in a shade so pale it defied categorization. She was twenty-seven, blond, a former actress/model/poet/singer whose trainer had told her just two days earlier that she had perhaps the most perfectly sculpted physique of any woman he'd ever worked with. Of course, he was paid to say things like that, but in her heart she suspected they were true, and she needed to hear them. She turned to her husband. "Yes," she said. "You did. But I pictured us in Kenya or Tanzania, to tell the truth."

"Yeah, yeah," he fired back impatiently, "yeah, yeah, yeah," the words coming so fast they might have been bullets squeezed from one of the glistening new big-bore rifles in the trunk, "but you know I can't take six weeks off from work, not now when the new Beverly Hills office is about to open up and the Montemoretto deal is all but in the bag . . . and besides, it's dangerous over there, what with the next revolution or war or whatever coming down every six minutes, and who do you think they're going to blame when the roof caves in? White people, right? And where do you think you'll want to be then?"

Mike Bender was a barely contained factory of energy, a steamroller of a man who had risen from receptionist to king and despot of his own real estate empire in the space of twelve short years. He was given to speechifying, the precious words dropping from his lips like coins from a slot machine, his fingertips alighting on his tongue, his hair, his ears, the crotch of his pants and his elbows as he spoke, writhing with the nervous energy that had made him rich. "And plus you've got your tsetse flies and black mambas and beriberi and the plague and god knows what all over there—I mean, picture Mexico, only a hundred times worse. No, listen, trust me—Gino swore this place is as close as it gets to the real thing, only without the hassles." He lowered his sunglasses to give her a look. "You're telling me you really want to get your ass chewed off in some lopsided tent in, in"—he couldn't seem to think of a place sufficiently grim, so he improvised—"Zambeziland?"

Nicole shrugged, giving him a glimpse of the pouty little half-smile she used to work up for the photographers when she was nineteen and doing the summerwear ads for JCPenney.

"You'll get your zebra-skin rug yet, you wait and see," Mike assured her, "and a couple lions' heads and gazelles or whatever for the wall in the den, okay?"

The Jaguar shot across the desert like a beam of light. Nicole lifted the knitting needles from her lap, thought better of it, and set them down again. "Okay," she said in a breathy little whisper, "but I just hope this place isn't too, you know, *tacky*."

A sudden harsh laugh erupted from the back seat, where Mike Bender's twelve-year-old daughter, Jasmine Honeysuckle Rose Bender, was stretched out supine with the last ten issues of *Bop* and a sixpack of New York Seltzer. "Get real, will you? I mean like shooting lions in Bakersfield? Tacky city. Tacky, tacky, tacky."

Up front, behind the wheel, his buttocks caressed by the supple kid leather of the seat and visions of bontebok leaping before his eyes, Mike Bender was mildly annoyed. He'd had an itch to hunt lion and elephant and rhino since he was a kid and first read *Confessions of a White Hunter* and the Classic Comics version of *King Solomon's Mines*. And this was his chance. So maybe it wasn't Africa, but who had the time to go on safari? If he could spare three days he was lucky. And you couldn't shoot anything over there anyway. Not anymore. Everything was a preserve now, a game park, a conservancy. There were no more white hunters. Just photographers.

He wanted to say "Give me a break, will you?" in his most imperious voice, the voice that sent his sales force scurrying for cover and his competitors into shock, but he held his peace. Nothing was going to ruin this for him. Nothing.

It was midafternoon. The sun hung overhead like an egg shirred in a cup. The thermometer in the feed shed was pushing a hundred and fifteen degrees, nothing was moving but for the vultures aloft in the poor bleached expanse of the sky, and the whole world seemed to have gone to sleep.

Except for Bernard. Bernard was beside himself—the Benders had been due at 10:00 A.M. and here it was quarter past two and still they hadn't arrived. He'd had Espinoza let the Tommies and eland out of their pens at nine, but he was afraid they'd all be lying up in the heat, and by noon he'd sent him out to round them up again. The giraffes were nowhere to be seen, and the elephant, tethered to a live oak Bernard had pruned to resemble an umbrella thorn, was looking as rumpled and dusty as a heap of Taiwanese luggage abandoned at the airport.

Bernard stood in the glare of the dried-up yard, squinting out on the screen of elephant grass and euphorbia he'd planted to hide the oil rig (if you knew it was there you could just detect the faintest motion of the big steel arm as it rose and fell and rose and fell again). He felt hopeless. For all the effort he'd put into it, the place looked like a circus camp, the bombed-out remains of a zoo, a dusty flat baking former almond ranch in the sun-blasted southeast corner of the San Joaquin Valley—which is exactly what it was. What would the Benders think? More important, what would they think at six hundred dollars a day, payable in advance, plus prices that ranged from a thousand a pop on the gazelles on up to twelve thousand for a lion and "priced as available" for the elephant? Real estate people had balked on him before, and business hadn't exactly been booming lately.

The vultures wheeled overhead. He was running sweat. The sun felt like a firm hand steering him toward the cool of the kitchen and a tall glass of quinine water (which he drank for effect rather than therapeutic value: there wasn't a malarial mosquito within a thousand miles). He was just about to pack it in when he caught the distant glint of sun on safety glass and saw the Benders' car throwing up dust clouds at the far end of the drive.

"Roland!" he bellowed, and every mortal ounce of him was in motion now, "Let the monkeys out into the trees! And the parrots!" Suddenly he was jogging across the dusty lot and up the path to where the elephant lay collapsed beneath the tree. He was working at the slip of the tether to set her loose and wondering if Roland would have the sense to stir up the lions and hyenas for the sake of sound effects, when suddenly she rose to her feet with a great blowing snort and gave a feeble trumpet.

Well. And that was a break—at least now he wouldn't have to use the ivory goad.

Bernard looked up at the old elephant in wonder—she still had a bit of showmanship in her, after all. Either that, or it was senile dementia. She was old—Bernard didn't know quite how old, though he did know she was a veteran of thirty-eight years with the Ringling Bros. and Barnum & Bailey Circus who'd performed under the name "Bessie Bee" and responded to "Shamba"—that is, if you happened to have the ivory goad in your hand. Bernard shot a glance up the drive, where a white Jaguar sedan was beginning to define itself against a billowing backdrop of dust, and then he heard the screech of the monkeys as they shot out of their cages and up into the trees, and he began to compose himself. He forced a smile, all red-cheeked and long-toothed, cinched the leopard-skin belt, squared his pith helmet and marched forward to greet his guests.

By the time the Benders rolled up to the veranda, the parrots were in the trees, the marabou stork was pecking at a spot of offal in the dirt, and the lions were roaring lustily from their hidden pens out back. Roland, decked out in his Masai toga and lion's-tooth necklace, bounded down the steps with alacrity to hold open the door for Bender, while Bessie Bee shambled around in the near distance, flapping her ears and blowing about in the dust. "Mr. Bender," Bernard cried, extending his hand to a fortyish man in sunglasses and polo shirt, "welcome to Africa."

Bender sprang out of the car like a child at the zoo. He was tall, lean, tanned—why did they all have to look like tennis pros? Bernard wondered—and stood there twitching a moment in the heat. He pumped Bernard's hand professionally and then launched into a lip-jerking, ear-tugging, foot-thumping apology: "Sorry we're late, Bernard, but my wife—have you met my wife?—my wife just had to get a couple rolls of film and we wound up buying out half of Reynoso's Camera in Bakersfield—you know it?—good prices. Real good prices. Hell, we needed a new video camera anyway, especially with"—he gestured to take in the house, the outbuildings, the elephant, the monkeys in the trees and the sun-blasted plains beyond—"all this."

Bernard was nodding, smiling, murmuring agreement, but he was on autopilot—his attention was fixed on the wife, whom Roland was fussing over now on the far side of the car. She raised her lovely white arms to fluff her hair and imprison her eyes behind a pair of sunglasses and Bernard called out a greeting in his best British-colonial accent (though he was British by ancestry only and had never in his life been east of Reno). The second wife, of course, he was thinking as she returned his greeting with a vague little pouting smile.

"Yes, yes, of course," Bernard said in response to some further idiocy from the husband's lips, his water blue eyes shifting to the daughter now—as black-headed as an Indian, and nearly as dark—and he saw right away that she was trouble, the sort of child who cultivates ugliness as a weapon.

Nicole Bender gave him a long slow appraisal over the hood of the car, and in the next moment he was ducking round the grille to squeeze her hand as if he were trying on a glove for size. "Beastly day," he said, proud of the Britishism, and then he was leading her up the broad stone steps and into the house, while her husband fumbled with an armload of guns and the daughter slouched along behind, already complaining about something in a nagging querulous little whine of a voice.

"I'm not saying that, Mike—you're not listening to me. I *said* the gazelles are very nice and they'll be perfect for the office, but I wanted something, well, *bigger* for the front hall and at least three of the zebra—two for the den, I thought, and we're going to need one for the ski lodge . . . you know, to hide that ugly paneling behind the bar?"

Mike Bender was deep into his fourth gin and tonic. Already the elation he'd felt over his first kill had begun to dissipate, replaced now by a gnawing sense of frustration and anger—why couldn't Nikki shut her face, even for a second? No sooner had they changed clothes and got out there on the savannah or veldt or whatever you wanted to call it, than she'd started in. He'd squeezed off a clean shot at a Thomson's gazelle at two hundred yards and before the thing's head had hit the ground, she was running it down. *Oh,* she gasped, as if she'd been surprised on the toilet, *but it's so small, isn't it?* And then she struck a pose for Puff and the colored guy who carried the guns and skinned out the carcasses. *Almost like a rabbit with horns.*

And now the great white hunter was leaning across the table to reassure her, his gut drawn tight against the khaki safari shirt, his accent so phony it was like something out of a Monty Python routine. "Mrs. Bender, Nicole," he began, mopping his blood blister of a face with a big checked handkerchief, "we'll go out for zebra in the morning, when it's cool, and if it's three you want, we'll get them, there's no problem with that. Four, if you like. Five. If you've got the bullets, we've got the game."

Mike watched as the canny crewcut head swiveled toward him. "And Mike," Puff said, as amenable as any tour guide but with just the right hint of stagery in his voice, "in the evening, it's the big stuff, the man-maker, old Simba himself."

As if in response, there was a cough and roar from somewhere out beyond the darkened windows, and Mike Bender could feel the wildness of it on the thin night air—lion, the lion he'd dreamed about since his aunt had taken him to the Central Park Zoo as a boy and the roar of the great shaggy yellow-eyed things had shaken him to his primordial root. To be out there, in that African night that was haunted with predators, big-headed and thick-skinned, the pounce, the slash, the crack of sinew and bone—it was at once terrifying and wonderful. But what was that smell of oil?

"What do you say, old man? Are you game?" Puff was leering at him now, and behind Puff's blocky leonine figure, the faces of his wife and daughter, arrayed like tribal masks.

Nothing fazed Mike Bender, the King of Encino. No seller could hold out against him, no buyer hope for more. His contracts were vises, his promotions sledgehammers, his holdings as solid as a mountain of iron. "I'm game," he said, touching his lips, running his fingers through his hair, jabbing at his elbows and underarms in a rising plume of metabolic excess. "Just oil up my H&H Magnum and point me toward 'em; it's what I've wanted all my life—"

There was a silence and his words seemed to hang in the air, empty of conviction. His daughter crouched over her plate, looking as if she were sucking on something rotten; his wife had that alert, let's-go-shopping look in her glittering little eyes. "Really. I mean, ever since I was a kid, and—how many are out there, anyway? Or do you keep count?"

Puff stroked the graying stubble of his head. There was another roar, muted this time, followed by the stabbed-in-the belly whoop of the hyena. "Oh, we've got a good-sized pride out there—twelve or fourteen, I'd say, and a few rogue males."

"Are there any big ones, with manes? That's what we want." He shifted his gaze to Nicole. "Maybe the whole thing, stuffed, standing up on its hind legs, what do you think, Nik? For maybe the reception room at the Beverly Hills office?" And then he made a joke of it: "Hey, if Prudential can get away with it—".

Nicole looked satisfied. So did Puff. But his daughter wasn't about to let him off so easily. She let out a snort of contempt, and the three of them turned toward her. "And so you go and kill some poor lion that isn't hurting anybody, and what's that supposed to prove?"

Puff exchanged a look with him, as if to say, *Now isn't that adorable?*

Jasmine Honeysuckle Rose pushed aside her salad plate. Her hair hung in her eyes in greasy black coils. She'd eaten nothing, having separated the tomatoes from the greens and the greens from the croutons and the croutons from the garbanzo beans. "Sting," she spat, "Brigitte Bardot, the New Kids, all of them say it's like animal deaths camps, like Hitler, and they're doing this special concert to save the animals in France, in Paris—"

"One lion more or less isn't going to hurt anybody," Nicole said, cutting the child off, and her mouth was drawn tight against the swell of her collagen-enhanced lips. "And I think your father's idea is super. An erect lion standing there as people come in the door—it's, it's symbolic is what it is."

Mike Bender couldn't tell if he was being ribbed or not. "Listen, Jasmine," he began, and his leg started to thump under the table as he tugged at his ear and fooled with his cutlery.

"Jasmine Honeysuckle Rose," she fired back.

Mike knew she'd always hated her name, an inspiration of her mother, the sort of crackbrained woman who saw spirits in the sunset and believed that he was the reincarnation of John D. Rockefeller. To throw it up to him, and to remind him of his ex-wife and all the mistakes he'd ever made or contemplated, his daughter insisted on her full name. Always.

"Okay: Jasmine Honeysuckle Rose," he said, "listen to me. All of this hippie-dippy save-the-environment crap might be all right if you're twelve, but you've got to realize hunting is as natural a part of man as, as—"

"Eating or drinking," Puff put in, rounding off the participle with a pseudo-Etonian ring.

"*Right!*" Jasmine cried, on her feet now, her eyes like sinkholes, her mouth twitching at the corners. "And so's shitting, farting and, and *fucking!*" And then she was gone, stamping down the trophy-hung hallway to her room, where she flung the door to with a thunderous crash.

A moment of silence descended on the table. Puff's eyes lingered on Nicole as she raised her arms to stretch and show off her breasts and the prim white pockets of shaved flesh under her arms. "Cute kid, huh?" he said. There was no mistaking the sarcasm this time.

"Real cute," Nicole said, and they were in league.

Turning to Mike as the colored guy came through the door with a platter of gazelle steaks and mesquite-roasted ears of corn, Puff let his voice grow warm and confidential. "Zebra in the morning, Mike," he said. "You'll like that." He leveled his watery gaze on him. "And then"—the gazelle steaks hitting the table, little dollops of blood-running flesh— "and then we load up for lion."

It wasn't that he bolted, actually—Bernard had seen worse, much worse— but he was on the verge of it. Either that or he was about to pass out. Any way you sliced it, it was a bad situation, the kind of encounter that made Bernard wish he'd never heard of Africa, lions, game parks or real estate people.

They'd come on the lion in the old almond grove. The trees there were like twisted antlers, leafless and dead, set out in rows as far as you could see, and the ground beneath them was littered with fallen branches. "Not too close now," Bernard had warned, but Bender wanted to be sure of the shot, and he got himself in a bind. In the next moment he was standing there knee-keep in the litter, jerking and shrugging like a spastic, the gun to his shoulder and nowhere to go, and the lion was coming at him with as much pure malice as Bernard had seen in his fourteen years as proprietor of Puff's African Game Ranch. And while Bernard didn't like to intervene—it always caused hard feelings after the fact—Mrs. Bender was a heartbeat away from being an aggrieved widow and his own insurance rates were about to go through the roof, never mind the lawsuits. It was a moment, no doubt about it.

The night before, after the Benders had gone off to bed, Bernard had had Espinoza go out and stir up the lions a bit and then set them loose—without their supper. That always put them in a mood, no matter how old, toothless and gimpy they might be. Let them go a night without horse meat and they were as savage as anything you'd encounter anywhere on earth. For Bernard, it was standard practice. Give the guests their money's worth, that was his motto. If they suspected that the lions were penned up ninety-nine percent of the time, none of them let on—for all they knew the beasts lived out there among the drought-ravaged almond trees and camouflaged oil rigs. And besides, it wasn't as if they had anywhere to go—the entire property was circumscribed by a twenty-foot-deep dry moat with a twelve-foot-high electrified fence rising up behind it. The ones the guests didn't put holes in would just wander back to their cages in a day or so, roaring their bellies out for horse meat and offal.

In the morning, after a breakfast of kippers and eggs and while the daughter slept in, Bernard had taken the Benders out after their zebra. They'd driven out to the water hole—an abandoned Olympic-sized swimming pool Bernard had planted up to look natural—and, after some discussion of price, the Benders—or, rather, the wife—decided on five. She was something, the wife. As good-looking a woman as Bernard had ever laid eyes on, and a better shot than her husband. She took two of the zebra at a hundred and fifty yards, barely a mark on the hides. "You can shoot, little lady," Bernard said as they sauntered up to the nearest of the fallen zebra.

The zebra lay there on its side beneath the knifing sun, and already the first flies had begun to gather. Bender was crouched over one of the carcasses in the near distance, inspecting it for bullet holes, and Roland was back in the Jeep, whetting his skinning knife. From the hills beyond, one of the starved lions let loose with an irascible roar.

Nicole smiled at him, pretty—awfully pretty—in her Banana Republic shorts and safari shirt. "I try," she said, unbuttoning her shirt to reveal a peach-colored halter top decorated with a gold pin in the shape of a rifle. He had to bend close to read the inscription: *Nicole Bender, Supermarksman Award, N.R.A., 1989.*

Then it was lunch and siesta, followed by gin and bitters and a few hands at canasta to while away the waning hours of the afternoon. Bernard did everything he could to amuse the lady, and not just in the interest of business—there was something there, something beating hot and hard beneath the mask of blusher and eyeliner and the puffed-up lips, and he couldn't help feeling the tug of it. It had been tough since Stella Rae had left him, and he took his tumbles where he could find them—after all, *that* came with the territory too.

At any rate, they took the Jeep Wrangler, a cooler of beer, Bender's .375 Holland & Holland, the lady's Winchester .458 Mag and his own stopper—the .600 Nitro—and headed out to where the twisted black branches of the orchard raked the flanks of the hills in the far corner of the ranch. It was where the lions always went when you set them loose. There was a little brook there—it was a torrent in season, but now it wasn't much more than a trickle. Still, they could lap up some water and roll in the grass and find a poor striped shade beneath the naked branches of the trees.

From the start, even when they were still on the gin and bitters and waiting out the heat, Bender had seemed edgy. The man couldn't sit still, rattling on about escrows and titles and whatnot, all the while tugging at his lips and ears and tongue like a third-base coach taking signals from the dugout. It was nerves, that's what it was: Bernard had taken enough dudes out there to recognize a fellow measuring out his own manhood against that big tawny thing stalking his imagination. One guy—he was a TV actor; maybe a fag, even—had got himself so worked up he'd overloaded on the gin and pissed his pants before they got the Jeep started. Bernard had seen him a hundred times since on the flickering tube, a hulking muscular character with a cleft chin and flashing eyes who was forever smashing crooks in the face and snaring women by the waist, but he could never forget the way the guy's eyes had vanished in his head as the piss stain spread from his crotch to his thighs and beyond. He took one look at Bender and knew there was trouble on the horizon.

They'd agreed on $11,500 for a big male with a mane, Bernard knocking off the odd five hundred because they'd taken the two extra zebra and he figured he'd give them a break. The only male he had of any size was Claude, who must have been something in his day but was now the leonine equivalent of a nonagenarian living on a diet of mush in a nursing home. Bernard had picked him up for a song at a flea-bitten circus in Guadalajara, and he must have been twenty-five years old if he was a day. He was half-blind, he stank like one of the walking dead and the molars on the lower left side of his jaw were so rotten he howled though his food when he ate. But he looked the part, especially at a distance, and he still carried some of the flesh he'd put on in his youth—and the pain in his jaw made him cranky; savage, even. He would do, Bernard had thought. He would do just fine.

But there was Bender, stuck in a morass of dead black branches, trembling all over like a man in an ice bath, and the lion coming at him. The first shot skipped in the dirt at two hundred feet and took Claude's left hind paw off at the joint, and he gave out with a roar of such pure raging claw-gutting bone-crunching nastiness that the idiot nearly dropped his rifle. Or so it seemed from where Bernard was standing with the Mrs. and Roland, fifteen yards back and with the angle to the right. Claude was a surprise. Instead of folding up into himself and skittering for the bushes, he came on, tearing up the dirt and roaring as if he'd been set afire—and Bender was jerking and twitching and twitter-ing so much he couldn't have hit the side of a beer truck. Bernard could feel his own heart going as he lifted the Nitro to his shoulder, and then there was the head-thumping blast of the gun and old Claude suddenly looked like a balled-up carpet with a basket of ground meat spread on top of it.

Bender turned to him with a white face. "What the—?" he stammered, and he was jerking at his fingers and flailing his arms. "What do you think you're doing?"

It was Bernard's moment. A jetliner rode high overhead, bound for the northwest, a silver rivet in the sky. There was an absolute, unutterable si-lence. The wife held her peace, the remaining lions cowered somewhere in the grass and every bird on the ranch was holding its breath in the dy-ing wake of that rolling cannonade. "Saving your bloody life," Bernard snarled, hot and disgusted and royally pissed off, but proud, as always, of the Britishism.

Mike Bender was angry—too angry to eat his kippered whatever and the deep-fried toast and runny eggs. And where was the coffee, for god's sake? They were in Bakersfield, after all, and not some canvas tent in Uganda. He barked at the colored guy—all tricked up to look like a na-tive, but with an accent right out of Compton—and told him he wanted coffee, black and strong, even if he had to drive to Oildale for it. Nicole sat across the table and watched him with mocking eyes. *Her* zebra had been perfect, but he'd fouled up two of the three he'd shot: *But Mike,* she'd said, *we can't hang these—they'll look like colanders.* And then the busi-ness with the lion. He'd looked bad on that one, and what was worse, he was out eleven and a half thousand bucks and there was nothing to show for it. Not after Puff blew the thing away. It was just meat and bone, that's all. Shit, the thing didn't even *have* a head after the great white hunter got done with it.

"C'mon, Mike," Nicole said, and she reached out to pat his hand but he snatched it away in a rage. "C'mon, baby, it's not the end of the world." He looked at her in that moment, the triumph shining in her eyes, and he wanted to slap her, choke her, get up from the table, snatch a rifle from the rack and pump a couple slugs into her.

He was about to snap back at her when the swinging doors to the kitchen parted and the colored guy came in with a pot of coffee and set it on the table. Roland, that was his name. He was surprised they didn't call him Zulu or Jambo or something to go along with the silly skirts that were supposed to make him look like a native. Christ, he'd like to get up and drill him too, for that matter. About the only break he'd had on this trip was that Jasmine Honeysuckle Rose had taken to sleeping till noon.

"Mike," Nicole pleaded, but he wouldn't hear her. Brooding, burning, plotting his revenge on every lender, shopkeeper and homeowner from the San Fernando Valley to Hancock Park, Mike Bender sipped moodily at his tepid instant coffee and awaited the great white hunter.

Puff was late to breakfast, but he looked rejuvenated—had he dyed his hair, was that it?—beaming, a fountain of energy, as if he'd stolen the flame from the King of Encino himself. "Good morning," he boomed in his phony West End accent, practically inhaling his mustache, and then he gave Nicole a look that was unmistakable and Mike felt it all pouring out of him, like lava from a volcano.

"No more lions, right?" Mike said, his voice low and choked.

"Afraid not," Puff answered, sitting himself down at the head of the table and smearing a slab of toast with Marmite. "As I told you yesterday, we've got all the females you want, but the males are juveniles, no manes at all to speak of."

"That stinks."

Bernard regarded Bender for a long moment and saw the child who'd never grown up, the rich kid, the perennial hacker and duffer, the parvenu stifled. He looked from Bender to the wife and back again—what was she doing with a clown like that?—and had a fleeting but powerful vision of her stretched out beside him in bed, breasts, thighs, puffy lips and all. "Listen, Mike," he said, "forget it. It happens to everybody. I thought we'd go for eland today—"

"*Eland*. Shit on eland."

"All right, then—water buff. A lot of them say Mbogo is the most dangerous animal in Africa, bar none."

The sunny eyes went dark with rage. "This isn't Africa," Bender spat. "It's Bakersfield."

Bernard had tried hard, and he hated it when they did that, when they punctured the illusion he so carefully nurtured. It was the illusion he was selling, after all—close your eyes and you're in Africa—and in a way he'd wanted the place to *be* Africa, wanted to make the old stories come alive, wanted to bring back the thrill of the great days, if only for a moment at a time. But it was more than that, too: Puff's African Game Ranch stood as a testament and memorial to the towering figure of Bernard's father.

Bernard Puff, Sr., had been one of the last great white hunters of East Africa—friend and compatriot of Percival and Ionides, host to some of the biggest names of American cinema and European aristocracy. He married an American heiress and they built a place in the White Highlands, dined with Isak Dinesen, ate game the year round. And then the war turned the place on its head and he sought refuge in America, losing himself in the vastness of the Southwest and the pockets of his in-laws. As a boy, Bernard had thrilled to the stories of the old days, fingering the ragged white scar a bush pig's tusks had left on his father's forearm, cleaning and oiling the ancient weapons that had stopped rhino, elephant, leopard and lion, gazing for hours into the bright glass eyes of the trophies mounted on the wall in the den, the very names—sable, kudu, bushbuck, kongoni—playing like an incantation in his head. He'd tried to do it justice, had devoted his life to it, and now here was this sorehead, this condominium peddler, running it all down.

"All right," he said. "Granted. What do you want me to do? I've got more lions coming in at the end of the month, prime cats they've trapped and relocated from Tsavo East . . ." (He was fudging here: actually, he had an emaciated sack of bones lined up at the San Francisco Zoo, a cat so old the public was offended by it, and another that had broken its leg three times jumping through a hoop with a West German circus.) "Eland we have, water buff, oryx, gazelle, hyena—I've even got a couple ostrich for you. But unless you want a female, no lion. I'm sorry."

And then, a light shining up from the depths, the glitter came back into the dealmaker's eyes, the smile widened, the tennis pro and backyard swimmer climbed out from behind the mask of the petulant real estate wonder boy. Bender was grinning. He leaned forward. "What about the elephant?"

"What about it?" Bernard lifted the toast to his lips, then set it down carefully again on the edge of his plate. The wife was watching him now, and Roland, refilling the coffee mugs, paused to give him a look.

"I want it."

Bernard stared down at the plate and fussed a moment with the coffeepot, the sugar, the cream. He hated to part with her, though he was pretty sure he could replace her—and the feed bills were killing him. Even in her dotage, Bessie Bee could put away more in an afternoon than a herd of Guernseys would go through in a winter. He gave the wife a cool glance, then shot his eyes at Bender. "Eighteen grand," he said.

Bender looked uncertain, his eyes glittering still, but sunk in on themselves, as if in awe at the enormity of the deal. "I'll want the head," he said finally, "the whole thing, stuffed and mounted—and yes, I know it's big, but I can deal with that, I've got the space, believe me . . . and the feet, I want the feet, for those, uh, what do you call them, umbrella stands?"

They found her in a brushy ravine, just beyond the swimming-pool-cum-water-hole. She was having a dust bath, powdering her pitted hide with fine pale dirt till she looked like an enormous wad of dough rolled in flour. Bernard could see where she'd trampled the high grass that hid the blue lip of the pool and uprooted half a ton of water lily and cattail, which she'd mounded up in a festering heap on the coping. He cursed under his breath when he saw the stand of eucalyptus she'd reduced to splinters and the imported fever tree she'd stripped of bark. It was his policy to keep her tethered—precisely to avoid this sort of wholesale destruction—but when there were guests on the ranch, he let her roam. He was regretting it now, and thinking he'd have to remember to get Espinoza to call the landscaping company first thing in the morning, when

Bender's voice brought him back to the moment. The voice was harsh, petulant, a rising squawk of protest: "But it's only got one tusk!"

Bernard sighed. It was true—she'd broken off half her left tusk somewhere along the line, but he'd gotten so used to her he hardly noticed. But there was Bender, sitting beside him in the Jeep, the wife in the back, the guns stacked up and the cooler full, and Bender was going to try to gouge him on the price, he could see it coming.

"When we said eighteen, I assumed we were talking a trophy animal," Bender said, and Bernard turned to him. "But now, I don't know."

Bernard just wanted it over with. Something told him he was making a mistake in going after Bessie Bee—the place wouldn't seem the same without her—but he was committed at this point, and he didn't want any arguments. "Okay," he sighed, shifting the weight of his paunch from left to right. "Seventeen."

"Sixteen."

"Sixteen-five, and that's as low as I'm going to go. You don't know what it's like to skin out something like this, let alone disposing of the carcass."

"You're on," Bender said, swiveling his head to give the wife a look, and then they were out of the Jeep and checking their weapons. Bender had a .470 Rigby elephant rifle and Bernard his Nitro—just in case the morning brought a reprise of the lion fiasco. The wife, who wasn't doing any shooting, had brought along a video camera. Roland was back at the house with a truck, a chain saw and a crew of Mexicans to clean up the mess once the deed was done.

It was still early, and the heat hadn't come up full yet—Bernard guessed it must have been eighty, eighty-five or so—but he was sweating already. He was always a little edgy on a hunt—especially with a clown like Bender twitching at his elbow, and most especially after what had happened with the lion. Bender was writhing and stamping up a storm, but his eyes were cool and focused as they strolled through the mesquite and tumbleweed and down into the ravine.

Bessie Bee was white with dust, flapping her ears and blowing up great clouds of it with her trunk. From a hundred yards you couldn't see much more than flying dirt, as if a tornado had touched down; at fifty, the rucked and seamed head of the old elephant began to take on shape. Though there was little more risk involved than in potting a cow in its stall, Bernard was habitually cautious, and he stopped Bender there, at fifty yards. A pair of vultures drifted overhead, attracted by the Jeep, which they knew as the purveyor of bleeding flesh and carrion. The elephant sneezed. A crow called out somewhere behind them. "This is as far as we go," Bernard said.

Bender gaped at him, popping his joints and bugging his eyes like a fraternity boy thwarted by the ID checker at the door of a bar full of sorority girls. "All I can see is dust," he said.

Bernard was deep inside himself now. He checked the bolt on the big gun and flipped back the safety. "Just wait," he said. "Find a spot—here, right here; you can use this rock to steady your aim—and just wait a minute, that's all. She'll tire of this in a minute or so, and when the dust settles you'll have your shot."

And so they crouched in the dirt, hunter and guide, and propped their guns up on a coarse red table of sandstone and waited for the dust to clear and the heat to rise and the vultures to sink down out of the sky in great ragged swoops.

For her part, Bessie Bee was more than a little suspicious. Though her eyes were poor, the Jeep was something she could see, and she could smell the hominids half a mile away. She should have been matriarch of a fine wild herd of elephants at Amboseli or Tsavo or the great Bahi swamp, but she'd lived all her fifty-two years on this strange and unnatural continent, amid the stink and confusion of man. She'd been goaded, beaten, tethered, taught to dance and stand on one leg and grasp the sorry wisp of a tail that hung from the sorry flanks of another sorry elephant like herself as they paraded before the teeming monkey masses in one forbidding arena after another. And then there was this, a place that stank of the oily secrets of the earth, and another tether and more men. She heard the thunder of the guns and she smelled the blood on the air and she knew they were killing. She knew, too, that the Jeep was there for her.

The dust settled round her, sifting down in a maelstrom of fine white motes. She flared her ears and trumpeted and lifted the standing timber of her right front foot from the ground and let it sway before her. She was tired of the goad, the tether, the brittle dry tasteless straw and cattle feed, tired of the sun and the air and the night and the morning: she charged.

She let her nose guide her till the guns crashed, once, twice, three times, and a new sort of goad tore into her, invasive and hot, but it just made her angry, made her come on all the harder, invincible, unstoppable, twelve feet at the shoulder and eight standing tons, no more circuses, no more palanquins, no more goads. And then she saw them, two pitiful sticklike figures springing up from behind a rock she could swallow and spit up three times over.

It wasn't panic exactly, not at first. Bender shot wide, and the heavy shock of the gun seemed to stun him. Bessie Bee came straight for them, homing in on them, and Bernard bit down on his mustache and shouted, "Shoot! Shoot, you idiot!"

He got his wish. Bender fired again, finally, but all he managed to do was blow some hair off the thing's back. Bernard stood then, the rifle to his shoulder, and though he remembered the lion and could already hear the nagging whining mealy-mouthed voice of Bender complaining over lunch of being denied *this* trophy too, the situation was critical; desperate, even—who would have thought it of Bessie Bee?—and he squeezed the trigger to the jerk and roar of the big gun.

Nothing. Had he missed? But then all at once he felt himself caught up in a landslide, the rush of air, the reek of elephant, and he was flying, actually flying, high out over the plain and into the blue.

When he landed, he sat up and found that his shoulder had come loose from the socket and that there was some sort of fluid—blood, his own blood—obscuring the vision in his right eye. He was in shock, he told himself, repeating it aloud, over and over: "I'm in shock, I'm in shock." Everything seemed hazy, and the arm didn't hurt much, though it should have, nor the gash in his scalp either. But didn't he have a gun? And where was it?

He looked up at the noise, a shriek of great conviction, and saw Bessie Bee rubbing her foot thoughtfully, almost tenderly, over Mike Bender's prostrate form. Bender seemed to be naked—or no, he didn't seem to be wearing any skin, either—and his head had been vastly transformed, so much more compact now. But there was something else going on too, something the insurance company wouldn't be able to rectify, of that he was sure, if only in a vague way—"I'm in shock," he repeated. This something was a shriek too, definitely human, but it rose and caught hold of the tail of the preceding shriek and climbed atop it, and before the vacuum of silence could close in there was another shriek, and another, until even the screams of the elephant were a whisper beside it.

It was Mrs. Bender, the wife, Nicole, one of the finest expressions of her species, and she was running from the Jeep and exercising her lungs. The Jeep seemed to be lying on its side—such an odd angle to see it from— and Mrs. Bender's reedy form was in that moment engulfed by a moving wall of flesh, the big flanks blotting the scene from view, all that movement and weight closing out the little aria of screams with a final elephantine roll of the drums.

It might have been seconds later, or an hour—Bernard didn't know. He sat there, an arm dangling from the shoulder, idly wiping the blood from his eye with his good hand while the naked black vultures drifted down on him with an air of professional interest. And then all at once, strange phenomenon, the sun was gone, and the vultures, and a great black shadow fell over him. He looked up dimly into the canvas of that colossal face framed in a riot of ears. "Bessie Bee?" he said. "Bessie Bee? Shamba?"

Half a mile away, fanned by the gentle breeze of the air conditioner, Jasmine Honeysuckle Rose Bender, two months short of her thirteenth birthday and sated with chocolate and dreams of lean spike-haired adolescents with guitars and leather jackets, shifted her head on the pillow and opened her eyes. She was, in that waking moment, sole inheritor of the Bender real estate empire, and all the monies and houses and stocks and bonds and properties that accrued to it, not to mention the beach house and the Ferrari Testarossa, but she wasn't yet aware of it. Something had awakened her, some ripple on the great pond of life. For just a moment there, over the drone of the air conditioner, she thought she'd heard a scream.

But no. It was probably just some peacock or baboon or whatever. Or that pitiful excuse for an elephant. She sat up, reached into her cooler for a root beer and shook her head. Tacky, she thought. Tacky, tacky, tacky.

A boy and his uncle try to sneak up on a flock of Canadian geese who are passing through a small town in North Carolina. The author's perceptions of the meaning of family are as elemental as the landscape. In 1999 the New Yorker *named Tony Earley one of the best young writers in America. This story, originally published in* Witness, *appears in his collection,* Here We Are in Paradise *(1994).*

Tony Earley

THE SIMPLE PRESENCE OF GEESE (1994)

WE SAW THE GEESE FROM the road at dusk, a flock of maybe forty or fifty. They dropped suddenly out of the sky, miles from the nearest flyway, and landed in a bottom on one of our farms, just outside Aliceville, North Carolina. This was in December, on one of those still evenings in the new part of winter when you cannot decide whether it is a good thing to inhale deeply, the air is so clear and sharp.

Uncle Zeno and I were headed home—I don't remember now where we had been—and the geese came down on us like a revelation: a single gray and black goose shot from out of nowhere directly into the path of our truck, flying faster than you would imagine anything that big could fly. It was so low to the ground that we heard the whistle of its wings over the sound of the engine. And before we were even through jumping in our seats, the air around us exploded with honking geese, so close and flying so fast that they seemed in danger of crashing into the truck. Their rising shouts and the rushing sound of their wings, coming on us so suddenly, were as loud and frightening as unexpected gunshots, and as strange to our ears as ancient tongues. Uncle Zeno slammed on the brakes so hard that the truck fishtailed in the gravel and left us crosswise in the road, facing the bottom.

The geese flew across the field and turned in a climbing curve against the wooded ridge on the other side of the creek, back the way they had come, toward Uncle Zeno and me. They spread out their great wings, beating straight downward in short strokes, catching themselves in the air, and settled into the short corn stubble, probably a half mile from the road. And they disappeared then, in the middle of the field as we watched, through the distance and the dim winter light, as completely as if they had been ghosts. Uncle Zeno turned off the headlights, and then the engine, and we leaned forward and stared out into the growing darkness, until the ridge was black against the sky. Canadian geese just did not on an ordinary day fly over the small place in which we lived our lives. We did not speak at first, and listened to our blood, and the winter silence around us, and wondered at the thing we had seen.

We decided on the way home, the sounds of flight still wild in our ears, that the geese bedded down in the bottom would be our secret, one that we would not share with Uncle Coran and Uncle Al, who were Uncle Zeno's brothers. My uncles were close, but they were competitive in the way that brothers often are—they could not fish or hunt without keeping score—and Uncle Zeno said that we could get a good one over on Uncle Coran and Uncle Al, who were twins, if we walked in at breakfast the next morning carrying a brace of Canadian geese. He hoped that we could sneak up on the flock just before dawn, while they were still bedded and cold, and thought that he could drop or two, maybe three if he could reload fast enough, before they managed to get into the air and climb away from the bottom. He was as excited on the way home as I had ever seen him.

My mother was also to be excluded from our plans, because Uncle Zeno said that if she even looked at Uncle Coran and Uncle Al, they would know something was up, and would gang up on her until she told them our secret. My mother was fourteen years younger than Uncle Al and Uncle Coran, and twenty-one years younger than Uncle Zeno. They called her Sissy, and knew—even after she was a grandmother, and they were men of ancient and remarkable age—exactly what to say to make her mad enough to fight. It was impossible for her to lie to them about anything. We lived with Uncle Zeno on Depot Street, and Uncle Coran and Uncle Al lived on either side of us, in houses of their own. The five of us together ate as a family three times a day, at the long table in Uncle Zeno's dining room, meals that my mother cooked.

I managed to keep quiet about the geese during supper, although Uncle Coran and Uncle Al more than once commented on the possum-like nature of my grin. Uncle Zeno twice nudged me under the table with his foot, and narrowed his eyes in warning. The whole family knew something was up, and that Uncle Zeno was behind it. I enjoyed every minute of letting them know that I knew what it was. It was a position I was not often in. My mother slipped into my room that night after I went to bed, bearing in her apron a rare stick of peppermint. She broke it in two and presented me with half, which I accepted. We sucked on our candy in silence, staring at each other, until she asked, misjudging my allegiances, just what exactly Uncle Zeno and I were up to. I told her that we were going to see a man about a dog, which is what Uncle Zeno would have said in reply to such a transparent attempt at bribery. My mother smiled—she always considered it a good sign to see parts of her brothers, particularly parts of Uncle Zeno, coming out in me—and told me to make sure that the dog would bark at a stranger, which was one of the many appropriate responses. After she kissed me and left the room, I heard Uncle Zeno in the kitchen loudly proclaiming that he didn't know what in the world they were talking about, that we weren't up to anything at all.

That night on their way back to their houses, Uncle Coran and Uncle Al stopped outside my window, pressed their faces against the glass, and growled like bears. I treated their performance with the disdain it deserved. I could not know then what the next day would bring, what Uncle Zeno and I would discover on our hunt. Most of the things that make you see the world and yourself in it differently, you do not imagine beforehand, and I suppose that is the best way. It enables us to live moment to moment in the things we hope to be true. I went to sleep that night possessor, along with my uncle, of what we thought to be a magnificent secret: in the morning a flock of Canadian geese would rise up before us into the air. They would be waiting, there in the frozen field, when we sneaked up on them in the new light.

In what seemed like only minutes, Uncle Zeno pulled my toe and held a finger to his lips. It was dark outside, for all I knew the deepest part of the night. I thought briefly about going back to sleep, into the dreams I had traveled through, and whose thresholds were still close by, but the thought of the geese exploding into the air, the secret adventure that I would share with Uncle Zeno, brought me fully awake. I kicked back the covers and gathered up my clothes and shoes and ran into the kitchen to dress beside the fire. Uncle Zeno was already wearing his hunting coat, and the legs of his overalls were stuffed down into the tall, black rubber boots he wore when he fed the stock. He was grinning. "Get a move on, Doc," he whispered, blowing on a cup of coffee. "Tonight me and you'll be eating a big old goose for dinner. You think we should let anybody else have any?" His shotgun was broken open and lying on the table. Neither his stock boots nor the gun, by my mother's decree, were supposed to be in the kitchen. I shook my head no. Let the rest of the world find their own geese.

When I was dressed, still shivering from my dash between sleep and the fire, Uncle Zeno and I started down the hall toward the darkness outside, and the things that waited for us in it, most of which we did not know. As we tiptoed past my mother's open door, she coughed, which stopped Uncle Zeno in his tracks. He shifted his gun to the other hand and dragged me by the collar back into the kitchen. From out of the straw basket that sat on the second shelf of the cupboard, he removed a piece of corn bread left over from supper the night before. "Here, Doc," he said, "you better eat this." He also poured me a glass of buttermilk. I gulped it all down. When we passed my mother's room a second time, we didn't hear a thing.

Once we made it out of the house, Uncle Zeno and I left in a hurry, pausing only long enough to scrape the ice off the windshield. If Uncle Al and Uncle Coran heard the sound of the truck starting in the yard, they did not dash barefoot out of their houses to see where we were going. And if our flight woke any of the hounds and pointers and assorted feists that divided their time and allegiances between our three houses, they did not crawl from out of their beds beneath the porches to investigate. We escaped cleanly, down the single block of Depot Street to the state highway.

Aliceville was still asleep as far as I could tell, the houses dark, and before Uncle Zeno even finished shifting into high gear we were out of town completely and into the open country. There is a surveyor's iron stake driven into the ground underneath the depot that marks the exact center of Aliceville—I suppose that small boys still play games whose rules involve crawling through the spiderwebs and imagined snakes beneath the building to touch the stake, there at the center of things—and from that point the imaginary line marking the city limits is only a half mile away in any direction. Aliceville is a small but perfect circle on a map, and it sits in the middle of the fields that surround it like a small idea in danger of being forgotten. We lived our lives inside that circle, and made it a town by saying that it was.

The stars were still bright and close above us, but strange somehow, stopped at some private point in their spinning that I had never seen. The state highway was white in the beams of our headlights, and black beyond, and the expansion strips in the concrete bumped under our tires in the countable rhythm of distance passing. There was no sign yet of the coming day, although in the east, down close to the tops of the trees beyond the fields, there was a faint purple tint that disappeared if you stared at it very long and tried, in your wishing for light and warmth, to turn it into dawn. The fields beside the highway were white with a hard frost.

Two miles outside town, Uncle Zeno turned off the state highway onto the dirt road that ran past the bottom where the geese waited for us in the dark. He cut the headlights and slowed the truck to a stealthy crawl, the engine barely above idle. We crept along the road in the starlight until he stopped the truck and turned off the engine a mile or more away from the bottom, at the place where the creek that ran on the other side of it forded the road. "Don't slam the door, Doc," Uncle Zeno whispered. "From here on out, if we poot, they'll hear it. If we make a sound, we'll never see them."

Uncle Zeno loaded his double barrel with two shells out of the pocket of his hunting coat, and gingerly clicked it shut. We were going to sneak up on the flock by walking in the creek, which had high banks and was hidden from view on both sides by thick underbrush. When we got close enough, we would run up out of the brush like Indians, and into the middle of the sleeping geese. They would explode into the frozen air around us for Uncle Zeno to shoot. I did not have any rubber boots, so I climbed onto Uncle Zeno's back—my uncles were tall, strong men who ran their last footrace down Depot Street on Uncle Zeno's sixtieth birthday—and I looped my arms around his neck and my legs around his waist. He shrugged once to get me higher on his back, and stepped over the thick mush ice that grew up out of the bank, and into the cold creek.

Uncle Zeno carried his gun in his right hand, and I felt its stock against my hip. We moved slowly downstream, and in a few steps the brush and trees that grew on the sides of the creek closed above our heads and hid us from whatever might have been watching. Uncle Zeno slid each foot in and out of the creek so quietly that I could not distinguish his steps from the noise made by the water.

We ducked beneath low-hanging vines and limbs and the trunks of trees that had fallen across the creek. I looked up through the thick branches and vines that were tangled above our heads, and could only occasionally see a star. They were dimmer, though it was still night, than when we had left home. I rested my chin on Uncle Zeno's shoulder and closed my eyes and listened to the sound of the creek moving by us in the dark. I might've even dozed off. When I opened my eyes I could sense the bottom on my left, its openness beneath the sky, but I could not see it yet through the laurel and briars. We were still a long way from the geese. Uncle Zeno tilted his head back until the stubble of his beard brushed my cheek, and he said "Shh" so softly that I almost couldn't hear it.

To this day, I do not know what sound we made that caused the geese to fly—how they knew we were there. We never saw them. We were still four or five hundred yards away when they took off, but I knew when it happened it was because of something we had done. We had been silly to think we could get close. When they rose from the bottom their wings pushing against the air sounded like a hard rain, one that might wake you up in the middle of the night. Their shouted cries were as exotic and urgent as they had been the night before, and I heard inside those cries frozen places we would never see. Uncle Zeno and I didn't move when they went up—we were so far away that it didn't startle us, but seemed inevitable somehow—and we stood still in the creek, with our heads cocked upward, listening. We could hear them a long time after they took off, spiraling upward in the sky, calling out, until they were high above us, almost out of earshot, and leaving our part of the world for good.

We listened to those last fading calls until even the possibility of hearing them again was gone, until not even our wishing could keep the familiar sounds we tried not to hear from returning into our lives. The creek moved around us as if we weren't there, along the edge of the bottom toward the river. A truck bound for New Carpenter on the state highway downshifted in the distance. A dog barked. I hid my face against Uncle Zeno's neck, suddenly ashamed of what we had wanted to do, of the dark thing we had held in our hearts. At that moment I would have said a prayer to bring the geese back, to hide them again in the field, had I thought it would work. But I knew there was nothing I could do, no desperate bargain I could make, that it was over, just over. The simple presence of the geese had made our world seem less small, and we were smaller than we had been, once they were gone.

When Uncle Zeno finally moved, I was surprised to see that it was daylight. The trunks of the trees around us had changed from black to gray, as if the day had been waiting only for the geese to climb back into the sky. I could make out the faint red of the sand on the bottom of the creek, the dark green of the laurel on its banks. It was like waking up. Uncle Zeno let out a long breath and turned toward the bottom and waded out of the creek. I slid down onto the ground. "Well, Doc," he said, "I guess me and you might as well go on home." Through the undergrowth I saw the gray sky curving down toward the field. Somewhere a crow called out a warning. There was nothing remarkable about any of it, not that I could tell, not anymore.

*This touching story of a man facing death was written shortly before the au-
thor's own death, in 1969. A hunter walks with his dog into a golden past
that is far more real, far warmer and more enticing than the briefly sketched,
painful present. Corey Ford (1902–1969) is best known for his humor column in* Field and Stream, *called "The Lower Forty." He also wrote for* Life,
Vanity Fair, *and the* Saturday Evening Post *and authored several books.
Ford was a close friend of Harold Ross, the founder of the* New Yorker, *and
was responsible for naming Eustace Tilly, the magazine's monocle-holding,
top-hatted mascot. This story was reprinted in* Field and Stream's *100-year
issue, 1895–1995.*

Corey Ford

THE ROAD TO TINKHAMTOWN (1970)

IT WAS A LONG WAY, but he knew where he was going. He would follow the road through the woods and over the crest of a hill and down
the hill to the stream, and cross the sagging timbers of the bridge, and
on the other side would be the place called Tinkhamtown. He was going
back to Tinkhamtown.

He walked slowly at first, his legs dragging with each step. He had not
walked for almost a year, and his flanks had shriveled and wasted away

from lying in bed so long; he could fit his fingers around his thigh. Doc Towle had said he would never walk again, but that was Doc for you, always on the pessimistic side. Why, now he was walking quite easily, once he had started. The strength was coming back into his legs, and he did not have to stop for breath so often. He tried jogging a few steps, just to show he could, but he slowed again because he had a long way to go.

It was hard to make out the old road, choked with alders and covered by matted leaves, and he shut his eyes so he could see it better. He could always see it when he shut his eyes. Yes, here was the beaver dam on the right, just as he remembered it, and the flooded stretch where he had picked his way from hummock to hummock while the dog splashed unconcernedly in front of him. The water had been over his boot tops in one place, and sure enough, as he waded it now his left boot filled with water again, the same warm squidgy feeling. Everything was the way it had been that afternoon, nothing had changed in ten years. Here was the blowdown across the road that he had clambered over, and here on a knoll was the clump of thornapples where a grouse had flushed as they passed. Shad had wanted to look for it, but he had whistled him back. They were looking for Tinkhamtown.

He had come across the name on a map in the town library. He used to study the old maps and survey charts of the state; sometimes they showed where a farming community had flourished, a century ago, and around the abandoned pastures and in the orchards grown up to pine, the birds would be feeding undisturbed. Some of his best grouse covers had been located that way. The map had been rolled up in a cardboard cylinder; it crackled with age as he spread it out. The date was 1857. It was the sector between Cardigan and Kearsarge Mountains, a wasteland of slash and second-growth timber without habitation today, but evidently it had supported a number of families before the Civil War. A road was marked on the map, dotted with Xs for homesteads, and the names of the owners were lettered beside them: Nason, J. Tinkham, Allard, R. Tinkham. Half the names were Tinkham. In the center of the map—the paper was so yellow that he could barely make it out—was the word "Tinkhamtown."

He had drawn a rough sketch on the back of an envelope, noting where the road left the highway and ran north to a fork and then turned east and crossed a stream that was not even named; and the next morning he and Shad had set out together to find the place. They could not drive very far in the Jeep, because washouts had gutted the roadbed and laid bare the ledges and boulders. He had stuffed the sketch in his hunting-coat pocket, and hung his shotgun over his forearm and started walking, the setter trotting ahead with the bell on his collar tinkling. It was an old-fashioned sleighbell, and it had a thin silvery note that echoed through the woods like peepers in the spring. He could follow the sound in the thickest cover, and when it stopped he would go to where he heard it last and Shad would be on point. After Shad's death, he had put the bell away. He'd never had another dog.

It was silent in the woods without the bell, and the way was longer than he remembered. He should have come to the big hill by now. Maybe he'd taken the wrong turn back at the fork. He thrust a hand into his hunting coat; the envelope with the sketch was still in the pocket. He sat down on a flat rock to get his bearings, and then he realized, with a surge of excitement, that he had stopped on this very rock for lunch ten years ago. Here was the waxed paper from his sandwich, tucked in a crevice, and here was the hollow in the leaves where Shad had stretched out beside him, the dog's soft muzzle flattened on his thigh. He looked up, and through the trees he could see the hill.

He rose and started walking again, carrying his shotgun. He had left the gun standing in its rack in the kitchen when he had been taken to the state hospital, but now it was hooked over his arm by the trigger guard; he could feel the solid heft of it. The woods grew more dense as he climbed, but here and there a shaft of sunlight slanted through the trees. *And there were forests ancient as the hills,* he thought, *enfolding sunny spots of greenery.* Funny that should come back to him now; he hadn't read it since he was a boy. Other things were coming back to him, the smell of dank leaves and sweetfern and frosted apples, the sharp contrast of sun and cool shade, the November stillness before snow. He walked faster, feeling the excitement swell within him.

He paused on the crest of the hill, straining his ears for the faint mutter of the stream below him, but he could not hear it because of the voices. He wished they would stop talking, so he could hear the stream. Someone was saying his name over and over, "Frank, Frank," and he opened his eyes reluctantly and looked up at his sister. Her face was worried, and there was nothing to worry about. He tried to tell her where he was going, but when he moved his lips the words would not form. "What did you say, Frank?" she asked, bending her head lower. "I don't understand." He couldn't make the words any clearer, and she straightened and said to Doc Towle: "It sounded like Tinkhamtown."

"Tinkhamtown?" Doc shook his head. "Never heard him mention any place by that name."

He smiled to himself. Of course he'd never mentioned it to Doc. Things like a secret grouse cover you didn't mention to anyone, not even to as close a friend as Doc was. No, he and Shad were the only ones who knew. They had found it together, that long ago afternoon, and it was their secret.

They had come to the stream—he shut his eyes so he could see it again—and Shad had trotted across the bridge. He had followed more cautiously, avoiding the loose planks and walking along a beam with his shotgun held out to balance himself. On the other side of the stream the road mounted steeply to a clearing in the woods, and he halted before the split-stone foundations of a house, the first of the series of farms shown on the map. It must have been a long time since the building had fallen in; the cottonwoods growing in the cellar hole were twenty, maybe thirty years old. His boot overturned a rusted ax blade and the handle of a china cup in the grass; that was all. Beside the doorstep was a lilac bush, almost as tall as the cottonwoods. He thought of the wife who had set it out, a little shrub then, and the husband who had chided her for wasting time on such frivolous things with all the farm work to be done. But the work had come to nothing, and still the lilac bloomed each spring, the one thing that had survived.

Shad's bell was moving along the stone wall at the edge of the clearing, and he strolled after him, not hunting, wondering about the people who had gone away and left their walls to crumble and their buildings to collapse under the winter snows. Had they ever come back to Tinkhamtown? Were they here now, watching him unseen? His toe stubbed against a block of hewn granite hidden by briars, part of the sill of the old barn. Once it had been a tight barn, warm with cattle steaming in their stalls, rich with the blend of hay and manure and harness leather. He liked to think of it the way it was; it was more real than this bare rectangle of blocks and the emptiness inside. He's always felt that way about the past. Doc used to argue that what's over is over, but he would insist Doc was wrong. Everything is the way it was, he'd tell Doc. The past never changes. You leave it and go on to the present, but it is still there, waiting for you to come back to it.

He had been so wrapped in his thoughts that he had not realized Shad's bell had stopped. He hurried across the clearing, holding his gun ready. In a corner of the stone wall an ancient apple tree had littered the ground with fallen fruit, and beneath it Shad was standing motionless. The white fan of his tail was lifted a little and his backline was level, the neck craned forward, one foreleg cocked. His flanks were trembling with the nearness of grouse, and a thin skein of drool hung from his jowls. The dog did not move as he approached, but the brown eyes rolled back until their whites showed, looking for him. "Steady, boy," he called. His throat was tight, the way it always got when Shad was on point, and he had to swallow hard. "Steady, I'm coming."

"I think his lips moved just now," his sister's voice said. He did not open his eyes, because he was waiting for the grouse to get up in front of Shad, but he knew Doc Towle was looking at him. "He's sleeping," Doc said after a moment. "Maybe you better get some sleep yourself, Mrs. Duncombe." He heard Doc's heavy footsteps cross the room. "Call me if there's any change," Doc said, and closed the door, and in the silence he could hear his sister's chair creaking beside him, her silk dress rustling regularly as she breathed.

What was she doing here, he wondered. Why had she come all the way from California to see him? It was the first time they had seen each other since she had married and moved out West. She was his only relative, but they had never been very close; they had nothing in common, really. He heard from her now and then, but it was always the same letter: why didn't he sell the old place, it was too big for him now that the folks had passed on, why didn't he take a small apartment in town where he wouldn't be alone? But he liked the big house, and he wasn't alone, not with Shad. He had closed off all the other rooms and moved into the kitchen so everything would be handy. His sister didn't approve of his bachelor ways, but it was very comfortable with his cot by the stove and Shad curled on the floor near him at night, whinnying and scratching the linoleum with his claws as he chased a bird in a dream. He wasn't alone when he heard that.

He had never married. He had looked after the folks as long as they lived; maybe that was why. Shad was his family. They were always together—Shad was short for Shadow—and there was a closeness between them that he did not feel for anyone else, not his sister or Doc even. He and Shad used to talk without words, each knowing what the other was thinking, and they could always find one another in the woods. He still remembered the little things about him: the possessive thrust of his jaw, the way he false-yawned when he was vexed, the setter stubbornness sometimes, the clownish grin when they were going hunting, the kind eyes. That was it: Shad was the kindest person he had ever known.

They had not hunted again after Tinkhamtown. The old dog had stumbled several times, walking back to the jeep, and he had to carry him in his arms the last hundred yards. It was hard to realize he was gone. He liked to think of him the way he was; it was like the barn, it was more real than the emptiness. Sometimes at night, lying awake with the pain in his legs, he would hear the scratching again, and he would be content and drop off to sleep, or what passed for sleep in these days and nights that ran together without dusk or dawn.

Once he asked Doc point-blank if he would ever get well. Doc was giving him something for the pain, and he hesitated a moment and finished what he was doing and cleaned the needle and then looked at him and said: "I'm afraid not, Frank." They had grown up in town together, and Doc knew him too well to lie. "I'm afraid there's nothing to do." Nothing to do but lie here and wait till it was over. "Tell me, Doc," he whispered, for his voice wasn't very strong, "what happens when it's over?" And Doc fumbled with the catch of his black bag and closed it and said well he supposed you went on to someplace else called the Hereafter. But he shook his head; he always argued with Doc. "No, it isn't someplace else," he told him. "It's someplace you've been where you want to be again." Doc didn't understand, and he couldn't explain it any better. He knew what he meant, but the shot was taking effect and he was tired.

He was tired now, and his legs ached a little as he started down the hill, trying to find the stream. It was too dark under the trees to see the sketch he had drawn, and he could not tell direction by the moss on the north side of the trunks. The moss grew all around them, swelling them out of size, and huge blowdowns blocked his way. Their upended roots were black and misshapen, and now instead of excitement he felt a surge of panic. He floundered through a pile of slash, his legs throbbing with pain as the sharp points stabbed him, but he did not have the strength to get to the other side and he had to back out again and circle. He did not know where he was going. It was getting late, and he had lost the way.

There was no sound in the woods, nothing to guide him, nothing but his sister's chair creaking and her breath catching now and then in a dry sob. She wanted him to turn back, and Doc wanted him to, they all wanted him to turn back. He thought of the big house; if he left it alone it would fall in with the winter snows and cottonwoods would grow in the cellar hole. And there were all the other doubts, but most of all there was the fear. He was afraid of the darkness, and being alone, and not knowing where he was going. It would be better to turn around and go back. He knew the way back.

And then he heard it, echoing through the woods like peepers in the spring, the thin silvery tinkle of a sleighbell. He started running toward it, following the sound down the hill. His legs were strong again, and he hurdled the blowdowns, he leapt over fallen logs, he put one fingertip on a pile of slash and sailed over it like a grouse skimming. He was getting nearer and the sound filled his ears, louder than a thousand churchbells ringing, louder than all the choirs in the sky, as loud as the pounding of his heart. The fear was gone; he was not lost. He had the bell to guide him now.

He came to the stream, and paused for a moment at the bridge. He wanted to tell them he was happy; if they only knew how happy he was, but when he opened his eyes he could not see them anymore. Everything else was bright, but the room was dark.

The bell had stopped, and he looked across the stream. The other side was bathed in sunshine, and he could see the road mounting steeply, and the clearing in the woods, and the apple tree in a corner of the stone wall. Shad was standing motionless beneath it, the white fan of his tail lifted, his neck craned forward and one foreleg cocked. The whites of his eyes showed as he looked back, waiting for him.

"Steady," he called, "steady, boy." He started across the bridge. "I'm coming."

PERMISSIONS ACKNOWLEDGMENTS

T. Coraghessan Boyle, "Big Game," from *Without a Hero,* ©1994 by T. Coraghessan Boyle. Reprinted by permission of Viking Penguin, a division of Penguin Putnam, Inc.

Tony Earley, "The Simple Presence of Geese," from *Here We Are in Paradise,* ©1994 by Tony Earley. Originally published in *Witness.* Reprinted by permission of Little, Brown and Company, Inc.

Corey Ford, "The Road to Tinkhamtown," originally published in *Field and Stream,* June, 1970. Reprinted by permission of Times Mirror Magazines, Inc.

Also available from Chicago Review Press:

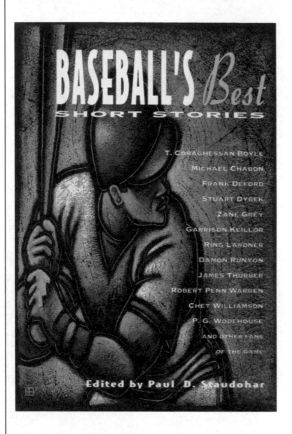

BASEBALL'S BEST SHORT STORIES
Edited by Paul D. Staudohar

"This outstanding anthology is a testament to baseball's enduring drawing power as subject matter for some of our most renowned authors."　　　*—Booklist*

"Staudohar has hit it out of the park."　　　*—Publishers Weekly*

Enjoy nostalgic reveries and thoughtful reflections on the great American pastime in this superb collection of 27 short stories and one poem. There's the extra-inning contest, the flamethrower versus the great slugger, the hot prospect who can't keep his mind on the game, the exhilarating win, and the heartbreaking loss. This wonderful anthology attests to baseball's place in our hearts, from "My Roomy," written by Ring Lardner in 1914, to Damon Runyon's "Baseball Hattie," written in the baseball-mad 1930s, to Garrison Keillor's 1988 story "Three New Twins Join Club in Spring."

404 pages, 6 × 9
paper, $16.95
ISBN 1-55652-319-X

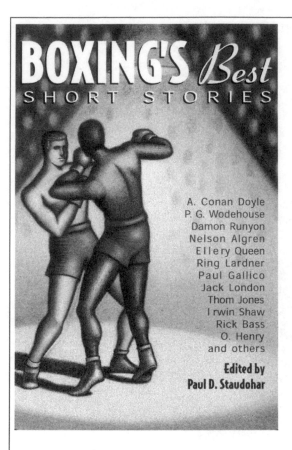

BOXING'S BEST SHORT STORIES

Edited by Paul D. Staudohar

"At once brutish and artistic, primitive and spellbinding, prizefighting provides rich material for talented writers. . . . This collection will delight fight fans, as well as those who just love a good story." —*School Library Journal*

Boxing has always had its share of violence, disreputable characters, and shattered dreams, but as an inspiration for great writing it is unsurpassed. The bone-jarring crack as a glove smashes into a jaw . . . endless seconds as the referee barks "one, two, three" . . . the roar of the crowd as the winner lifts his pulpy face in victory . . . *Boxing's Best Short Stories* brings the action of the ring to life with 22 classic tales.

352 pages, 6 × 9
cloth, $24.00
ISBN 1-55652-364-5

FISHING'S BEST SHORT STORIES
Edited by Paul D. Staudohar

These twenty-five takes by outstanding authors offer a bounty of fishing adventures: the solitary sportsman casting in a fast trout stream; expensive ocean charters seeking permit and grouper; a couple of kids with bamboo poles and high hopes for the big one. The scenery is as varied as the catch, and passion for the sport goes hand-in-hand with humor, chicanery, surprise endings, friendships between young and old, and romance in unexpected places.

384 pages, 6 × 9
cloth, $24.00
ISBN 1-55652-403-X

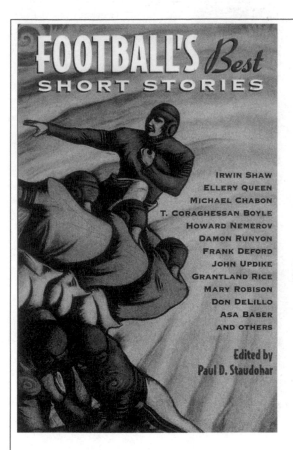

FOOTBALL'S BEST SHORT STORIES
Edited by Paul D. Staudohar

"An exciting collection of some of the best 20th-century writers venturing into some unexpected venues."   —J. C. Martin, *The Arizona Daily Star.*

There are no rookies here—some of America's best writers have penned short stories on football. In this lively anthology of 21 stories and one classic poem about football, fathers and sons tackle their issues, coaches and quarterbacks collide, and ordinary heroes emerge from the blitz. Each decade of the 20th century is tackled, from Ralph D. Paine's 1909 moving story of a down-on-his-luck father who goes to see his son play a big game for Yale, to Ellery Queen's 1940s detective story set in the Rose Bowl, to Frank Deford's spoof on the media hysteria of the Superbowl, written in 1978.

336 pages, 6 × 9
cloth, $22.00, ISBN 1-55652-330-0
paper, $16.95, ISBN 1-55652-365-3

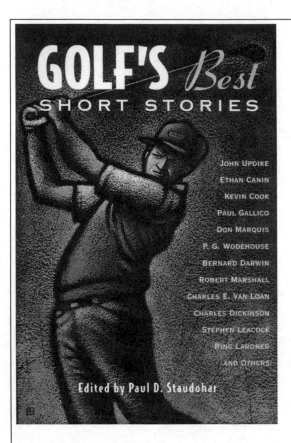

GOLF'S BEST SHORT STORIES
Edited by Paul D. Staudohar

Twenty-four gems from many great writers, including P. G. Wodehouse, Paul Gallico, Don Marquis, and John Updike, are represented in these great tales of golf. British duffers, amateur sleuths, pros, hustlers, plodders, cheaters, starry-eyed lovers, and crass finaglers people these stories, which range from comedy to tragedy, mystery, action, introspection, and romance. Each reveals a true love of the game and a wry understanding of golf's frustrations, perplexities, embarrassments, and moments of pure delight.

416 pages, 6 × 9
cloth, $24.00 ISBN 1-55652-321-1
paper, $16.95 ISBN 1-55652-325-4

These books are available from your local bookstore or from Independent Publishers Group by calling (312) 337-0747 or (800) 888-4741.